Praise for *To the Top of Denali*:

"*To the Top of Denali* is a fascinating account of historic, tragic, and contemporary climbs on the mountain."

—*Juneau Empire*

"Sherwonit has produced 'Denali in a Nutshell.' . . . The author has [created] an incredibly accurate portrait of the mountain and the climbers. . . . *To the Top of Denali* is fat with information . . . and some seldom seen photos. . . . So read this book before you go. Better yet, take it with you (or it will take you) to the top of Denali, where you'll salute Bill Sherwonit for the world that opens up at your feet."

—Jonathan Waterman

"Here in one book are the great moments of mountaineering on Denali. . . . [It] offers insight and tales of great adventure for both advanced climbers and all the armchair explorers who wonder why people climb mountains."

—Excerpt from the Foreword by Art Davidson

"Bill Sherwonit tells the story of McKinley through the high and cold experience of those who were there. These tales will keep you up long evenings and perhaps make you shiver in your warm living room. They are as timeless as the mountain itself. . . . I haven't read anything about McKinley that tells the history of the mountain so easily and naturally."

—Galen Rowell

"Sherwonit describes some of the best-known personalities and eccentrics associated with the mountain—Bradford Washburn, Ray Genet, John Waterman, Vern Tejas, and Naomi Uemura, a Japanese climber who disappeared in 1984 after becoming the first person to climb McKinley alone during the winter. . . . You don't need to be a climber to appreciate the stories."

—*Fairbanks Daily News-Miner*

"Books like [*To the Top of Denali*] should be assigned reading for anybody contemplating the climb."

—Bradford Washburn

Renny Jackson

A CLIMBER ASCENDS MOUNT MCKINLEY'S CASSIN RIDGE,
A STEEP ICE AND ROCK SPINE THAT'S CONSIDERED ONE OF
NORTH AMERICA'S GREAT MOUNTAINEERING CHALLENGES.

THIRD EDITION

TO THE TOP OF DENALI

CLIMBING ADVENTURES ON NORTH AMERICA'S HIGHEST PEAK

BILL SHERWONIT

WITH A FOREWORD BY ART DAVIDSON

ALASKA NORTHWEST BOOKS®

Third edition 2012

Library of Congress Cataloging-in-Publication Data:
Sherwonit, Bill, 1950-
To the top of Denali : climbing adventures on North America's highest peak / Bill Sherwonit ; with a foreword by Art Davidson. — 3rd ed.
p. cm.
Includes bibliographical references and index.
ISBN 978-0-88240-894-1 (pbk.)
1. Mountaineering—Alaska--McKinley, Mount—History. 2. McKinley, Mount (Alaska)—Description and travel. I. Title.
GV199.42.A42M3256 2012
796.52'2'097983—dc23
2012034427

Book design and maps by Cameron Mason
Cover design by Elizabeth Watson

Cover photos: Front cover—Mount McKinley, photo by Fred Hirschmann. Back cover—Author Bill Sherwonit explores Anchorage's "backyard wilderness," Chugach State Park, in 2011 with his beloved hiking companion, Coya. Photo by Tom Englehart.

With the permission of the *Anchorage Times*, nine articles by the author are reprinted here, whole or in part: "McKinley Rangers Fight Battle with Trash on Mountain" (May 19, 1985); "Mountain Doctors Set Up Shop on McKinley" (March 29, 1987); "Writer Begins His Assault on Denali" (May 30, 1987); Climbing McKinley," three-part series (July 19 and 26 and August 2, 1987); "Following in Uemura's Footsteps" (April 10, 1988); "Anguished Tejas Couldn't Have Known Climber's Trouble" (May 29, 1988); "Determination to Succeed Killed Climber" (May 29, 1988); "McKinley Mountaineering, 1988" (January 22, 1989); and "McKinley Masterpiece" (March 19, 1989). "The Deadliest Season: 1992" first appeared in the *Anchorage Daily News* (July 12, 1992), in slightly different form.

Alaska Northwest Books®
An imprint of Turner Publishing Company
4507 Charlotte Avenue, Suite 100
Nashville, TN 37209
(615) 255-2665

www.turnerbookstore.com

For Helene and Mom,
and in memory of Dad

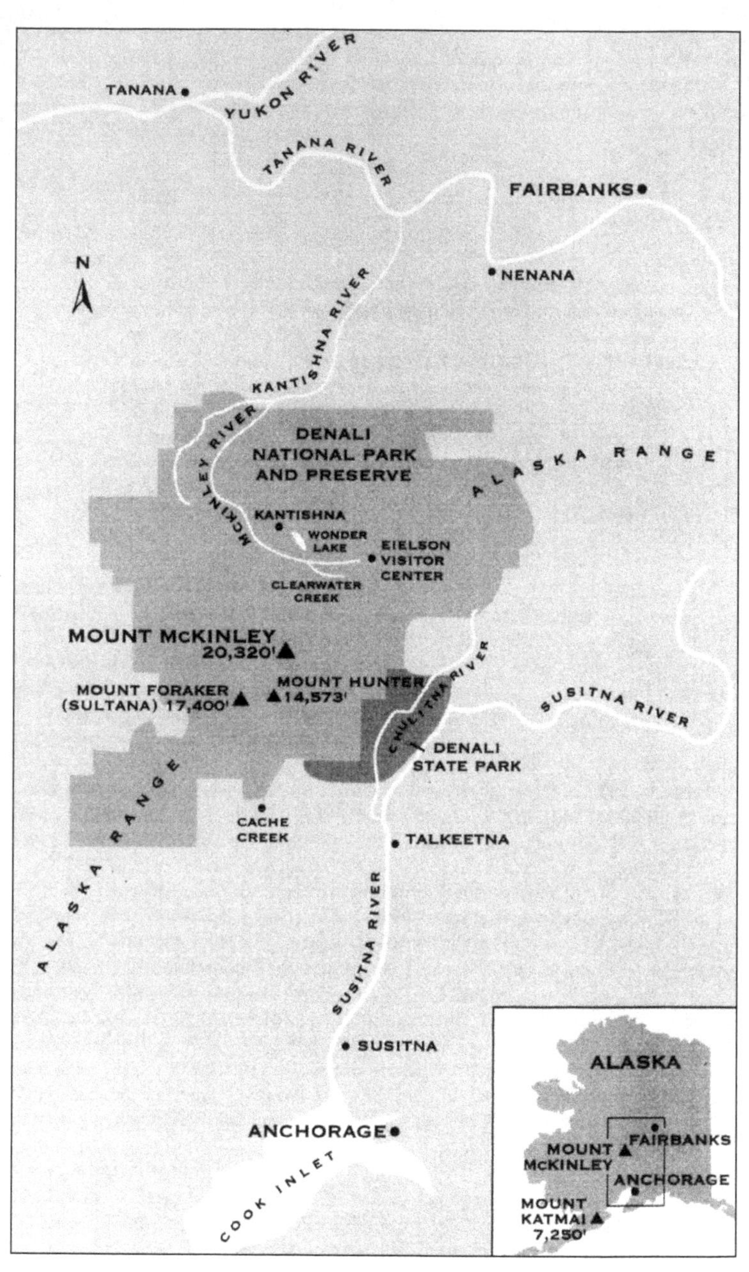

DENALI NATIONAL PARK AND PRESERVE
(SEE INSET FOR LOCATION IN ALASKA)

Contents

FOREWORD

LIKE OTHER MOUNTAINEERS, I am often asked, "Why do you climb?"

The question is posed as if going out into the mountains is one of the most bizarre and inexplicable things men or women might do.

I think there are mountains in all of our lives. Whether we climb the earth's highest peaks, hike in gentle hills, or explore the metaphorical ranges of the psyche, most of us are drawn by the archetypal power, beauty, and exquisite wildness of mountains. In the mountains of the world, we can venture into wilderness, connect with nature, seek ultimate challenges, or simply have a good time with friends in the outdoors.

Of the earth's wild places, Denali, towering over all the glaciers and high ridges of the Alaska Range, is one of the wildest and most intriguing. In my five expeditions to Denali, once making the first winter ascent, I have found myself drawn into its tremendous presence. It is not only the highest peak in North America, but it is one of the highest mountains in the world, from its base. It spawns more than a dozen glacial rivers. Enormous avalanches rake its exposed slopes. Storm winds reach hurricane force–more than 150 miles per hour. And the unpredictable weather and ever-changing mountain light envelop Denali in a mysterious, awesome beauty.

Few of us will ever have the opportunity to climb Denali, but writer Bill Sherwonit can take all of us to the mountain's highest reaches. An Alaskan, Sherwonit lives close to the mountain's presence. A climber himself, he has scaled Denali. As a writer, Sherwonit transports us not only to the mountain, but into the drama of the great expeditions. In an informative, fast-paced narrative, he brings alive the heroics of the pioneers who tried to make the first ascent and of those who followed, putting up ever more harrowing routes on the mountain's steep ridges and walls.

Here in one book are the great moments of mountaineering on Denali. Sherwonit allows us to share the adventures of those who have risked their lives trying to reach its summit. He lets us share the excitement of their success, and unflinchingly lays bare the tragic accidents that have claimed the lives of climbers. It is a pleasure to welcome this book, which offers insight and tales of great adventure for both advanced climbers and all the armchair explorers who wonder why people climb mountains.

ART DAVIDSON

Author of numerous books including *Minus 148°: The First Winter Ascent of Mt. McKinley*, *Alakshak: The Great Country*, and *In the Wake of the* Exxon Valdez.

Preface

The roots of this book can probably be traced back to high school, when I was captivated by Maurice Herzog's classic, *Annapurna*. But more directly, the book is tied to a couple of events in my life in 1985.

First, I changed jobs at the *Anchorage Times*, switching from sportswriter to outdoors writer. Instead of covering athletic events like basketball or baseball, I was reporting on such activities as fishing, hunting, camping–and mountain climbing. Though not a mountaineer, I'd always loved the mountains and been intrigued by the people who climb them. Now, suddenly, it was my job to write about climbing activities in our country's Last Frontier. In a way, it was a dream come true.

About two months after changing jobs, I met Mike Howerton, an experienced Alaskan climber who was organizing a benefit expedition to Mount McKinley to raise money for a cancer-care unit in an Anchorage hospital. In preparing a feature on that expedition, I spent three days in the Alaska Range with Howerton's four-member party. Although I didn't ascend higher than about 7,500 feet that visit (two years later I did climb to the summit), my firsthand introduction to McKinley's Kahiltna Glacier Base Camp and its cast of characters whetted my enthusiasm for both the 20,320-foot mountain and the mountaineers drawn to it. Over the next five years, McKinley became one of my favorite newspaper beats. And that journalistic interest led to this project.

Originally, I was asked to write a mountaineering adventure book that included all of Alaska's major ranges. But in talking to climbers and researching the state's mountaineering literature, I found myself pulled more and more toward Denali, "The High One," as North America's highest peak has traditionally been known to Alaska's Natives, and to its wealth of history. There are so many compelling stories about the mountain, most of them unknown except within the narrow confines of the climbing community. Stories of struggle and achievement, of triumph and tragedy, of climbing controversies and issues unique to this special high place. I discovered enough information to fill several volumes, and in doing so, narrowed the scope of my project to Denali.

In writing the book, I focused on several of the more significant attempts—whether successful or not—to reach the mountain's top, from the earliest expeditions in 1903 to the winter solo ascents of Vern Tejas and Dave Staeheli in the late 1980s. Most of the expeditions included were milestones of one sort or another.

I also chose to include my 1987 trip up the West Buttress Route—hardly a milestone, except from a personal perspective—because that account describes the path now followed by the majority of McKinley climbers (more than 80 percent in recent years), and presents the perspective of someone who has made a summit ascent but is not a hard-core mountaineer. As appealing as they are, adventure stories paint only a partial picture of climbing on Denali. The peak's lofty status, together with improved access, government management, and the steady growth of adventure travel, have dramatically changed the nature of McKinley mountaineering over the past two decades. Several of the mountain's most important issues and controversies, which have received little attention except within the Alaska media, are discussed at length in this book, including the evolution of Denali's mountain-guide industry; trash and sanitation problems and the growth of environmental awareness; National Park Service regulation of mountaineering and guiding activities; climber self-sufficiency; and the coordination and high costs of rescue operations.

One final issue presented a special dilemma in my writing: what name to use for the mountain, "McKinley" or "Denali"? As explained in the book, a growing number of Alaskans—climbers and non-climbers alike—use the Native name. "Denali" is certainly my preference. Yet "McKinley" remains the peak's "official" name, the one used by Congress and recognized by most Americans. So a compromise seems best. The book became *To the Top of Denali*, but "McKinley" is used throughout most of the text. Backgrounds for both names are discussed, and an argument for an official name change is presented in Chapter 4. Most of the people in this book live (or lived) within sight of Denali. One of my great joys in writing this book was the opportunity to present an Alaskan perspective of Denali, through the words and images of people whose lives are intimately tied to The High One.

September 1999: Ten years have elapsed since I began work on the first edition of *To the Top of Denali.* Over the past decade, more than 11,200 people have attempted to reach McKinley's summit–only slightly fewer than had walked the mountain's slopes in the previous seventy-seven years. We have witnessed the deadliest season in Denali's history; the removal of its most famous guide company, Genet Expeditions; the institution of a mountaineering user fee; and an unprecedented January ascent. We've also seen the easing of a disturbing trend: after many years in which foreign climbers accounted for an inordinately high percentage of McKinley rescues and deaths, there were signs in the late 1990s that they'd begun to take fewer risks–or at least required less assistance from rescuers. While I haven't returned to Denali's slopes since my one ascent in 1987, I remain as enthralled as ever by the great peak. Here again, with updated information, are stories of the mountain and its mountaineers.

Summer 2012: Another thirteen years have passed since I last documented mountaineering changes and trends on The High One. Nearly a century after Hudson Stuck, Walter Harper, Harry Karstens, and Robert Tatum stood atop the roof of North America, Mount McKinley–Denali–is as popular as ever with climbers (more than ever I wish the mountain's older and more fitting name would be officially restored).

At least 1,100 people have attempted to reach the mountain's summit every year since 2000, including an all-time high of 1,340 people in 2005. A growing number of those McKinley mountaineers have little or no high-altitude climbing experience, so increasingly they depend on guides; in fact the number of guided climbers increased by 33 percent between 2002 and 2012, while independent sorts declined by 32 percent. Whether guided or not, more mountaineers than ever follow the path blazed by Bradford Washburn. In recent years as many as 90 percent (or more) have taken the West Buttress Route. Washburn first predicted that the West Buttress would become the safest, easiest, and fastest way to the summit in 1947; sixty years later, the climbing world was saddened to lose McKinley's greatest visionary, when he died on January 10, 2007.

The first decade of the 2000s was also marked by some notable new regulations: looking ahead to the possibility of an even more crowded mountain, the National Park Service capped the number of climbers who may annually walk upon McKinley at 1,500. And McKinley mountaineers are now required to follow leave-no-trace policies that include the use of Clean Mountain Cans (learn more about that in Chapter 14, "Mountain of Trash").

Among the more encouraging trends: though still an "issue," illegal guiding is not nearly as prevalent as it had been in the 1980s and '90s. On the other hand, NPS rescue expenses have continued to rise, an usually high number of guided clients have perished on McKinley's slopes, and climbers seem to be increasingly dependent–and less self-sufficient–since the turn of the century. The latter trend especially troubles Denali's mountaineering rangers.

This year also marks a quarter-century since my own lone ascent of Denali, at age thirty-seven. I was never anything more than a novice mountaineer and today my most ambitious "climbs" are strenuous uphill hikes–I do love walking high ridgelines, whether in the Alaska Range, Brooks Range, or the Chugach

Mountains that border my adopted hometown of Anchorage—but I still have vivid memories of my guided journey up the West Buttress. Sometimes when walking in the hills, a sharp gust of chilling wind, or something about the light or sky, will transport me back to Denali's slopes. In some ways it seems a lifetime ago, but there are moments when it feels like yesterday. Perhaps because I've been on the mountain, in re-reading the stories in this book, I remain in awe of the pioneering achievements of people like Brad Washburn, Hudson Stuck, and the Sourdoughs; and I applaud the efforts of more ordinary climbers who face great challenge and sometimes, great hardship, on Denali's slopes. Some day, I tell myself, I will return to the Kahiltna Glacier for another glimpse of that world, though I have no aspirations to go far beyond base camp. For now I'm content to admire The High One, and its mountaineers, from afar.

Acknowledgments

MANY PEOPLE, IN many different ways, helped with this project. I'm indebted to all those who took the time to share their Denali-mountaineering opinions, experiences, and/or expertise, most notably Gary Bocarde, Doug Buchanan, Steve Davis, Andy Embick, Peter Hackett, Jim Hale, Harry Johnson, Mike Howerton, Dave Johnston, Todd Miner, Brian Okonek, Bob Seibert, Dave Staeheli, and Vern Tejas. I'd also like to acknowledge two climbers who talked with me at length about other mountains before I finally focused on Denali, Bob Jacobs and Willy Hersman.

Special thanks to Art Davidson for writing the foreword and providing inspiration; to Bradford Washburn for sharing his McKinley expertise; to Daryl Miller for his gracious help while I worked on the revised edition of this book; to Sara Juday for her confidence in my writing skills; and to Ellen Wheat for her wonderful editing, infectious enthusiasm, and unwavering encouragement.

Thanks also to my editors at the *Anchorage Times* who allowed me to reprint all or parts of several of my stories that originally appeared in the *Times*; to those who contributed photographs; and to authors whose work served as valuable sources. I'm deeply grateful to the many people who supported my book-writing effort; their positive energies and good wishes are much appreciated. Gordon Jones, Bob Pelz, and Kenny Powers deserve special mention for helping me through some writer's crises. Mike Burwell, John Strasenburgh, and Todd Miner helped by reading portions of my manuscript. And Dulcy Boehle gave me great encouragement, patience, and love throughout the initial writing and publication of the book.

For help with this newest edition of *To the Top of Denali*, I extend thanks to Denali National Park's lead mountaineering ranger, John

Leonard, and several other Denali employees: Roger Robinson, Kirk Dietz, Kris Fister, Missy Smothers, and Maureen McLaughlin. I'm also grateful to climber/guide Colby Coombs for his contributions. Thanks also to Tim Frew and Doug Pfeiffer, who recognized the need to update the book and encouraged the new edition; and to other staff at Graphic Arts Books, who helped in its production, including editor Kathy Howard and designer Vicki Knapton.

Finally, I extend my deep gratitude to Helene Feiner, who for the past half-dozen or so years has not only supported my writing, but joined me on many adventurous and loving times spent hiking and exploring the hills and mountains of Alaska and beyond.

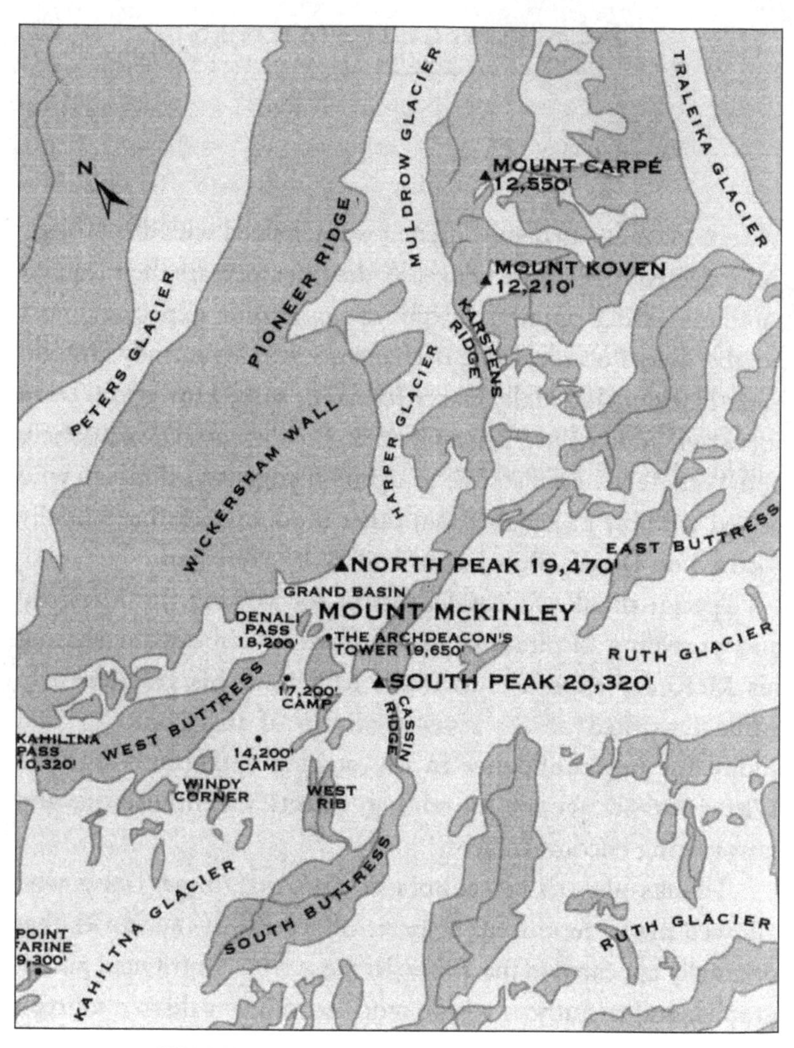

MOUNT MCKINLEY—DENALI, THE HIGH ONE

Chapter One

The Mountain

Rising 20,320 feet above sea level, Mount McKinley is a perfect symbol of Alaska. In a land of superlatives and extremes, this monumental granite monolith is the state's most dominating feature.

Towering over its Alaska Range neighbors, McKinley is a wild, desolate world of ice, snow, and extreme cold year-round. The mountain looms more than 18,000 feet above the surrounding tundra plains and river valleys and its vertical rise is among the highest in the world.

The peak's great height, combined with its subarctic location, make it one of the coldest mountains on earth, if not *the* coldest. Halfway to the summit, McKinley's climate equals the North Pole's in severity. Even in May, nighttime temperatures on its upper slopes may reach −30° to −40° Fahrenheit. In winter, temperatures below −60°F have been recorded.

McKinley is so massive it creates its own weather systems. Some storms have produced winds exceeding 150 miles per hour. The mountain is also frequently battered by storms originating in the North Pacific. Long periods of clear and calm weather are rare, particularly on its upper slopes. Because of McKinley's northerly location, scientists have estimated that the available oxygen at its summit is equal to that of Himalayan mountains 2,000 to 3,000 feet higher. For all of these reasons, McKinley has earned a reputation as the ultimate challenge in North American mountaineering.

Adding to the mountain's magnetism is its high visibility and, since the advent of commercial bush-pilot services in the 1950s, its remarkable accessibility. The centerpiece of six-million-acre Denali National Park and Preserve, McKinley can be seen from Alaska's two largest cities as well as the George Parks Highway, which offers countless splendid views. For those seeking a closer view, the mountain is only a half-hour plane ride from Talkeetna. This small town (population about 900 as of 2011), located about 120 highway miles from Anchorage, has justifiably earned a reputation as the "Gateway to Denali." Four Talkeetna air-taxi services provide both sightseeing opportunities and transportation to the Kahiltna Glacier, which since the late 1960s has served as base camp for the majority of McKinley's mountaineering expeditions. From the 7,200-foot base camp, it's about sixteen miles and 13,000 vertical feet to the summit.

Several routes can be followed to the top of McKinley, but by far the most popular is the West Buttress. Although mountaineers agree that this route does not require great technical climbing expertise, success rates on the West Buttress are comparatively low; most years, nearly half of McKinley's West Buttress climbers fail to reach the summit, and many people have died on the route. McKinley's other ridges and faces offer even longer or more difficult routes.

By late July of 2012, 38,529 climbers had walked on McKinley's slopes; 20,062 actually reached the summit (about 52 percent). The large majority of those attempts and successes have occurred since the early 1970s, more than half of them since the mid-1990s.

Improved access, the availability of professional guiding services, and advances in climbing gear, clothing, and food supplies have attracted increasing numbers of adventure-seekers to McKinley, many of whom hardly qualify as mountaineers. It's been proven that climbers with little or no previous high-altitude climbing experience can reach McKinley's top when benefiting from expert guidance and state-of-the-art equipment. Yet a mastery of basic mountaineering skills, excellent physical conditioning, good judgment, and a willingness to endure pain are required.

Those who underestimate McKinley's dangers suffer the consequences: altitude sickness, broken bones, hypothermia, frostbite, or even death. Since the mountain was first attempted in 1903, 120 people have died on its slopes and hundreds more have been seriously injured.

Because McKinley is located on federal parklands, the National Park Service is charged with managing the mountain's use. Federal regulations require all climbers to pay a $350 fee (as of 2012; the cost is $250 for climbers twenty-four or younger) that helps fund the park's mountaineering program expenses. It is not a rescue-fund fee. McKinley mountaineers are also required to register at least sixty days before their expedition (exceptions are made for those who've previously climbed McKinley since 1995) and team leaders must report to rangers after completing an expedition. The National Park Service has also capped the number of climbers who can annually walk the great peak's slopes at 1,500, but the climbing crowds have not yet approached that number (the all-time high is 1,340 people in 2005).

Though McKinley is enormously popular and easily accessible today, only a century ago North America's tallest peak was terra incognita. A foreboding and mysterious mountain, it was unclimbed, unexplored, and unknown to most Americans.

It wasn't unknown to Alaska's Native people, however. Among several Athabascan tribes, the great mountain was a familiar and revered landmark. Koyukon Indians living in Alaska's Interior called the mountain *Deenaalee,* "The High One." The anglicized version, *Denali*, is the most widely recognized Native name for the peak, but it wasn't the only one used by local residents. Linguist James Kari has identified at least eight names historically used by Native residents of the region, whose translations mean either "The High One" or "Big Mountain."[1]

A Native legend that explains the mountain's creation is recounted by climber Art Davidson in his book *Minus 148°: The Winter Ascent of Mt. McKinley*, which documents the first winter expedition to Denali in 1967. According to Davidson, an old, blind Indian sage named Hoonah recalled:

> Before this great mountain was raised into the sky, Yako–the peaceful "Athabascan Adam" whose powers changed wicked men into animals, birds and bees and who gave creatures of the forest immortality through vernal reproduction–journeyed to the sunset land in the distant west to find himself a wife. When he stroked his canoe to the shore of the village ruled by Totson, the raven war chief who delighted in killing animals and men, a mother with a happy face walked to the edge of the water and gave her beautiful young daughter to be Yako's wife. Totson, grown jealous and mean, sharpened his magic war spear, then pursued Yako across the sea. Totson's magic caused a great storm to blow in Yako's path, but the magic of the gentle giant Yako cleared a smooth passage through the wind and waves. Totson grabbed his spear, which had never missed its mark, and flung it at Yako's back. Yako, seeing the spearhead glint in the sun as it rose and arched toward him, called on his most powerful magic stones to send an enormous wave into the sky to deflect the spear. As the wave flew into the air it turned into a great rock mountain. The spearhead splintered into little pieces when it struck near the

summit of the peak, and as Totson's canoe smashed into a sharp angular wall of the mountain, the war chief changed into a croaking raven. Yako traveled safely beyond the great mountain to his home in the east, where he fathered many children and allowed none of his people to possess a warlike spirit. Descendants of Yako, the Tena Indians, call the mountain *Denali*, the high one.[2]

Two other Native stories associated with Denali are briefly mentioned by Robert Hixson Julyan in his book *Mountain Names*: "An Alaskan Indian legend tells that the snow and ice on McKinley [or Denali] were created to keep the mountain sheep from escaping the wolves; another says flying geese crash into the mountain's side so that the ravens might feed."[3]

And in his autobiography, *My Life of High Adventure*, former park superintendent Grant Pearson recounts:

> Some people will tell you [Denali] also means "Home of the Sun." The natives have a legend about it: long ago a party of hunters were camping in mid-summer on the south side of the range, and saw the sun apparently disappear right into the mountain—then come out the other side in the morning. They returned to their village and reported, "We have found the sun's home! He goes into it at night and comes out in the morning."[4]

Generations of Indians had regarded the mountain as a holy place, treating it with a distant reverence and using it as a point of reference. Only after non-Native pioneers—with their passion for discovery, exploration, and conquest—learned of the mountain's existence did humans attempt to unravel its secrets. In doing so, it was only natural that they'd find a route to its top.

Courtesy of the Alaska State Library, Wickersham Collection, PCA277-18-43

JAMES WICKERSHAM, A US DISTRICT JUDGE BASED IN ALASKA'S INTERIOR, LED THE FIRST ATTEMPT TO CLIMB MOUNT MCKINLEY IN JUNE 1903.

Chapter Two

The Pioneers

Alaska was "discovered" by European explorers in 1741, but North America's tallest peak remained hidden from non-Natives for another half century. The first recorded sighting was made by the British explorer Capt. George Vancouver. While sailing through Cook Inlet's Knik Arm on May 6, 1794, he spotted "distant stupendous mountains covered with snow, and apparently detached from one another."[1] Vancouver's description is generally accepted as the first written reference to Mount McKinley and its companion peak, 17,400-foot Mount Foraker.

Some seventy years later, twenty-one-year-old William Dall of Boston became the first American scientist to study Alaska's Interior. While traveling along the Yukon River in 1866, Dall noted a long mountain chain that he later identified as the Alaska Range, but from a distance of 150 miles or more he failed to note any singularly spectacular peak. Dall, in fact, left Alaska believing 18,008-foot Mount St. Elias to be the territory's highest mountain and reported as much upon his return to Boston.[2]

Nine years after Dall's expedition up the Yukon, an Irish-born prospector and trader named Arthur Harper became the first known white to travel along Interior Alaska's Tanana River. After that rafting trip, he reported seeing "the great ice mountain to the south."[3] Harper's observation is of special interest since his son Walter later became the first to set foot on "the ice mountain's" summit, in 1913.

American prospectors working along the Tanana and Yukon Rivers were responsible for giving the peak its first English name. And it wasn't McKinley. In 1889, a party of gold-seekers led by Frank Densmore enjoyed a spectacular view of the great ice mountain from Lake Minchumina, north of the Alaska Range. According to Terris Moore, "We are told it was Densmore's enthusiastic descriptions of the mountain which led the Yukon pioneers to name it 'Densmore's Mountain.'"[4]

Moore credits Princeton-educated prospector William A. Dickey as the first person to closely approximate the mountain's true height, give it the name by which it is officially known today, and bring the peak to national attention in 1897. Dickey's Alaskan experiences were reported in the January 24, 1897, edition of the *New York Sun*. His most significant news was of a "great mountain . . . far in the interior from Cook's Inlet and almost due north of Tyonick. All of the Indians of Cook's Inlet call it the 'Bulshoe' Mountain, which is their word for anything very large." Proclaiming that it "compelled our unbounded admiration," Dickey said nothing he'd ever seen could compare with this Alaskan peak.[5,6]

Dickey's party named the peak "Mount McKinley," after William McKinley of Ohio, "who had been nominated for the presidency and that fact was the first news we received on our way out of that wonderful wilderness. We have no doubt that this peak is the highest in North America and estimate that it is over 20,000 feet high," a remarkably accurate guess.

Grant Pearson's book offers a slightly different version of McKinley's naming:

> In 1896, [Dickey] and a friend were hunting gold on the Susitna River where there are fine views of the mountain. They fell in with a couple of other prospectors who were rabid promoters of Democratic Candidate William Jennings Bryan's free silver idea. They bent Dickey's ears for days on the subject and to get even, Dickey named the mountain after the Republican champion of the gold standard [McKinley], wrote a newspaper article describing the great peak and the name stuck.[7]

The summer after Dickey's "discovery" was reported in the *Sun*, a US Geological Survey (USGS) team was assigned to measure the mountain's height, which had been estimated to be anywhere from 20,000 to 25,000 feet. Robert Muldrow confirmed McKinley's altitude to be greater than 20,000 feet,[8] and his calculated summit elevation of 20,464 feet came extremely close to the figure of 20,320 feet determined by Bradford Washburn and the National Geodetic Survey several decades later, using much more sophisticated equipment. (During the summer of 1989, a team of Alaskan scientists using state-of-the-art technology determined McKinley's height to be 20,306 feet–fourteen feet less than Washburn calculated. The new measurement is considered more accurate, because it was recorded with satellite equipment that took into account gravitational distortions caused by McKinley's huge mass. Official approval of the new figure would have to come from the National Geodetic Survey; but as of 2012, 20,320 feet was still the mountain's widely accepted height and the number used by the National Park Service.)

Measuring the mountain from afar was one thing. Exploring it was quite another. It wasn't until 1902 that another USGS scientist, Alfred Brooks, became the first person known to walk on McKinley's lower slopes. He was also the first to suggest a plan for reaching its summit. In his report for the Geological Survey, Brooks wrote:

> A two hours' walk across the valley, through several deep glacial streams, brought me to the very base of the mountain. . . . My objective point was a shoulder of the mountain about 10,000 feet high; but at three in the afternoon, I found my route blocked by a smooth expanse of ice. With the aid of my geologic pick I managed to cut steps in the slippery surface, and thus climbed a hundred feet higher; then the angle of slope became steeper, and as the ridge on which the glacier lay fell off at the sides in sheer cliffs, a slip would have been fatal. Convinced at length that it would be utterly foolhardy, alone as I was, to attempt to reach the shoulder for which I was headed, at 7,500 feet I turned and cautiously retraced my steps. . . .
>
> I gazed along the precipitous slopes of the mountain and tried again to realize its great altitude, with a thrill of satisfaction at being the first man to approach the summit, which was only nine miles from where I smoked my pipe.[9]

In addition to his USGS report, Brooks wrote an article in 1903 for *National Geographic* magazine titled "Plan for Climbing Mount McKinley."[10] In that story, he suggested that a northern approach would offer the best chance for success. Any attempt from Cook Inlet to the south would require too much time and effort during the trek to the mountain's base.

Brooks proved to have remarkable foresight. Of nine McKinley expeditions staged over the next decade, those approaching from the south exhausted themselves, their time, or supplies before making any serious summit try. But teams attacking from the north side pioneered a route that eventually led to the mountain's first ascent.

The first two attempts to reach McKinley's summit took place in 1903. The first party was led by Judge James Wickersham, who had been appointed US district judge for Alaska in 1901; later he would serve fourteen years as Alaska's lone representative in Congress.[11] Wickersham began organizing an expedition in May 1903, after moving his court from Eagle to Fairbanks, where a mining-boom camp had sprung up following a gold strike in 1902. Wickersham quite accurately figured that Fairbanks would eventually become Interior Alaska's commercial center.

With two months until the next scheduled court session, Wickersham began looking for a challenge to occupy his time. He settled on a trip to "that monarch of North American mountains, Mount McKinley." The judge picked four young and energetic companions for his expedition. He then added two thoroughbred Kentucky mules for packing supplies, which included flour, bacon, beans, dried apples, prunes, 300 feet of rope, alpenstocks (crude ice axes), footwear, and 100 pounds of rolled oats and a bale of hay for the mules.

The group took a river steamer down the Tanana River to the Kantishna River, which they followed until the boat ran out of fuel, then headed cross country to the base of the mountains. By June 18, they'd established a permanent camp in the upper McKinley River drainage at an elevation of about 4,000 feet. Two days later, four team members left camp with provisions for three or four days, plus rope and ice axes.

The climbers hiked about five miles up the main glacier that led from camp, then chose to follow a side glacier that seemed to offer a more direct route to their destination. Unfortunately, that tributary glacier turned into a dead end. Wickersham wrote that, after traveling about nine hours, "[We reach] a tremendous precipice beyond which we cannot go. Our only line of further ascent would be to climb the vertical wall of the mountain at our left and that is impossible." Frustrated by their blocked path and worried that warm weather was melting and weakening the mountain's snowpack, thus making it more susceptible to avalanches, the climbers reluctantly concluded that they'd better turn back. Reaching higher ground seemed impossible, at least for that season.

The main glacier that Wickersham's party had followed was the Peters Glacier (named by Brooks in 1902); the tributary glacier they ascended to 8,000 feet was the Jeffrey Spur. And the enormous, steep face that stopped the Wickersham team was later appropriately named the Wickersham Wall. The route they followed remained unclimbed until 1963.

Less than two months after the Wickersham party's departure, another expedition–this one led by Dr. Frederick Cook–came upon the earlier group's abandoned base camp.[12] Cook organized his 1903 attempt with funding support from *Harper's* magazine. Several years later, he would achieve great notoriety and spark endless debate with his claims of reaching both McKinley's summit and the North Pole.

Among Cook's teammates was journalist Robert Dunn, whose book chronicling the expedition, *The Shameless Diary of an Explorer*,[13] is considered a classic example of exploration exposé writing. According to Dunn, the six-member, fourteen-horse expedition approached McKinley from Cook Inlet (named much earlier for another explorer, Capt. James Cook). As Brooks had predicted in *National Geographic*, it wasn't the best way to go. Only after traveling "some 450 miles through trail-less forests and over tundra, under the curse of mosquitoes and bulldog flies," wrote Dunn, did the party reach Wickersham's camp at the base of the Peters Glacier. The nine-week cross-country trek left the team low on both supplies and time.

Because it was mid-August and the party wasn't prepared to spend the winter in Alaska, the climbers had only a few days before they'd have to begin their return trip to Cook Inlet. After reaching an estimated height of 11,300 feet, this second party, like its predecessor, was "thwarted by an insurmountable wall," according to Cook. (It was, however, a different wall, since Cook had attempted to climb the mountain's Northwest Buttress.)

Despite his failure to climb McKinley, Cook was favorably received upon his return to the eastern United States. Moore writes, "He was honored with memberships in various learned societies, geographical and alpine clubs, including the presidency of the Explorers Club in New York." So, when Cook announced plans to attempt another climb of McKinley in 1906, several qualified applicants sought to join the expedition.[14] Those finally joining the team were Herschel Parker, a physics professor at Columbia University; Belmore Browne, an artist, outdoorsman, and experienced climber; topographer Russell Porter; photographer Walter Miller; and horsepackers Fred Printz and Ed Barrill.

After two months of exploring and mapping the Yentna, Chulitna, and Kahiltna Rivers—all of which drain McKinley's southern glaciers—the party returned to Cook Inlet in mid-August, convinced that the mountain could not be climbed from the south.

Just as the group was breaking up, a peculiar thing happened. Cook sent a telegram to New York City stating, "Am preparing for a last desperate attempt on Mount McKinley," and returned to the Alaska Range accompanied only by Barrill. A few weeks later, upon rejoining Browne in Seldovia, as they'd previously arranged, Cook announced that he'd indeed pulled off a mountaineering coup by climbing McKinley.

Cook also sent a telegram to one of his financial backers in New York: "We have reached the summit of Mount McKinley by a new route from the north." That wondrous news was, of course, relayed to the press, and made major headlines.

Browne, however, had trouble accepting Cook's story. Later, he explained:

> I now found myself in an embarrassing position. I knew the character of the country that guarded the southern face of the big mountain, had travelled in that country, and knew that the time that Dr. Cook had been absent was too short to allow his even reaching the mountain. I knew that Dr. Cook had not climbed Mount McKinley. . . . This knowledge, however, did not constitute proof and I knew that I should have to collect some facts.

Browne's misgivings soon became common knowledge within the mountaineering community, but the public and media continued to believe Cook's account. And in the May 1907 issue of *Harper's Monthly*, Cook offered visual proof of his alleged conquest: a map showing his purported route to McKinley's summit, as well as a photograph supposedly showing Barrill on the mountain's top, waving an American flag.

Browne and Parker were convinced that Cook could never have completed the published route in twelve days, but were unable to publicly confront the explorer before he left the United States on an arctic expedition.

After Cook's departure, publishing companies in New York and London released yet another account of his McKinley climb, *To the Top of the Continent.* The book gave Cook's doubters even more reason to dispute his claim. As Moore explains:

> It now appeared that the "summit" photograph in the magazine must have been cropped or retouched along its right-handed edge. For in the book's "summit" picture, not cropped or retouched in this way, a bit of another peak now emerged in the right-hand background. . . . Parker and Browne were now persuaded that Dr. Cook's "summit" photograph had not been taken anywhere near the top of Mount McKinley.

Any controversies about Cook's McKinley expedition were brushed aside on September 1, 1909, with the announcement that Cook had reached the North Pole on April 21, 1908. While members of the Explorers Club were no longer willing to accept Cook's claims at face value, most everyone else seemed quite happy to, and his latest success made headlines around the world.

Cook's polar exploits were soon openly questioned, however. On September 6, 1909, Robert Peary announced that he had reached the North Pole in April and told the Associated Press, "Cook's claims should not be taken too seriously. The two Eskimoes who accompanied him say he went no distance north and not out of sight of land. Other members of the tribe corroborate their story."

Within two months, the various groups that had earlier honored Cook began to call for proof of his polar triumph. It soon became clear he had none, other than his own statements and observations.

Even as the North Pole controversy began heating up, Cook appeared before the Explorers Club, where he was asked to respond to Browne and Parker's accusations. Cook requested, and received, two weeks' time to prepare a reply. But before his scheduled reappearance, Cook disappeared. (He finally showed up about one year later, still asserting that he'd made the first ascent of McKinley.)

By the end of 1909, Cook's once highly regarded reputation had taken a severe beating. Several organizations, including the Explorers Club and The American Alpine Club, dropped him from membership while at the same time honoring Peary. The public, however, still considered Cook to be very much a hero; in opinion polls taken by several newspapers across the country, he easily outpolled Peary as the first to reach the North Pole.

Not satisfied with expelling Cook from membership, the Explorers Club, in conjunction with the American Geographical

Society, organized an expedition to investigate Cook's McKinley claims. And so, in 1910, Browne and Parker returned to the mountain.[15] The expedition's task was simple, but not necessarily easy: to find the peak where Cook had taken his alleged summit photo of McKinley. It probably would have helped to bring Barrill, who'd accompanied Cook in September 1906. But he too had become a controversial figure.

Though Barrill had originally gone along with Cook's claims, he later recanted and stated in a notarized document that the famous summit photograph published by Dr. Cook was actually made on a peak only 8,000 feet high and twenty miles away from the mountain.

While Cook's attackers used Barrill's admission as further evidence of the explorer's dishonesty, Cook supporters argued that Barrill had been bribed to make his statement. His integrity, as well as Cook's, was being challenged. Seeking to avoid further controversy, Browne and Parker left Barrill out of their expedition. Instead they chose six other qualified men who had taken no stand in the Cook debate.

While heading up the Susitna drainage toward the Alaska Range, the Explorers Club party encountered another McKinley expedition, representing the Mazama Mountaineering Club of Oregon. Ironically, unlike Browne and Parker, the Mazama party leader, C. E. Rusk—an expert mountaineer and an attorney known for his integrity—hoped to find evidence that would validate, rather than disprove, Cook's McKinley account.

Following Cook's map, the Parker-Browne expedition began traveling up the Ruth Glacier, which Cook had named for his daughter, on May 31. On June 16, the party spotted a mountain very similar to the one in Cook's photographs. The next task was to locate the exact site, if possible, where Cook had taken his now-notorious summit picture.

COURTESY OF THE FARQUHAR COLLECTION, ELMER E. RASMUSON LIBRARY, UNIVERSITY OF ALASKA FAIRBANKS

IN 1910, BELMORE BROWNE TAKES A PHOTO OF A TEAM MEMBER STANDING ATOP THE "FAKE PEAK" WHICH FREDERICK COOK HAD CLAIMED TO BE MCKINLEY'S SUMMIT IN 1906.

After several days of storms, the party resumed its investigation. By carefully matching photos to topography, Browne said, "we could trace him peak by peak and snowfield by snowfield, to within a foot of the spot where he had exposed his negatives." The group's painstaking detective work paid off on June 22, when, according to Browne, "we heard Professor Parker shout, 'We've got it!' An instant later we saw that it was true–the little outcrop of rock below the saddle was the rock peak of Dr. Cook's book, under which he wrote, 'The Top of our Continent–The Summit of Mount McKinley.'" A short while later the party located the distant peak that had appeared in the untouched version of Cook's alleged summit photo. As Barrill had testified, Cook's "summit" was located about twenty miles from McKinley, on a ridge well below 10,000 feet.

Now only one final task remained: to reach McKinley's summit, where a picture of North America's true high point could be taken for comparison with Cook's photos. Despite their determination, Browne and Parker were unable to find a route through the area's icefalls and near-vertical rock faces, and were stopped far short of the top.

The Mazama party also found it impossible to negotiate the immense granite walls bordering the Ruth Glacier and were forced to retreat while still nine miles and 14,000 vertical feet from McKinley's summit. But before leaving the Alaska Range, Rusk encountered sufficient evidence to disprove rather than support Cook's story and demonstrate the absurdity of his claim.[16]

The Parker-Browne and Mazama parties were not the only groups to investigate Cook's claims during the summer of 1910. A group of Alaskan miners, to become known as the Sourdoughs, climbed McKinley to discredit Cook. In doing so, they pulled off one of the most amazing and controversial feats in Alaska's climbing history. Their expedition is recounted in the following chapter.

For now, we'll stay with Parker and Browne, who, after disproving Cook's claim in 1910, made one final attempt of their own to reach McKinley's summit in 1912.[17] Convinced by their previous attempts that climbing McKinley was impossible from the south, they decided to shift their energies to the Muldrow Glacier on the mountain's northeast flank. Joined by Merl La Voy and Arthur Aten, who had participated in their 1910 expedition, Parker and Browne reached the Alaska Range's northern side in mid-April. After establishing camp, they hunted caribou and Dall sheep for food; then, via sled-dog team, they hauled several hundred pounds of supplies up the Muldrow Glacier. After caching food, climbing gear, and other provisions at 11,000 feet, they returned the dog team to base camp.

Following several weeks of rest, Parker, Brown, and La Voy began their ascent while Aten remained in camp with the dogs. By early June, the climbers had reached the upper Muldrow cache.

On June 8, after three days of heavy snowfall, the glacier's usual creaks and groans caused by shifting ice were accompanied by loud booming noises, like thunder or distant cannon fire. Though puzzled by the unfamiliar sounds, the climbers assumed it was caused by the glacial ice settling beneath the heavy snow load. Only much later did they learn that the booms were made by the violent eruption of Mount Katmai, several hundred miles away on the Alaska Peninsula.

From the Muldrow Glacier, the team ascended the northeast ridge (later named Karstens Ridge), which led to an upper glacier bowl known as the Big Basin. Though exhausting because of the new snow, the route was not technically difficult. On June 27, after relaying their supplies to successively higher camps, Parker, Browne, and La Voy reached their high camp, located between McKinley's North and South Peaks at an elevation of about 16,600 feet. The next day dawned crystal clear and the party began its final assault at 6 A.M. Upon reaching the ridge leading to McKinley's summit, the climbers noticed a dense sea of clouds approaching from the south, rising against the range's foothills.

A short while later, just below 19,000 feet, Parker, Browne, and La Voy got their first clear look at the summit. As Browne later recalled, "It rose as innocently as a tilted, snow-covered tennis court and as we looked it over we grinned with relief—we knew the peak was ours!" Yet even as the climbers grinned, the weather quickly began deteriorating. The wind increased, the sky darkened under a mass of storm clouds, and snow began falling heavily.

Not ready to give up, the group continued on. Shortly after they reached 20,000 feet (by Parker's altimeter reading), Browne topped a small rise. He recalled:

> I was struck by the full fury of the storm. The breath was driven from my body and I held to my axe with stooped shoulders to stand against the gale; I couldn't go ahead. As I brushed the frost from my glasses and squinted upward through the stinging snow I saw a sight that

> will haunt me to my dying day. The slope above me was no longer steep . . . we were close to the top!

Browne returned to the others and explained it was impossible to walk into the gale above. They agreed it would be suicide to try. Only a few hundred vertical feet from the mountain's top, the three men were forced to retreat. The descent to high camp took two hours, and the team finally reached the safety of their tent at 7:35 P.M. after what Browne called "as cruel a day as I trust I will ever experience."

Stormy weather wasn't the only cruelty the climbers faced. Pemmican, a Native American food consisting of dried meat and melted fat that was popular with explorers, had proved inedible above 15,000 feet. As Browne explained:

> In both our 16,000 and 16,615 foot camps we had tried to eat cooked pemmican without success. We were able to choke down a few mouthfuls of this food, but we were at last forced to realize that our stomachs could not handle the amount of fat it contained. . . . We were now living, as in fact we had been living since leaving our 15,000 foot camp, on tea, sugar, hardtack, and raisins. Our chocolate was finished. We had lost ten days' rations in useless pemmican!

(Medical studies have since demonstrated that fatty foods indeed become difficult, if not impossible, to digest at high altitudes.) The climbers could count on no more than four days' rations. Time had nearly run out.

Following a rest day, the group began its final attempt. Leaving camp at 3:00 A.M., Parker, Browne, and La Voy began their race against yet another dark storm front moving in from the south. By 7:30, they'd reached 19,300 feet. But already the clouds were wrapping the team in wind-driven sheets of snow.

The trio endured the storm for as long as possible. After an

COURTESY OF THE ALASKA STATE LIBRARY, EARLY PRINTS, 01-3441

BELMORE BROWNE MADE THREE ATTEMPTS TO REACH MCKINLEY'S SUMMIT. HE, HERSCHEL PARKER, AND MERL LA VOY NEARLY SUCCEEDED IN 1912, BUT WERE STOPPED BY A STORM.

hour, they had no choice but to give up, or risk losing their lives. According to Browne's account:

> When we had fought the blizzard to the limit of our endurance we turned and without a word stumbled downward. I remember only a feeling of weakness and dumb despair. . . . We reached camp at 3:00 P.M. and after some hot tea we felt a wild longing to leave the desolate spot.

They began their descent, and two days later the three climbers rejoined Aten back at base camp.

On July 6, they witnessed an avalanche like no other they'd seen. A deep rumbling came from the Alaska Range and the earth around them began to roll, moving huge boulders several feet. A few minutes later, the entire western flank of Mount Brooks—

located about ten miles from the camp—began to avalanche, plunging down the mountain like a gigantic wave. That wave tumbled thousands of feet onto the glaciers below, filling the range with a thunderous roar and creating a giant white cloud that Browne estimated to be up to 4,000 feet high:

> We knew that the cloud was advancing at a rate close to sixty miles an hour and that we did not have much time to spare. But with boulders to hold the bottom and tautened guy-ropes, we made the tent as solid as possible and got inside before the cloud struck us. The tent held fast, but after the 'wullies' passed, the ground was spangled with ice-dust that only a few minutes before had formed the icy covering of a peak ten miles away!

Months later, the climbers learned that the earthquake causing the immense avalanche and snow cloud had been related to Mount Katmai's earlier eruption.

Not all of the earthquake's effects were noticed by members of the Parker-Browne party, however. Unknown to them, the quake had made some major changes in the route they'd nearly followed to McKinley's summit—changes that would be discovered by the Hudson Stuck Expedition in 1913. It had torn large sections of Karstens Ridge apart, ripping off huge chunks of ice and bedrock and turning the slope into a jumble of ice blocks. Had members of the Parker-Browne party been descending the ridge when the ground shook, in all likelihood they would have been killed.

Ironically, the pemmican diet and stormy weather that hindered the climbers' attempt on McKinley's summit may also have saved their lives by driving them off the mountain before the earthquake struck.

MAGAZINE SECTION

The New York Times.

MAGAZINE SECTION

FIRST ACCOUNT OF CONQUERING MT. McKINLEY

Thomas Lloyd, Leader of the Successful Expedition, Tells How He and His Comrades Planted the Stars and Stripes on the Heretofore Baffling Peak, the Highest Point on the American Continent

DRAMATIC STORY OF THOMAS LLOY

COURTESY OF THE ALASKA STATE LIBRARY, WICKERSHAM COLLECTION, PCA277-18-43

ON JUNE 5, 1910, THE *NEW YORK TIMES MAGAZINE* REPRINTED THE ACCOUNT OF THE SOURDOUGH'S SUCCESSFUL ASCENT OF MOUNT MCKINLEY ON APRIL 3, WRITTEN BY W. F. THOMPSON, EDITOR OF THE *FAIRBANKS DAILY NEWS-MINER*.

Chapter Three

The Sourdough Expedition, 1910

Choosing the most significant mountaineering accomplishment in Alaska's climbing history is an imposing, if not impossible, task.

As Valdez physician and climber Andy Embick once explained, "There are just so many categories to consider. Are you talking about big-wall climbs? First ascents? Solo ascents? Winter climbs? Comparing those different kinds of climbs is like comparing apples and oranges. It just can't be done."

Perhaps. But, believing it would be fun–and educational–to try, I conducted an informal and quite unscientific telephone poll of approximately twenty veteran Alaska mountaineers to see if those most devoted to climbing and exploring Alaska's high places could reach some consensus. I asked participants to name the mountaineering feat(s) they considered to be the most significant or noteworthy, with no limit on the number and types of choices.[1]

The variety of responses was enormous. More than thirty expeditions received mention. Some, such as the first winter ascent of Mount McKinley by Art Davidson, Ray Genet, and Dave Johnston in 1967, are well-publicized mountaineering masterpieces. Others, such as John Waterman's five-month solo of Mount Hunter in 1978, have received little public attention but are considered classics within the mountaineering community. From the many opinions offered, one expedition stood out from all the rest: the Sourdough Expedition of 1910.[2] A handful of other climbs received as much mention, but none was so enthusiastically endorsed. The Sourdoughs were the first or second choice of about a third of all those polled.

Steve Davis's response was typical of Sourdough supporters. "It's phenomenal, what they did," said Davis, an Anchorage-based marine fisheries biologist and mountaineer, who has served several years on the American Alpine Club's board of directors. "The Sourdoughs pulled off one of the best pioneering efforts ever. Their ascent (from 11,000 feet to the summit of McKinley's 19,470-foot North Peak) was the equivalent of an alpine-style climb; they did it so quickly. And carrying a huge spruce pole, no less."

Former McKinley guide Jim Hale added, "For those guys to reach the top with homemade equipment and so little climbing experience, while hauling a spruce pole, is just incredible. It's superhuman by today's standards. Those guys had to be tough as nails."

More than any other group of climbers, past or present, the Sourdoughs seem to symbolize the pioneering spirit and adventurous nature of what is often called the Alaskan mystique. Over the past century, their ascent has become the stuff of legend, and rightly so. This group of four gold miners challenged North America's highest peak with the most rudimentary gear and no technical climbing experience, simply to disprove explorer Frederick Cook's claim of reaching the mountain's summit in 1906 and to demonstrate that Alaskans could outdo the exploits–whether real or imagined–of any "Easterners."

That they succeeded in a brazen style uniquely their own delights Todd Miner, who calls their ascent a "climbing masterpiece." "To me, one of the most appealing aspects of the expedition is that it was a bunch of locals doing it," said Miner, a mountaineer who for several years coordinated the University of Alaska-Anchorage's Alaska Wilderness Studies Program. "It's a classic case of Alaskans showing Outsiders how it's done."

The expedition reached its literal high point on April 3, 1910, when Sourdoughs Billy Taylor and Pete Anderson reached the top of McKinley's 19,470-foot North Peak, widely recognized as a more difficult ascent than the higher–and ultimately more prestigious–20,320-foot South Peak. The Sourdoughs' reason for choosing the North Peak seemed quite logical at the time; the miners hoped that the fourteen-foot spruce pole, complete with a six-by-twelve-foot American flag they'd lugged up McKinley, would be seen from Kantishna, the mining community north of the mountain, and serve as visible proof of their conquest.

Taylor and Anderson made their summit push from 11,000 feet. Hauling their flagpole, they climbed more than 8,000 vertical feet and then descended to camp in eighteen hours' time–an outstanding feat by any mountaineering standard. (By comparison, most present-day McKinley expeditions climb no more than 3,000 to 4,000 vertical feet on summit day, which typically lasts ten to fifteen hours.) Yet the Sourdoughs' final incredible ascent is merely one chapter in an altogether remarkable story that for many years was steeped in controversy and, as historian Terrence Cole notes, "is still shrouded in mystery."

As seems to be the case with so many legendary Alaskan adventures, the Sourdough Expedition began with some barroom braggadocio. Or so the story goes. The expedition's leader and instigator was Tom Lloyd, a Welshman and former Utah sheriff who came to Alaska during the Klondike gold rush, eventually settling in the Kantishna Hills north of Mount McKinley. In the fall of 1909, Lloyd and several other patrons of a Fairbanks bar joined in a discussion that focused on Frederick Cook's claim that he'd reached McKinley's summit in 1906. As the *Fairbanks Daily Times* noted in 1909, "Ever since Dr. Cook described his ascent of Mount McKinley, Alaskans have been suspicious of the accuracy of this explorer."[3] Although Cook's account was later demonstrated to be a hoax, in 1909 there was still no definitive proof that he'd lied.

According to Lloyd's official account of the Sourdough Expedition, which appeared in the *New York Times Magazine* on June 5, 1910, "[Bar owner] Bill McPhee and me were talking one day of the possibility of getting to the summit of Mount McKinley and I said I thought if anyone could make the climb there were several pioneers of my acquaintance who could. Bill said he didn't believe that any living man could make the ascent."[4]

McPhee argued that the fifty-year-old Lloyd was too old and overweight for such an undertaking, to which the miner responded that "for two cents" he'd show it could be done. To call Lloyd's bluff, McPhee offered to pay $500 to anyone who would climb McKinley and "prove whether that fellow Cook made the climb or not."

After two other businessmen agreed to put up $500 each, Lloyd accepted the challenge. The proposed expedition was big news in Fairbanks, and before long it made local headlines. In his official account, Lloyd admitted, "Of course, after the papers got hold of the story we hated the idea of ever coming back here defeated."

A seven-member party left Fairbanks in December 1909, accompanied by four horses, a mule, and a dog team. Their send-off included an editorial in the *Fairbanks Daily Times*, which promised, "Our boys will succeed . . . and they'll show up Dr. Cook and the other 'Outside' doctors and expeditions."

Original team members included Tom Lloyd, Billy Taylor, Pete Anderson, Charles McGonagall, C. E. Davidson, Bob Horne, and a person identified as W. Lloyd. But the latter three men quit before the actual climbing began, following a dispute between Tom Lloyd and Davidson, a talented surveyor/photographer whose role with the expedition, according to Cole, was "to map the route and keep track of elevations."

In his account of the Sourdough Expedition, Terris Moore writes that Lloyd antagonized Davidson after the first of the team's mountain camps had been established, further noting that one report mentions a fistfight. After that confrontation, Davidson departed for Fairbanks accompanied by Horne and W. Lloyd. The expedition was left with four members, all miners from the Kantishna District: Taylor was Lloyd's mining partner; McGonagall and Anderson each had worked several years for the two property owners.

The Sourdoughs spent most of February establishing a series of camps in the lowlands and foothills on the north side of McKinley. By the end of the month, they'd set up their mountain base of operations near the mouth of Cache Creek at an elevation of about 2,900 feet, which they called the Willows Camp.

On March 1, the team began "prospecting for the big climb," Lloyd wrote in his expedition diary. "Anderson and McGonagall examined the [Muldrow] glacier today. We call it the 'Wall Street Glacier,' being enclosed by exceedingly high walls on each side." Three days later, they set up their first glacier camp. Lloyd, who'd lost the barometer loaned him by Davidson, estimated the camp's elevation at 9,000 to 10,000 feet, but it was probably much lower. Team members then descended and spent the next several days cutting firewood and hauling it up the glacier, along with a wood-burning stove.

Traversing the Muldrow proved to be quite intimidating. As Lloyd explained in his diary:

> For the first four or five miles there are no crevasses in sight, as they have been blown full of snow, but the next eight miles are terrible for crevasses. You can look down in them for distances stretching from 100 feet to Hades or China. Look down one of them and you never will forget it. . . . Most of them appear to be bottomless. These are not good things to look at.

Despite the danger of a crevasse fall, the climbers traveled unroped, a practice most contemporary McKinley mountaineers would consider foolhardy. There's no way to know whether the Sourdoughs' decision was made in ignorance or disdain for such protection. Years later, when asked why the team chose not to use climbing ropes, Taylor simply answered, "Didn't need them."[5] Such an attitude seems to reflect the Sourdoughs' style. With the notable exception of their fourteen-foot flagpole, they chose to travel light.

The team had "less 'junk' with them than an Eastern excursion party would take along for a one-day's outing in the hills," wrote W. F. Thompson, editor of the *Fairbanks Daily News-Miner*, who prepared Lloyd's story for publication in the *New York Times*. The Sourdoughs' climbing gear consisted of only the bare essentials: snowshoes; homemade crampons, which they called "creepers"; and crude ice axes, which Lloyd described as "long poles with double hooks on one end–hooks made of steel–and a sharp steel point on the other end." Their high-altitude food supplies included bacon, beans, flour, sugar, dried fruits, butter, coffee, hot chocolate, and caribou meat. To endure the subzero cold, they simply wore bib overalls, long underwear, shirts, parkas, mittens, shoepacs (insulated rubber boots), and Indian moccasins. (The moccasins that the pioneer McKinley climbers wore were like Eskimo mukluks: tall, above-the-calf footwear, dry-tanned, with a moose-hide sole and caribou-skin uppers. Worn with insoles and at least three pairs of wool socks, they were reportedly very warm and provided plenty of support.)[6]

Even their reading material was limited. The climbers brought only one magazine, which they read from end to end. "I don't remember the name of the magazine," Lloyd later commented, "but in our estimation it is the best magazine published in the world."

Other essentials included wooden stakes for trail marking and poles for crevasse crossings. The poles were placed across crevasses too wide to jump; the men then piled snow between the poles, which hardened and froze, creating a bridge over which the climbers could travel on snowshoes.

The team reached the site of its third and final camp on March 17, at the head of the Muldrow Glacier. Lloyd estimated the elevation at "not less than 15,000 feet," though later McKinley explorers determined the camp's altitude could have been no higher than 11,000 feet. The climbers spent the next several days digging a protective tunnel into the snow, relaying supplies from lower camps, cutting steps into the ice along what is now called Karstens Ridge, and enduring stormy weather.

On April 1, the Sourdoughs made their first summit attempt. But they were forced by stormy weather to turn back. Two days later, they tried again. Outfitted with a bag of doughnuts, three thermos bottles of hot chocolate (and caribou meat, according to some accounts), and their fourteen-foot spruce pole, Taylor, Anderson, and McGonagall headed for the summit at 3:00 A.M. Lloyd apparently had moved down to the Willows Camp; exactly why isn't clear, but he may have been suffering from altitude sickness. Unroped, without the benefit of any climbing aid other than their crude homemade crampons and ice axes, the three climbers ascended Karstens Ridge, crossed the Grand Basin–later to be named the Harper Glacier–and headed up a steep couloir now known as the Sourdough Gully.

A few hundred feet below the summit, McGonagall stopped. Years later, in a conversation with alpine historian Francis Farquhar, he explained, "No, I didn't go clear to the top–why should I? I'd finished my turn carrying the pole before we got there. Taylor and Pete finished the job–I sat down and rested, then went back to camp." Grant Pearson suggests otherwise in his book *My Life of High Adventure*, claiming that McGonagall fell victim to altitude sickness.[7]

Taylor and Anderson continued on, however, still hauling their spruce pole. And sometime late in the afternoon, they concluded their unprecedented ascent by standing atop the North Peak's summit. Twenty-seven years later, in an interview eventually published in *The American Alpine Journal*, Taylor recalled that he and Anderson spent two and a half hours on top of the mountain, though the temperature reached as low as −30°F that day. "It was colder than hell," he reported. "Mitts and everything was all ice."

Before descending back to camp, the Sourdoughs planted their pole, complete with American flag. Said Taylor, "We . . . built a pyramid of [rocks] about fifteen inches high and we dug down in the ice so the pole had a support of about thirty inches and was held by four guy lines–just cotton ropes. We fastened the guy lines to little spurs of rock." Though they'd planned to leave their flagpole at the summit, the climbers were forced to plant it on the highest available rock outcropping, located a few hundred feet below the top.

Taylor and Anderson returned to the high camp late that night, completing their climb in eighteen hours. The next day, all mem-

COURTESY OF NATIONAL PARK SERVICES, DENALI NATIONAL PARK & PRESERVE, DENA 1963

MEMBERS OF THE SOURDOUGH EXPEDITION. FROM LEFT TO RIGHT: CHARLES MCGONAGALL, THOMAS LLOYD, PETE ANDERSON, AND BILLY TAYLOR.

bers of the party were reunited at the Willows Camp. No attempt to climb the South Peak was made.

Their mission accomplished, Taylor, Anderson, and McGonagall returned to Kantishna. Lloyd, meanwhile, traveled to Fairbanks with news of the history-making ascent. Unfortunately, the Sourdough Expedition's team leader decided to mix fantasy with fact, and the team's true feat was transformed into an Alaskan tall tale. Returning to a hero's welcome on April 11, Lloyd proclaimed that the entire party had reached the summits of both the North and South peaks. Furthermore, they'd found no evidence to substantiate Cook's claims.

Word of the team's success quickly spread. On April 12, the *Fairbanks Daily Times* published an account of the historic climb, and the story quickly made headlines around the country.

According to historian Cole, "Congratulations poured in, including a telegram from President William Howard Taft."

Not everyone took Lloyd's word at face value, however. On April 16, the *New York Times* ran a story in which naturalist/explorer Charles Sheldon challenged Lloyd's claims:

> It is clearly the duty of the press . . . not to encourage full credibility in the reports of the alleged ascent until the facts and details are authoritatively published. Only Tom Lloyd apparently brought out the report, the other members of the party having remained in the Kantishna District 150 miles away; so we haven't had their corroborative evidence.[8]

Despite such published doubts, the *New York Times* successfully bid for first rights to a detailed report of the climb. And on June 5, the newspaper devoted three pages of its Sunday magazine section to the Sourdough Expedition; the package included a story of the ascent written by W. F. Thompson plus Lloyd's own firsthand account, which featured entries from his daily record. A day later, the story ran in London's *Daily Telegraph.*

Even as Thompson was preparing his *New York Times* article, the challenges to Lloyd's account increased. Other evidence of the ascent was demanded, but photos taken during the expedition proved unsatisfactory. Lloyd felt enough pressure that he asked Taylor, Anderson, and McGonagall to repeat the climb and secure additional photos. In a little-known but fascinating adventure, the three climbers reascended McKinley in May. They reached Denali Pass (elevation about 18,200 feet) and took additional photographs of the mountain. Nearly forty years later, McGonagall recalled: "We didn't camp—we just kept going for three days—it was light enough and we were all skookum [an Indian word meaning strong or heroic]."[9] The photos resulting from the second climb remain one of the Sourdough Expedition's many mysteries, because apparently they were never published.

With no solid proof to back up Lloyd's boasts, skepticism continued to build, such doubts being reinforced in part by the Sourdough leader's age and overweight condition; according to Taylor, Lloyd was "awful fat." Before long, the Sourdoughs were looked on no more favorably than Cook, the man they'd hoped to discredit. According to Cole:

> The contradictions in [Lloyd's] story and the fact that he supposedly admitted in private to some of his friends that he had not climbed the mountain himself, eventually discredited the entire expedition. Soon the Sourdoughs and their flagpole were regarded as just one more fascinating frontier tale, about as believable as an exploit of Paul Bunyan.

Back in Kantishna, the other Sourdough team members were unaware that Lloyd's false claims had caused their mountaineering feat to fall into disrepute. When interviewed in 1937, Taylor said, "He [Lloyd] was the head of the party and we never dreamed he wouldn't give a straight story. I wish to God we hadda been there. . . . We didn't get out till June and then they didn't believe any of us had climbed it."

Taylor also said that he didn't give prior approval to Lloyd's account of the climb that appeared in the *New York Times*. Yet on June 11, each of the Sourdoughs signed a notarized statement that "a party of four in number known as the Lloyd party" had reached the North Peak at 3:25 P.M. on April 3, 1910. Whether they knew in advance of Lloyd's fictitious account, or chose to go along with his claims because of some misplaced loyalty, none of the Sourdoughs publicly challenged their leader's story until years later.

(There's an interesting historical side note to the Sourdough Expedition. At least partly because of embarrassment about its role in the promotion of Lloyd's story, the *Fairbanks Daily Times* organized its own McKinley expedition in 1912. Led by Ralph Cairns, the newspaper's telegraph editor, the party reached McKinley's base in late February. The climbers failed to find McGonagall Pass, which provides the easiest access to the Muldrow Glacier, and instead set up base camp on the Peters Glacier, following a similar route to that taken by Wickersham in 1903. Like the Wickersham party, the Cairns Expedition was turned back at about 10,000 feet by apparently unclimbable ice walls. On April 10, 1912, the *Times* ran a front-page story reporting the team's failure.)

A final blow to the Sourdoughs' believability was struck in 1912, when Belmore Browne and Herschel Parker reported that they saw no evidence of the fourteen-foot flagpole during their attempt to climb McKinley. Because Browne and Parker carefully documented their own ascent, great credibility was given to their point of view. In his report of the 1912 climb, Browne wrote:

> On our journey up the glacier from below we had begun to study the North Peak. . . . Every rock and snow slope of that approach had come into the field of our powerful binoculars. We not only saw no sign of the flagpole, but it is our concerted opinion that the northern peak is more inaccessible than its higher southern sister.[10]

Though Browne intended only to disprove the Sourdoughs' claims, he ultimately paid them a great compliment by noting the greater difficulty faced in climbing the North Peak. Parker, meanwhile, was quoted as saying, "Dr. Cook didn't have anything on the Lloyd party when it comes to fabrications." Case closed. Or so it seemed at the time. The Sourdough story became generally accepted as nothing more than an Alaskan tale, until the following year.

In 1913, after a decade of unsuccessful attempts to reach the pinnacle of North America, an expedition led by Episcopal missionary Hudson Stuck placed all four of its members on McKinley's 20,320-foot summit. And en route to the top, they spotted the Sourdoughs' flagpole.

The climbers made their exciting discovery from the Grand Basin, located between the North and South Peaks. In his mountaineering classic, *The Ascent of Denali*, Stuck recalls:

> While we were resting . . . we fell to talking about the pioneer climbers of this mountain who claimed to have set a flagstaff near the summit of the North Peak–as to which feat a great deal of incredulity existed in Alaska for several reasons–and we renewed our determination that if the weather permitted when we had reached our goal and ascended the South Peak, we would climb the North Peak also to seek for traces of this earlier exploit on Denali. . . . All at once Walter [Harper] cried out: "I see the flagstaff!" Eagerly pointing to the rocky prominence nearest the summit–the summit itself covered with snow–he added: "I see it plainly!" [Harry] Karstens, looking where he pointed, saw it also and, whipping out the field glasses, one by one we all looked, and saw it distinctly standing out against the sky. With the naked eye I was never able to see it unmistakably, but through the glasses it stood out, sturdy and strong, one side covered with crusted snow. We were greatly rejoiced that we could carry down positive confirmation of this matter.[11]

When Stuck returned to Kantishna and told members of the Sourdough party about his team's sighting, "there was a feeling expressed that the climbing party of the previous summer [Belmore and Parker's group] must have seen it also and had suppressed mention of it." But Stuck concluded:

> There is no ground for such a damaging assumption. It would never be seen with the naked eye save by those who were intently searching

> for it. Professor Parker and Mr. Belmore Browne entertained the pretty general incredulity about the "Pioneer" ascent, perhaps too readily, certainly too confidently; but the men themselves must bear the chief blame for that. The writer and his party, knowing these men much better, have never [doubted] that some of them had accomplished what was claimed, and these details have been gone into for no other reason than that the honor may at least be given where honor is due.[12]

It's especially worth noting that Stuck's party was the only group ever to verify the flagpole's existence. The next expedition to climb the North Peak, two decades later in 1932, failed to find any evidence of the pole.

Except for the one chance sighting, the Sourdoughs' story might always have been regarded as a tall tale. But thanks to the efforts of the 1913 expedition, this group of skookum miners was finally and deservedly given credit for what Stuck called "a most extraordinary feat, unique—the writer has no hesitation in claiming—in all the annals of mountaineering."[13]

More than a century later, the Sourdoughs' achievement is still recognized as extraordinary. And certainly unique.

Courtesy of the Alaska State Library, Early Prints, 01-3192

HUDSON STUCK, AN EPISCOPAL MISSIONARY WHO CAME TO ALASKA IN 1904, ORGANIZED THE FIRST SUCCESSFUL ASCENT OF McKINLEY'S SOUTH PEAK IN 1913.

Chapter Four

Hudson Stuck and the First Ascent, 1913

The first decade of mountaineering on McKinley left North America's highest peak wrapped in a shroud of controversy. And confusion.

The triumphs asserted by Cook and Lloyd, once applauded, had been largely discredited. But not entirely. While Lloyd eventually backed off his claims, Cook continued to insist that he had indeed reached the top of the continent, despite the evidence to the contrary. And a substantial portion of the general public continued to believe him. As historian Terris Moore explains, there was so much uncertainty as to who'd really done what, McKinley became known as "The Mountain of Mystery."[1]

The confusion enveloping McKinley was admirably summed up in 1913 by Edwin Swift Balch, a prominent Philadelphia lawyer who later testified before a congressional committee investigating the mountain's controversies:

> Lloyd denies Cook. Browne denies Cook and Lloyd. Stuck denies Cook and Lloyd, and while not denying Browne, repeats over and over that Browne did not reach the top. There is a perfect epidemic of denials. So much so that it would be more accurate to nickname the peak Mount Denial instead of Mount Denali.[2]

By 1913, Cook, Lloyd, and Browne were familiar names within mountaineering circles. Not so Hudson Stuck. As he explains in the preface to his book *The Ascent of Denali*, Stuck was "no professed explorer, or climber or 'scientist,' but a missionary, and of these matters an amateur only."[3]

Stuck's amateur interest in mountaineering began in Great Britain. He later climbed in Colorado and the Canadian Rockies, but before his McKinley expedition, the greatest height he'd ever reached was the top of 14,410-foot Mount Rainier in Washington.

By his own admission, Stuck was concerned more with men than mountains. After arriving in Alaska in 1904, that concern became focused on Alaska's Natives, "a gentle and kindly race, now threatened with a wanton and senseless extermination." As archdeacon of the Yukon, the Episcopal missionary's work was centered in Alaska's Interior, where he traveled year-round visiting Native settlements. (Stuck's wintertime adventures are recorded in the book *Ten Thousand Miles with a Dog Sled*.)

In 1906, Stuck's passion for mountain climbing was rekindled by a view of McKinley from Pedro Dome, located near Fairbanks. As Stuck described it:

> Far to the southwest rose Mt. McKinley, or Tenali, as the Tanana natives call it . . . dominating the whole scene . . . as it shimmered in its pearly beauty and grew clearer and brighter as I gazed. What a glorious, broad, massive uplift that mountain is! The Mississippi is not so truly the father of waters as McKinley is the father of moun-

> tains. It is not a peak, but a region. I would rather climb that mountain than discover the richest goldmine in Alaska.

Five years after seeing that wondrous view, Stuck resolved to reach McKinley's summit, or at least make a serious attempt. The project was supported by his superior, Bishop Rowe of Alaska, who approved a leave of absence. That accomplished, Stuck went about recruiting a team. For companions, he picked three men experienced in dealing with ice and snow, though none was a mountaineer.

Stuck's first choice was Harry Karstens, who at age nineteen had been lured north from Illinois by the Klondike gold rush. In the sixteen years leading up to Stuck's expedition, Karstens had earned a reputation as a first-rate explorer, woodsman, and backcountry traveler. He'd mined for gold, delivered mail, and worked as a guide for noted naturalist and big-game hunter Charles Sheldon, who from 1906 to 1908 had studied the natural history of McKinley's northern foothills. (Those studies led to the creation of Mount McKinley National Park in 1917.) In 1906, Sheldon and Karstens had worked out a possible route to McKinley's summit—a route essentially the same as that later followed by the Sourdoughs in 1910. Afterward, Karstens had tried on several occasions to interest Sheldon in climbing the mountain. Sheldon, however, had declined. Finally given an opportunity to participate in such an expedition, Karstens enthusiastically accepted Stuck's invitation.

The expedition's other two climbing members were Robert Tatum and Walter Harper, both twenty-one years old. Tatum, from Tennessee, worked with Stuck at the Episcopal mission in Nenana, while Harper, part Native, had served as Stuck's attendant and interpreter. He was also the missionary's dog team driver in winter and boat engineer in summer. Stuck had high praise for Harper, who "took gleefully to high mountaineering, while his kindliness and invincible amiability endeared him to every member of the party."

Two Indian teenagers, known simply as Johnny and Esaias in Stuck's account, were non-climbing members of the expedition. Johnny kept watch over base camp during the ascent of McKinley; Esaias went as far as base, then drove one of the party's dog teams back to Nenana.

Stuck's plan called for supplies to be shipped into the McKinley region the summer preceding the climb and cached as close as possible to the mountain's base. Then, the following spring before breakup, dog teams would be used to transport food, fuel, and equipment onto the Muldrow Glacier.

Because no supplier of standard climbing gear could be found anywhere in the United States, Karstens arranged to have the team's ice axes and crampons made in Fairbanks. Another problem was footwear. Alpine boots sent through the mail proved useless, so team members ransacked Fairbanks for "boots of any kind in which three or four pairs of socks could be worn." They finally settled on rubber snow boots, to which leather soles were fastened. In all, the team spent $92 on six pairs of boots, money that Stuck considered entirely wasted because the climbers later discovered that moccasins used in combination with up to five pairs of socks "were the only practicable foot-gear." Although $92 may not seem like a big expense for a climbing expedition, Stuck didn't have many financial resources to fall back on. Food supplies, equipment, and incidentals eventually cost Stuck slightly less than $1,000, "a mere fraction of the cost of previous expeditions, it is true, but a matter of long scraping together for a missionary."

The team of six persons, two sleds, and fourteen dogs began its journey in mid-March, leaving Nenana on St. Patrick's Day, 1913. Among the supplies hauled in were seventy pounds of high-altitude food: meat, milk chocolate, Chinese tea compressed into tablets, rice, figs, and sugared almonds. Non-climbing gear included an eight- by ten-foot silk tent; three smaller silk tents for the high camps; a Yukon stove; pots, pans, and dishes; and a Primus stove for high elevations. Bedding consisted primarily of down quilts, favored over fur robes and blankets because of their lightness, warmth, and compressibility; however, two pairs of camel's hair blankets and a sleeping bag lined with down and camel's hair cloth were also taken. And Karstens brought along a twenty-five-pound wolf robe.

The group reached the gold camps at Kantishna on March 21, where more than a ton of supplies had been cached. (It was also here that the climbers acquired the moccasins to be used later on the mountain.) Supplies were then relayed some fifty miles cross-country to the base of the Alaska Range, using directions provided by members of the Sourdough Expedition.

The climbers put in a camp at timberline (elevation about 2,000 feet), where they cut wood to be used for fuel on the mountain, and then established a base camp at 4,000 feet on April 10. The team's top priority at this camp was to gather and preserve a sufficient meat supply for consumption on McKinley. Finding game was no problem; within a short time four caribou and a Dall sheep were killed. Not only did the animals provide meat; their hides were carried up the mountain for extra bedding layers.

The choicest portions of the meat were made into pemmican. Pemmican had contributed to the Parker-Browne Expedition's undoing in 1912, but Stuck's group apparently had less trouble digesting the fatty food, since he noted, "We never lost appetite for it or failed to enjoy and assimilate it."

When not preparing food or relaying loads of equipment and wood to the head of McGonagall Pass, which overlooks the Muldrow Glacier, team members had plenty to keep them busy at base camp. They adjusted snowshoes, fit crampons to moccasins, and tinkered with the party's scientific instruments, which included several barometers and thermometers.

On April 11, Stuck and Karstens got their first look at the Muldrow Glacier, "the road to the heart of the mountain," and as they viewed it, Stuck recalled, "Our spirits leaped up that at last we were entered upon our real task. . . . To both of us it had an infinite attractiveness, for it was the highway of desire." That highway was bounded by two steep walls, the right wall rising to the North Peak, the left eventually leading to their destination, the South Peak.

On April 15, the team finished ferrying its supplies to McGonagall Pass. Esaias returned to Nenana with several of the dogs, since two teams were no longer required. Three days later, a camp was established on the glacier. While moving up the Muldrow, the Stuck party sent three team members in an advance patrol to seek out and mark a safe route, while two others stayed with the remaining dog team.

The glacier's surface was a maze of crevasses, which made travel especially difficult for the dog team and sled. Though some fissures were mere surface cracks, others were wide, gaping chasms hundreds of feet deep with no visible bottom. Because so many crevasses were hidden by snow, members of the advance team roped themselves together and used a long pole to probe for hidden holes.

Above the first glacier camp, the six-dog team was divided into a couple of three-dog units, each pulling what Stuck described as a small Yukon sled. Even with the combination of dog- and manpower, transporting supplies and wood up the Muldrow became an exhausting, tedious grind. Temperatures varied greatly throughout the day. Stuck reported that the weather was often bitterly cold in the mornings, insufferably hot at noon, and then bitterly cold again at night.

During the traverse up the glacier, the party suffered a potentially disastrous loss when one of the caches caught fire. Smoking

COURTESY OF THE ARCHIVES OF THE EPISCOPAL CHURCH

AFTER ESTABLISHING THEIR BASE CAMP AT 4,000 FEET, MEMBERS OF THE STUCK EXPEDITION HUNTED GAME AND GATHERED A LARGE SUPPLY OF WOOD FOR THEIR ASCENT.

was the likely cause. While puffing on their pipes during a rest break, either Stuck or Karstens had apparently tossed away a still-lit match, which fell among the silk tents covering the cache. After the climbers left, the cache must have burst into flames. Lost in the fire was all of the expedition's sugar, powdered milk, baking soda, prunes, raisins and dried apples, and most of its tobacco, as well as a case of pilot bread, a sack of woolen socks and gloves, and a box of film.

Fortunately, all the high-altitude food had been spared. Still, Stuck admitted, "It was a great blow to us and involved considerable delay at a very unfortunate time. . . . Our carelessness had brought us nigh to the ruining of the whole expedition."

One day after the fire, the team established itself at the head of Muldrow Glacier, an elevation of about 11,500 feet. Then sled covers (for tent repair), old socks and mittens, and whatever food could be spared were retrieved from base camp, and the climbers got down to the task of repairing burnt clothing and tents.

Just beyond the expedition's 11,500-foot camp, the Muldrow came to an abrupt end. Above them rose a great icefall separating the lower and upper glaciers. From this point, the climbers would have to ascend the northeast ridge leading to the upper bowl. The dogs' usefulness ended here, so Johnny took them back to base camp on May 9, to await his teammates' return from the mountain.

Before leaving for the McKinley climb, the Stuck Expedition had read a magazine story on Parker and Browne's 1912 attempt. That story described the northeast ridge as a "steep but practicable snow slope" and included a photo of the ridge. To the Stuck party's surprise–and dismay–the ridge they faced offered almost no resemblance to the magazine description or the photograph. Though the upper third matched Browne's description, the remainder was split off by a sudden, sharp break in slope and everything below was a chaotic, jumbled mass of rock and ice blocks, many of them bigger than train cars.

After a few moments of confusion, the climbers solved the mystery before them; the ridge must have been shattered by the earthquake reported by Parker and Browne in 1912. Stuck said, "It was as though, as soon as the Parker-Browne party reached the foot of the mountain, the ladder by which they'd ascended and descended was broken up."

The quake's disturbance of the earth and ice had greatly increased the route's degree of difficulty. The same ridge that the Sourdoughs had climbed in less than a day while hauling a fourteen-foot pole, and that the Parker-Browne party had ascended in a few days while relaying supplies, would occupy the Stuck Expedition for a full three weeks, as team members laboriously carved a staircase up several miles–and 3,000 vertical feet–of shattered ice, rock, and snow.

Movement up the ridge was delayed by several days of whiteout, often mixed with high winds and heavy snows. Yet Stuck's team kept its humor, as he noted:

> The situation was not without its ludicrous side. Here were four men who had already passed through the long Alaskan winter, and now, when the rivers were breaking and the trees bursting into leaf, the flowers spangling every hillside, they were deliberately pushing themselves up into the winter still, with the long-expected summer but a day's march away.

While waiting out the storm, the team ran out of its final sugar reserves, which had been brought up from base camp following the cache fire. Deprived of sugar, team members soon began torturing themselves with sweet fantasies, until Karstens forcefully advised his partners to "forget it!" Still, Stuck admitted, "We all missed sugar sorely and continued to miss it until the end."

Later, while ascending the northeast ridge, the climbers suffered another significant food loss. As Stuck explained it, "a cold night killed the germ in the sour dough, and we were never again able to set up a fermentation in it." With the dough refusing to sour, and its baking powder supply lost in the fire, the team was left without bread, which the climbers missed nearly as much as the sugar.

Thanks to their roomy tent and large supply of wood, the team suffered few other discomforts. And though they often heard the thunder of nearby avalanches or the crash of discharges from the glacier's icefall, the party had placed its 11,500-foot camp in a site that was out of harm's way, so safety wasn't a continual concern.

As soon as the storm eased up, the climbers began their snail-like ascent. Steps carved into the ice and snow slope had to be made deep and wide enough so that they'd act as stable platforms while the men ferried heavy loads up the ridge. Off-and-on whiteout conditions constantly interrupted their work. Yet the hard, tedious effort and slow progress were balanced by the increasingly spectacular views. "From our perch on that ridge the lofty peaks and massive ridges rose on every side," Stuck reported. "We were within the hall of the mountain kings indeed; kings nameless here, in this multitude of lofty summits, but that elsewhere in the world would have each one his name and story."

After three weeks of camping at 11,500 feet and gradually carving their way upward, the team moved camp onto the ridge. Loaded down by heavy packs, they'd proceeded only a short distance before a storm drove them back down. The next day they tried again, but with only half the loads. And on May 25 the climbers completed their move, establishing a camp at 13,000 feet.

Above that camp, the ridge became steeper, more rugged, and increasingly chaotic. As expected, the deep cleavage separating the jumbled ice maze from the ridge above provided the most difficult and dangerous climbing. Stuck went so far as to call it the crux of the ascent. But on May 27, Karstens and Harper cleared that intimidating hurdle. "The way was clear to the top of the ridge now and that night our spirits were high," Stuck recalled, "and congratulations were showered upon the victorious pioneers."

By May 30, the party had established a camp at the pass that gives entrance to the upper glacier, then known as the Grand Basin. Across the glacier from the 15,000-foot campsite were the sheer, dark cliffs of the North Peak, while still high above on the left, barely visible, was the expedition's goal: the South Peak.

In his book, Stuck recommended that the pass be named for Professor Herschel Parker and the rock tower rising above it be named for Belmore Browne; he further suggested the northeast ridge be named after Karstens, whom he praised for "a brilliant piece of mountaineering" in leading the expedition through the jumbled chaos of ice. Parker Pass, Browne Tower, and Karstens Ridge are now three well-known landmarks on McKinley's Muldrow Glacier Route.

Once above the ice-jumbled ridge, the climbers knew from Browne and Parker's account that the most difficult portion of their ascent had been completed. Later climbers would agree with Stuck that an ascent of McKinley via the Muldrow Glacier Route is generally not so much a technical challenge as it is a test of endurance, strength, and good judgment. Yet, for the Stuck party, Karstens Ridge, in its shattered state, did offer "all the spice of sensation and danger that any man could desire."

Moving beyond Parker Pass, the team steadily and patiently worked its way upward while adjusting to decreased oxygen and increased cold. Nighttime temperatures within the Grand Basin ranged from a high of −10°F to a low of −21°F. Despite subzero temperatures, the climbers stayed plenty warm at night. They slept on top of sheep and caribou skins that provided excellent insulation and covered themselves with down quilts, camel's hair blankets, and Karstens's wolf robe.

A more difficult adjustment was the thin air. Stuck noted:

> The fatigue of packing in that thin atmosphere with the sun's rays reflected from ice and snow everywhere was most exhausting. . . . Those who have carried a pack only on the lower levels cannot conceive how enormously greater the labor is at these heights. . . . Put a forty-pound pack on a man's back, with the knowledge that tomorrow he must go down for another, and you have mountaineering in Alaska. In the ascent of this twenty-thousand-foot mountain every member of the party climbed at least sixty thousand feet [while relaying loads]. It is this going down and doing it all over again that is the heartbreaking part of climbing.

At altitudes above 15,000 feet, Stuck in particular became seriously bothered by the altitude. Though for several days he didn't experience any nausea, headaches, or other symptoms of high-altitude sickness, the fifty-year-old archdeacon admittedly suffered a severe shortness of breath. Even slight exertion would be followed by a spell of panting. Rest stops were required every dozen or so steps. In hopes of improving his wind, Stuck finally gave up his pipe-smoking habit while high on the mountain. But not even that sacrifice was enough. Eventually he was forced to reduce his load to a few scientific instruments; his other gear was distributed among Karstens, Harper, and Tatum.

The climbers established a series of camps while crossing the Grand Basin during the first week of June. It was during this traverse that Harper spotted the flagpole left in 1910 by the Sourdoughs. Finally, on June 6, they set up the team's high camp, at 18,000 feet. The four men had put themselves in a superb position to reach McKinley's summit. They sat less than 2,500 vertical feet from the mountaintop—a single day's climb—with a full two weeks' supply of food and fuel. If necessary, their provisions could be stretched as long as three weeks. Given that cushion, the team was prepared to wait several days, if necessary. But the weather remained clear and calm, ideal for a summit attempt.

On the night of June 6, Walter Harper cooked up a special presummit meal: using the unfermented sourdough, he made noodles for a stew. According to Stuck, Harper "made the noodles too large and did not cook them enough, and they wrought internal havoc upon those who partook of them. Three of the four of us were unwell all night. . . . Walter alone was at ease, with digestive and somnolent capabilities proof against any invasion."

Stuck was certainly correct in his observation that digestion is more delicate and more easily disturbed at high altitudes than at lower elevations. But he may have been wrong in blaming Harper's noodles for the climbers' discomfort; pemmican was a much more likely cause of the climbers' intestinal woes, despite Stuck's belief that he and the others had no problems digesting the fat-rich food.

In his book *High Alaska*, climber Jonathan Waterman comments on the Stuck group's distress:

> By the time they were at their eighteen-thousand-foot camp, [members of Stuck's party] had spent forty-eight days on the mountain. They should have been superbly acclimatized. However, according to Stuck's [account], everyone but Harper was turning sleeplessly in his caribou and down. . . . It is likely that they suffered from acute mountain sickness, brought on by their diet of high fat and protein.[4]

June 7 dawned bright and cloudless, though windy. Unwilling to sacrifice such clear weather, the team prepared for a summit try despite the continued ills of Stuck, Tatum, and Karstens. In his diary, Karstens admitted:

> I had one of the most severe headaches. If it were not the final climb I should have stayed in camp but being . . . such a promising day I managed to pull through. I put Walter in lead and kept him there all day with never a change. I took second place on the rope so I could direct Walter.[5]

The team left its high camp at about 5:00 A.M., carrying only lunch food and instruments to be used for a variety of summit measurements. Though outfitted in full winter hand- and footgear, the climbers' toes and fingers were quickly numbed by subzero temperatures and a steady breeze. (Stuck's footgear consisted of three pairs of heavy woolen socks, two pairs of camel's hair socks, and one pair of thick felt socks, all stuffed within his moccasins.)

Unwilling to sacrifice any part of their bodies to frostbite, the climbers paid close attention to their extremities. The slightest hint that anyone's hands or feet were beginning to freeze would have prompted the team's return to high camp. Fortunately no such difficult decision had to be made. Still, by late morning, the harsh conditions had taken a heavy toll on the men's energy and enthusiasm. Doubts began to creep in. Would they be able to endure the cold and wind long enough to reach the summit?

A round of hot tea during the team's lunch break provided needed warmth and also helped boost sagging spirits. With renewed confidence and determination, the party of four resumed its upward journey, and by 1:30 P.M. the climbers found themselves on the threshold of a mountaineering dream: McKinley's top stood just a few yards away.

Harper, who'd been in the lead all day, was the first to scramble onto the summit. Karstens and Tatum were right behind, but Stuck barely dragged himself to the top. By his own account:

> The last man on the rope, in his enthusiasm and excitement somewhat overpassing his narrow wind margin, had almost to be hauled up the last few feet and fell unconscious for a moment upon the floor of the little snow basin that occupies the top of the mountain. This, then, is the actual summit, a little crater-like basin, sixty or sixty-five feet long and twenty to twenty-five feet wide.

As soon as the climbers had regained their breath, they shook hands, said a prayer of thanks, and set up a small tent, in which a series of instrument readings were taken, using the party's aneroid and mercury barometers and the boiling-point, alcohol minimum-temperature, and mercury thermometers. Several summit photos were also taken, but most proved to be greatly disappointing.

Only after the scientific work was completed did the climbers allow themselves to enjoy the surrounding landscape. Among the jewels to be seen was 17,400-foot Mount Foraker, known also as "Sultana," "Denali's wife." But most impressive to Stuck were views to the east and south, where an "infinite tangle of mountain ranges filled the whole scene, until gray sky, gray mountain and gray sea merged in the ultimate distance. . . . The beautiful crescent curve of the whole Alaska Range exhibited itself from Denali to the sea."

Understanding that only once in their lifetime would they be privileged to witness such extraordinary sights, the climbers stayed on top as long as possible. But after one and a half hours on the top, they finally were forced to yield to the "miserable limitations of the flesh." At two minutes past 3:00, the team began its descent.

The climbers reached their 18,000-foot camp at about 5:00 P.M., ending a twelve-hour summit day. That night in his diary, Stuck wrote, "I remember no day in my life so full of toil, distress and exhaustion, and yet so full of happiness and keen gratification."

On June 8, after a morning prayer, the climbers departed high camp at 9:30 A.M. Before leaving the Grand Basin, they cached the minimum-temperature thermometer and an empty can, in which they placed a record of their ascent. At Stuck's request, that upper basin would be later renamed Harper Glacier to honor Walter Harper, the first person to stand on McKinley's summit.

After the basin came the most difficult avenue of descent, the northeast ridge. Nearly two feet of snow had fallen since the team last traveled along the ridge, and the steps they'd previously carved were wiped out, making it necessary to shovel out the old ones or, in some places, make new ones.

The climbers reached their upper Muldrow camp at 9:30 P.M. after twelve hours of travel, and resumed their descent the following morning. Tied together on one rope, the four teammates proceeded down the heavily crevassed glacier, which presented a much different face than it had in May. The lower stretch of the Muldrow proved to be a rather dirty sight in summer; streams of murky water flowed over melting and discolored ice and the snow was darkened by abundant rock debris.

The pass leading down from the glacier was free of snow and presented the climbers with their first view of vegetation in several weeks. As Stuck described it:

> The first thing that struck our eyes . . . was a brilliant trailing purple moss flower of such gorgeous color that we all exclaimed at its beauty. . . . If a man would know to the utmost the charm of flowers, let him exile himself among the snows of a lofty mountain during fifty days of spring and come down into the first full flush of summer.

A less pleasant discovery was the abundance of mosquitoes, which provided an enthusiastic welcoming committee. Expecting to have finished its expedition a month earlier, the climbers hadn't brought any insect repellent; now they had to face the prospect of a fifty- to sixty-mile cross-country trek, "subject all the while to the assaults of venomous insects." While extremely uncomfortable because of the mosquitoes, their main concern was for Johnny, the Indian teenager who'd been assigned to base camp with the dogs. But Johnny and the dogs proved to be in fine shape, thus removing the team's last anxiety. Johnny had saved the team a special treat–his own ration of sugar and milk–knowing that theirs had been destroyed in the fire. The four weary climbers experienced the pleasure of these luxuries with their coffee for the first time in almost two months.

The team devoted June 9 to rest and contentment before resuming their return journey. They had plenty of reason to be contented, for as Stuck noted, "Not a single mishap had occurred to mar the complete success of our undertaking–not a single injury of any sort to any one, not an illness [except, perhaps, for a short bout with altitude sickness]. All five of us were in perfect health."

On June 10, the team departed from base camp, leaving a tent with food and other unneeded items cached inside it. After some difficult stream crossings, they made a short stopover in the Kantishna mining district, then floated down the Kantishna, Tanana, and Yukon Rivers. On June 20, the team reached Tanana, thus ending an historic journey begun three months and four days earlier.

Based on his "McKinley" scientific studies, Stuck later determined the mountain's height to be 20,700 feet, about 400 feet higher than the now-accepted figure. He also returned from McKinley convinced that no other route would be found to the top.

One other issue is worthy of mention: Stuck's fanatical opposition to the use of "McKinley" as the name of the mountain. In the preface to his 1914 book, the archdeacon made an eloquent plea for "the restoration to the greatest mountain in North America of its immemorial native name." In Stuck's view, the use of "McKinley" was an affront to both the mountain and Alaska's Native people:

> There is, to the author's mind, a certain ruthless arrogance that grows more offensive to him as the years pass by, in the temper that comes to a "new" land and contemptuously ignores the native names of conspicuous natural objects, almost always appropriate and significant, and overlays them with names that are, commonly, neither the one nor the other.

Stuck felt confident that:

> Should the reader ever be privileged . . . [to] see these mountains revealed as the clouds of a passing snowstorm [are] swept away, he would be overwhelmed by the majesty of the scene and at the same time deeply moved with the appropriateness of the simple native names; for simplicity is always a quality of true majesty.

Though the continent's greatest mountain was known by several Native names, the one preferred by Stuck was Denali:

> It is probably true of every great mountain that it bears diverse native names as one tribe or another, on this side or on that of its mighty bulk, speaks of it. But the area in which, and the people by whom, this mountain is known as Denali, preponderate so greatly as to leave no question which native name it should bear.

In concluding his plea, Stuck addressed "the learned societies of the world, the geographical societies, the ethnological societies" that opposed the replacement of Native names. "To them," he noted, "the writer confidently appeals."

Stuck's confidence was, however, misplaced. Nearly a century after his book's publication, the mountain officially remains "McKinley," despite the fact that a large majority of Alaskans would prefer to have the peak renamed "Denali" (and a large and growing number of the state's residents call it by that name.)

The issue has flared several times since 1975, when the Alaska legislature issued a joint resolution requesting Congress to change the peak and surrounding national park's names from "McKinley" to "Denali." Congress, being the political body that it is, forged a compromise: Mount McKinley National Park, established in 1917, became "Denali National Park and Preserve" in 1980 (when the park also expanded), but the mountain remained "McKinley."

For more than three decades since then, Alaska's congressional delegates have repeatedly tried to get legislation passed that would restore the mountain's Native name, most recently in 2012, when US Sen. Lisa Murkowski introduced a bill that would officially change Mount McKinley to Mount Denali (the fate of that legislation is uncertain as this revised edition goes to press). Elected representatives from William McKinley's home state of Ohio have so far successfully opposed such attempts, but it's unlikely Alaskans will let the controversy die.

Merl La Voy, Courtesy of the Farquhar Collection, Elmer E. Rasmuson Library, Univ. of Alaska Fairbanks

ALFRED LINDLEY AND HARRY LIEK,
FOR WHOM THE 1932 LINDLEY-LIEK EXPEDITION WAS NAMED,
STAND TOGETHER AFTER THEIR SUCCESSFUL ASCENT
OF MCKINLEY'S NORTH AND SOUTH PEAKS.

Chapter Five

The 1932 Expeditions: Carpé and Lindley-Liek

Following his return from Mount McKinley in 1913, Hudson Stuck predicted that it would be a long time before anyone would return to the mountain, figuring that "while yet such a peak is unclimbed, there is constant goading of mountaineering minds to its conquest; once its top has been reached, the incentive declines."[1]

His prediction was right on the mark. Interest in climbing North America's highest peak declined dramatically after the Stuck expedition's successful ascent. Although nine different teams had attempted to reach McKinley's summit between 1903 and 1913, following its conquest, nearly two decades passed before another party walked upon the mountain's slopes. In 1932, a relative flurry of activity arose, when two groups attempted ascents in what proved to be a milestone year for McKinley mountaineering.[2]

Allen Carpé, a thirty-eight-year-old research engineer, spearheaded the first scientific climb of McKinley that year. His high-altitude study of cosmic radiation was part of a much larger program that included investigations in several mountainous areas around the world. Widely respected for both his scientific and climbing expertise, Carpé had already participated in the first ascents of three major North American peaks: 15,300-foot Mount Fairweather and 16,550-foot Mount Bona in Alaska; and 19,850-foot Mount Logan in Canada, the continent's second-highest mountain. To help run the cosmic-ray study, he recruited Edward Beckwith, a consulting engineer and former instructor at the Massachusetts Institute of Technology. Team members Theodore Koven, Percy Olton, and Nicholas Spadavecchia would also play supporting roles.

The second expedition was organized by Erling Strom of Norway and Alfred Lindley of Minnesota, who hoped to make the first ascent of McKinley on skis. As if that weren't challenge enough, they also planned to attempt both the North and South Peaks. Joining Strom and Lindley were Mount McKinley National Park superintendent Harry Liek and park ranger Grant Pearson.

According to Pearson's account of the expedition, Strom first saw McKinley during a 1928 visit to Alaska. A professional ski instructor who operated schools in New York and Canada, he immediately felt an overpowering desire to ski it from top to bottom. Over the next three years, Strom tried recruiting numerous people for his proposed ski climb and descent but couldn't find any takers. One of those he approached was Lindley, a recent law school graduate.

When first told of Strom's dream in 1931, Lindley listened with "polite interest" but made no commitment. Months later, during a visit to Alaska with his father, the Minneapolis attorney got his own look at McKinley, and he too became stricken with summit fever. In short order, he contacted Strom, and the two men agreed to organize an expedition the following spring.

While still in Alaska, Lindley stopped at McKinley National Park headquarters to get information on the mountain and permission to climb it. The federal government assumed management control over Mount McKinley following the park's creation in 1917, but no attempts were made over the next fourteen years. The 1932 expeditions were the first to require National Park Service approval to climb McKinley.

During a discussion of the proposed ascent, Liek expressed interest in joining the expedition. He explained that if park officials participated in the expedition, their sled dog teams could be used to haul supplies, thus cutting down on expenses. Lindley and Strom agreed to Liek's proposed package deal, which eventually included Pearson as well, and the four-member ski party became known as the Lindley-Liek Expedition.

After learning of Liek's agreement with Strom and Lindley, Carpé requested similar dog-team support for his cosmic-ray study, figuring that any government agency willing to help a "purely sporting event" would also lend assistance to a scientific endeavor. His reasoning proved correct. Though it had no policies that specifically addressed such issues, the Park Service agreed to haul several hundred pounds of cosmic-ray equipment up the Muldrow Glacier and cache it at 11,000 feet. (Such free assistance did not, however, evolve into standard Park Service practice.)

Accompanied by two dog teams and three handlers, the four ski mountaineers began ascending the Muldrow in early April, several weeks ahead of Carpé's group. To aid their ascent, the skiers used climbing "skins," made of seal fur, attached to the bottoms of the skis with straps. Strom explained their function: "The fur lies flat when you slide your ski forward, but it roughs up, like stroking a cat the wrong way, if your ski starts to slip back. Acts like a brake. You take 'em off, of course, going down."

Though Strom, Lindley, and Liek each had considerable experience, Pearson had been on skis only once as an adult and that was while being pulled—and steered—by a dog team. His ski trials and tribulations are humorously detailed in his book *My Life of High Adventure*, which devotes three chapters to the Lindley-Liek Expedition. Anyone who's learned to ski as an adult can probably empathize with his difficulties. Pearson wrote:

> I got my feet lashed onto my five-foot boards with their skin bottoms and began to plod around the camp, feeling as awkward as a duck in mud. . . . I shambled up to the top [of a hill near camp] and took off the skins. Then I started down. To my surprise, I found I could keep my balance by leaning forward. The skis carried me at a good clip and when I reached the bottom, my ski tips kept right on aiming downhill with the result that I plunged face forward into the soft snow, so deep I figured I wouldn't get out till summer.

Later, he learned that going uphill could be just as difficult:

> At the foot of the camp we faced a steep climb; and while I was striving to put one ski ahead of the other, and watching carefully to see it didn't take off sideways on its own, the others got far ahead of me. I would step forward and my skis would slide back in the soft snow, skins or no skins, first one ski then the other. 'These things,' I thought, falling over backwards, 'are just a fad.'

With Strom's guidance, Pearson eventually learned enough about both uphill and downhill skiing to keep pace with his teammates during their traverse of the Muldrow. The expedition soon discovered that the glacier was not the smooth highway it appeared to be from a distance. Rather, it was more like an icy obstacle course, booby-trapped with deep crevasses hidden beneath snow. To avoid falling in the crevasses, the skiers roped up to each other while breaking trail. Using a ski pole, at each step the leader would probe the snow for crevasses. "What with this constant poking and prodding about, we must have looked as if we were out on Muldrow hunting for clams," Pearson commented.

Though the skiers often had difficulty finding safe bridges across crevasses, the dog teams had even a worse time of it. Once, while relaying loads up to a camp at 9,000 feet, Pearson watched as the front end of one team disappeared from sight. While dog handler John Rumohr held on to the sled's brake, Pearson carefully leaned over the crevasse's edge and found two dogs dangling over the black hole below. Quickly he hooked his ski pole into their harness and pulled the dogs to safety.

The next morning, again approaching the 9,000-foot camp, Rumohr's sled broke through another bridge, this time after he and the dogs had crossed safely. It took a half hour for three men to pull the sled out of the crevasse. As Pearson later commented, Rumohr "must have grown to hate that stretch of trail."

By mid-April, the team had set up its third camp at 11,000 feet, near the head of the Muldrow Glacier and about a mile from an immense, 4,000-foot-high icefall. Pearson gives his readers a sense of scale:

> You could stack four Empire State Buildings one on top of the other alongside that Harper Ice Fall, and after you got out of the last elevator you'd still have a long climb, unless you inadvertently took the express down, aboard an avalanche. Those avalanches came thundering down over the headwall almost every half hour, shaking the whole glacier and setting up a five-minute snowstorm of pulverized ice.

At the 11,000-foot camp, Strom, Liek, Lindley, and Pearson parted company with the dog teams and replaced their skis with crampons and ice axes. Leaving the Muldrow Glacier, they began the difficult ascent of Karstens Ridge, which presented the expedition's first serious climbing challenge. Roped to each other, Strom and Pearson led the way up the steep and narrow ridge, taking turns at chopping steps into the snow and ice. Despite their reliance on ice-climbing tools, the mountaineers still hauled along their skis, in hopes of using them above. Pearson recalled, "We must have looked like the world's most fanatical winter sportsmen, climbing those ice steps . . . just to go skiing."

By April 24, the Lindley-Liek Expedition had established its fourth camp, at 12,000 feet. Carpé's group, meanwhile, was making last-minute preparations for its trip into the mountains. The scientists would be traveling to the Muldrow in a most unconventional way: by air. Never before had anyone landed an airplane on a glacier.

For the historic flight to the mountain, Carpé hired the services of Joe Crosson, the head pilot of Alaska Airways. Edward Beckwith described Crosson in *The American Alpine Journal* in 1933 as "an Alaskan airman of long experience . . . unconcerned at the prospect of attempting to land on the untried slopes of McKinley."[3] Raised on a Kansas farm, Crosson had moved from California to Alaska in 1926, to work as a pilot for the Fairbanks Airplane Company. Over the next decade, he built a reputation as one of Alaska's top aviators and was widely known as the "mercy pilot," for his participation in several highly publicized search-and-rescue missions. He was also the first to make a commercial flight to Barrow, Alaska's northernmost settlement. Like nearly all of Alaska's earliest bush pilots, Crosson suffered numerous crash landings, but according to Jean Potter's *The Flying North*, only one of his passengers was injured in more than 8,000 hours of flying.[4]

Carpé, Beckwith, and Koven met Crosson at Nenana, a village located along the Tanana River, about 120 air miles northeast of McKinley. (The other two team members, Olton and Spadavecchia, would fly in later.) On April 25, crammed into the single-engine

Fairchild monoplane on skis with several hundred pounds of gear, they headed for the Muldrow.

Upon reaching the glacier, Crosson flew across it several times, carefully inspecting its surface. As far as he could tell, it appeared smooth for several miles. After a brief discussion with Carpé, the pilot made one final approach and landed on the glacier without any difficulty, delivering his passengers to the Muldrow at an elevation of about 6,000 feet as though it were a routine matter, not an aviation first. "[It] was about the best we had hoped for," Beckwith reported. "Carpé was delighted, and shook hands with Crosson, who took it much as a matter of course and lit a cigar before leaving the plane."

After passengers and gear had been unloaded, Crosson got back in the plane and gunned it up-glacier. Ever so slowly, it began lifting off the snow. The climbers waited to see or hear the plane fly overhead, figuring their pilot would naturally circle and fly back. Seeing and hearing nothing, the men concluded he must have crashed.

While Beckwith began shuttling gear to the team's first campsite, Carpé and Koven traveled up the glacier to check on Crosson. Finding no sign of the plane, they concluded he'd flown off without turning around. But a few hours later, the pilot came snowshoeing down the Muldrow. Calmly, matter-of-factly, Crosson explained that he'd been unable to rise over the nearby ridge and had been forced to make an emergency landing several miles up the glacier. Luckily he'd done so without damage to the plane or himself.

The next morning, pilot and climbers hiked back to the plane, whose skis were now ice-covered and frozen in the snow. With three men rocking the wings and Crosson revving the engine, they finally pulled the plane out.

Once more, Crosson prepared for takeoff. This time, accompanied by Beckwith, who was going to take care of some logistical tasks back in Nenana, he got sufficient height to clear the ridge, though his passenger later wrote, "We had a tough, long ride before leaving the ice, the skis jumping from one frozen ridge to the next, and I thought surely one would break."

About a week later, Beckwith returned to McKinley with the team's remaining members and supplies. This time, two planes were used to transport climbers and gear from Fairbanks, partly to split up the load but also to increase the margin of safety. If one of the pilots had to make a forced landing somewhere between Fairbanks and the Muldrow Glacier, the other would be able to mark his position for rescuers.

With pilots Crosson and Jerry Jones at the controls, Beckwith, Spadavecchia, and Olton were treated to yet another couple of "routine" glacier landings. Upon reaching the team's campsite, Beckwith found a note stating that Carpé and Koven had gone to the head of the glacier to establish a camp at 11,000 feet. Having previously discussed the possibility of an airdrop with Carpé, as a way of saving time and energy, Beckwith asked Crosson if such an aerial maneuver might be feasible. The pilot agreed to try, so they loaded five boxes of supplies and Beckwith's duffel bag onto the plane, and headed for the upper Muldrow.

As Crosson circled camp, Beckwith dropped the boxes and his bag out the door of the plane, thus accomplishing in less than an hour what normally would have taken several days. A short while later, after Beckwith had been redelivered to the lower camp, both pilots were safely off the glacier and on their way back to town.

The historic airdrop was witnessed from above by members of the Lindley-Liek party, who'd reached the top of Karstens Ridge and established a camp at 15,000 feet. As Lindley later noted in his *American Alpine Journal* account:

> We were startled to see a red airplane come up the glacier, circle over the campsite, and drop bundle after bundle to [Carpé and Koven]. We had

> amused ourselves by leaving a tentative signal arrangement with Alaska Airways, in case they should be flying over the mountain, to let them know the precise day on which we thought we would be on the South Peak. Accordingly, we rushed around to pull out sleeping bags to make the signal, but the plane stuck strictly to its business of dropping supplies, and, once through, it went back down the glacier without coming up to our altitude.[5]

Crosson had in fact noticed the Lindley-Liek team, but either wasn't aware of the signal arrangement, or was too occupied below to attempt a flyover.

While at 15,000 feet, the party found the minimum-temperature thermometer that Stuck had cached nineteen years earlier. The thermometer's needle had been pushed as low as the instrument could register, −95°F, the coldest temperature ever recorded in North America. Lindley expressed some skepticism about the thermometer's accuracy, but when later tested in Washington, D.C., the instrument was found to be in perfect working order, according to Pearson.

After sitting out a storm for two days, the Lindley-Liek Expedition moved to its high camp on May 6. The snow remained icy, so skis stayed attached to the climbers' packs rather than to their feet. Once established at 17,000 feet, the climbers were in a position to climb both the North and South Peaks. They'd brought enough food and fuel for ten days, in case a storm should strike. But as in 1913, no waiting was necessary. May 7 dawned brilliantly clear and wonderfully calm. Though a day of rest seemed appealing, the team didn't dare let the opportunity slip past.

The four men began their summit approach at 9:00 A.M. Because the hard, crusty snow made walking easier than skiing, they left the skis at camp, "stuck in the snow like sentinels alongside the tents." Though Strom's dream of skiing to the summit hadn't been realized, he expressed satisfaction that the team had skied a bit at 17,000 feet, higher than anyone had ever done before.

Exhausted by the altitude, lungs searing as they struggled to catch their breath in the thin air, and blasted by winds that drove the windchill temperature to −65°F or colder, the climbers slowly and painfully inched their way upward. Every twenty-five paces, they stopped to rest, but didn't dare sit down because of the difficulty in standing back up. Eight hours after leaving camp, the team reached the top of the continent.

Though he felt rewarded for his hard work, Strom later wrote that there was "little to tell" about the view from McKinley's summit. "One is simply too high up," he explained. "Everything round about now appears almost flat. Only Mount Foraker was lying there, dark and mystic with sharp contours against a glorious sunset."[6]

Pearson, however, was enthralled with the view, which he described as "stupendous. A hundred thousand square miles of Alaska lay below us. It was sharply, beautifully clear; only the horizon was hazy."

The early-evening temperature at McKinley's top was −35°F. Fortunately there wasn't much wind. Despite such bitter cold, the climbers remained on the summit for a half hour, taking numerous photographs. Unfortunately, the camera shutters malfunctioned in the extreme cold and the film was overexposed.

While taking pictures, Strom removed his mittens. His bare hands were exposed to the air for only a few minutes, but that was long enough to freeze five fingertips. Several weeks later, the tips and nails from those frostbitten fingers fell off, and only after several months did what was left of the fingers begin to look normal again.

Once he'd used up his film, Pearson wandered away from his partners "to be alone for part of those thirty minutes, to savor them–thirty minutes of triumph after years of dreaming that went back to a boy sitting on a stump reading exciting tales of Alaska; that covered months of planning and weeks of backbreaking toil up the long white slopes I was now looking down upon."

The team cached a brass tube, in which they placed a notebook with their names and the date of the climb. Then, unroped, they began descending to camp. Ahead of the others, Pearson was crossing a patch of ice when the crampon on his right foot snagged his windpants, and he fell. He slid down the slope, rapidly picking up speed. Careening down the mountain out of control, Pearson slid about 200 yards before finally rolling over on his side. He attempted to stop the fall by jamming the point of his ice axe into the snow and using it as a brake. But just as his momentum was slowing, the axe struck a patch of ice and flew into the air. It came down on the other arm, burying its point in Pearson's left wrist and slicing a deep gash. In a flash, he pulled the axe out of his wrist and jammed it back in the snow, again trying to slow his fall. Finally the slope became gentler and he rolled to a stop.

Unaware of the fall, Pearson's teammates figured he'd pushed on ahead. Finally spotting him below, waving frantically, they worked their way down and found him to be "an awful sight," as Strom described it.

Indeed he was. During his tumble down the icy slope, Pearson had torn an ear, cut a cheek, sliced his wrist, and gashed his forehead above one eye. He was covered with frozen blood. Already, the eye was swelling shut, and blood was smeared in his other eye, making it difficult to see out of that one as well. On top of all that, his stocking cap had been knocked off; exposed to the cold, his ears had begun to freeze. Quickly, Strom offered him a spare hat.

With all of his bruises, cuts, and his frozen ear lobes, Pearson had gotten off lightly. He had, after all, survived. And in the process,

Merl La Voy, Courtesy of the Farquhar Collection, University of Alaska Fairbanks

MEMBERS OF A TEAM ORGANIZED TO RECOVER THE BODIES AND SCIENTIFIC JOURNALS OF ALLEN CARPÉ AND THEODORE KOVEN STAND BY THE MULDROW GLACIER CAMP.

he'd been given "by bloody experience, an example of the truth of the maxim that a mountain is never climbed until you are safely down. And for descending climbers, a mountain sets an ingenious trap. . . . After you've made the top, you have a feeling that all the hard part is over. This is the siren lure that leads to that one careless step." He'd also learned firsthand the dangers of traveling unroped.

The team got down to high camp by 9:00 P.M., twelve hours after starting out. After Pearson's wounds were cleaned, the climbers drank a hot rum to toast their success, then collapsed into their sleeping bags without eating dinner. They spent May 8 in camp, resting their exhausted–and in Pearson's case, battered–bodies for an attempt on the North Peak.

The next morning dawned both clear and remarkably warm, with a temperature of 10°F, after several days in the −25° to −35°F range. It was yet another beautiful day on the mountain.

Once more roped together, the four climbers followed the Harper Glacier to a steep ridge that led to the North Peak's summit. They had little trouble until reaching a section of slick, ice-coated rocks. Their progress slowed to about a quarter mile per hour, they carefully ascended the ridge, and finally reached its top at 6:00 P.M. Pearson described the climb as "drudgery," explaining, "There was no great inspiration to sustain us. After all, we had [already] climbed the main peak." But once at the summit, overlooking the foothills and tundra lowlands stretching north of McKinley, he "regained that mountaineer's special sense of excitement and achievement."

The team had hoped to search for some sign of the Sourdoughs' flagpole before returning to camp, but a strong wind, exhaustion, and difficult climbing prompted the group to leave any such search for future expeditions. That decision proved to be a wise one. A blizzard moved in just as the climbers reached the safety of their tents and continued through the next afternoon. High winds, heavy snowfall, and poor visibility forced the men to remain in their tents. Once the storm let up, the party began its descent.

Going down, the climbers didn't relay their gear as they had while ascending, so they were forced to carry much heavier loads, estimated by Pearson to weigh ninety-five pounds apiece. Left behind were the extra food and fuel that had served as blizzard insurance, as well as a tent and a gasoline stove.

Traveling all night, the climbers descended Karstens Ridge, and reached the upper Muldrow Glacier at 5:00 A.M. on May 11. There they found tents and equipment belonging to Carpé's cosmic-ray expedition, but no sign of life. Looking into one of the tents, Pearson found both sleeping bags and packs. "You don't leave either when you're going to be away overnight," he observed. "It looked queer. . . . We all had a feeling that something was wrong."

Searching the tents thoroughly for additional clues, members of the Lindley-Liek party found diaries belonging to both Carpé and Koven, as well as a scientific journal with data on the cosmic-ray experiments, but none of those satisfactorily explained the mystery they'd stumbled onto. The last entry had been dated May 9, two days earlier.

They also checked closely for tracks leading from Carpé's camp to Karstens Ridge, but found none. It seemed most likely that Carpé and Koven had descended the glacier to rendezvous with their teammates. But if so, why hadn't they taken their sleeping bags? And Strom noted that "other things in the tents [exactly what things, he didn't say] also indicated that they expected to return the same day, but had not returned."

More than eighteen hours had passed since they'd eaten or slept. But puzzled and worried by their discoveries at Carpé's camp, the four men decided to forgo the luxuries of a hot meal and nap. After a snack of bread and jam, they roped themselves together and cautiously began skiing down the heavily crevassed Muldrow, following the route they'd ascended, which was barely visible under recent snowfall.

About three miles below the camp, Strom spotted a dark object. The group stopped and approached. It was Theodore Koven's body, lying face down in the snow. He apparently had been there for several days. Injuries to his head and leg showed that he'd probably fallen into a crevasse, managed to climb out, but then died from loss of blood, exhaustion, and hypothermia.

Following the discovery of Koven's frozen corpse, the Lindley-Liek team searched among a maze of crevasses for some sign of Carpé. Now certain that he too must be dead, probably at the bottom of a nearby crevasse, they gave up after an hour of thorough looking.

Following that search, Strom and Lindley returned to 11,000 feet to retrieve a sled, to which they tied Koven's body. Then, with Strom tied to the front of the sled to pull it and Lindley roped in from behind as a rudder, the team resumed its journey down the glacier.

Because all the rope was being used to haul the sled, Liek and Pearson were unable to tie in with their teammates. To minimize the dangers of traveling unroped, they swapped skis for snowshoes, which they felt safer wearing, and took up positions at the rear of the procession.

Pearson wasn't particularly bothered by the new traveling arrangement, figuring that any snow bridge capable of supporting the sled would easily hold him or Liek. He figured wrong. The team had moved only a couple hundred yards when Pearson plunged out of sight. "I had time to let out a feeble shout. Then, for a couple of long, long seconds, I plummeted downward," he later recalled. "I remember thinking 'This is it, fellow.' Then my pack scraped against the side of the crevasse, my head banged hard against the ice wall and I came to a jarring stop."

His fall had been stopped by a pile of snow wedged between the crevasse walls. Forty feet above, a ray of sunlight slanted through the broken snow bridge. Below was nothing but pure blackness. And death. Pearson could hear his teammates yelling, "Are you hurt?" He wasn't sure of his condition. Once more his face had been smashed, his body ached. But at least he was alive and conscious.

His teammates had difficulty hauling him out of the deep hole, so Pearson, drawing on incredible reserves, pulled himself up the rope, hand over hand. More than an hour later he reached the crevasse's lip and, with a final tug from his partners, "flopped out on that open, blessed glacier top like a fish yanked ashore." His teammates carefully checked Pearson for serious injuries, but fortunately he'd only suffered a cut lip, scraped face, and "assorted bruises."

With more than six miles still to travel, the climbers knew they'd be foolish to take any additional risks. Two men had already died while traveling unroped on the glacier, and a third had barely escaped death. So they left Koven's body, wrapping it in a tent and marking its location with the eight-foot sled, and resumed their descent roped to one another.

After traveling about a half mile, the team found what Pearson described as "mute and shocking testimony of what had happened to those two men":

> At the edge of the crevasse lay an ice axe and a pair of crampons. Faint ski tracks told us that the man who was ahead had passed over the crevasse safely on the snow crust, that the man behind had fallen through, and that the man ahead had come back to help him out. The tracks showed that the skier ahead had sidestepped carefully up to the edge—and there the snow had caved in and hurled him into the crevasse. . . . The story was plainly written in the snow, a stark tragedy of two men, supposedly experienced mountaineers, betrayed by their eagerness to greet their friends [still camped lower on the glacier]. They had gone down the glacier unroped, over a trail they thought they knew, and one of the mountain's oldest traps had sprung shut on them—as it almost had on me.

Completing their journey down the Muldrow, the skiers reached McGonagall Pass at about 2:00 A.M. on May 12, after a day and a half of steady and sometimes traumatic travel. There they discovered two other members of Carpé's expedition: Ed Beckwith and Percy Olton. Another teammate, Nicholas Spadavecchia, had gone to seek help for Beckwith, who was seriously ill from suspected food poisoning.

The Lindley-Liek party stayed with Olton and Beckwith a short while, breaking the news of Carpé and Koven's deaths. Beckwith later recounted:

> It took us some time to really grasp the facts. It was especially hard to believe that anything could have happened to Carpé, for while he was an independent climber, he was extremely careful in

> his own way, and there were no serious technical difficulties on the mountain.

Realizing there was little they could do to help Beckwith, the skiers then continued to their base camp along Cache Creek, which they reached at 5:00 A.M. In the thirty-nine hours since leaving 17,000 feet, they'd eaten one small meal and taken only a couple of brief rests.

Liek fell asleep immediately, but the others stayed awake long enough to consume a sumptuous meal of oyster stew, sausages, canned chicken, biscuits, spinach, and cocoa. Out of danger, with their struggle finally behind them, the men celebrated the successful end of their expedition and the glorious taste of new beginnings. As Strom later described it:

> There was spring in the air. A few bare spots here and there and ptarmigan cackling all around us. It was as if we were starting a new life with only summer and sun and as if the last days and nights were the end of everything hard, cold and sad in this world. Never had we felt so happy to be alive.

Once back at park headquarters, the Lindley-Liek team sent an emergency radio message to Fairbanks, requesting airplane assistance in rescuing Beckwith and Olton from the Muldrow Glacier. By early May, all the snow had melted in Fairbanks, making it difficult if not impossible for a ski-equipped plane to take off. But the Fairbanks Fire Department solved the problem by hosing down the available landing strip until it was all mud.

According to Pearson, pilot Jerry Jones "whooshed the ski plane through the slop until it was airborne, flew to Mount McKinley and picked up the sick man waiting in a tent on the glacier. His splasho return landing is probably the only one on record ever accomplished in a man-made mud pie."

And what happened to Spadavecchia, Beckwith's teammate who'd been sent to find help? A newcomer to the McKinley area, he'd become thoroughly lost. After several days spent wandering through the wilderness, Spadavecchia found his way back to McGonagall Pass, but the camp had already been abandoned. Eventually he was found by a rescue party.

Interest in the cosmic-ray expedition didn't end with the rescues of Beckwith and Spadavecchia, however. In August 1932, Koven's body and Carpé's scientific notebooks were recovered by a three-member party that included Grant Pearson. And the first climbers to die on McKinley were later memorialized by the naming of two neighboring peaks: Mount Koven, 12,210 feet; and Mount Carpé, 12,550 feet.

Bill Sherwonit

CLIMBERS ASCENDING MCKINLEY'S WEST BUTTRESS ROUTE TAKE A REST STOP WHILE TRAVERSING THE RIDGELINE THAT LEADS TO HIGH CAMP AT 17,200 FEET.

Chapter Six

Bradford Washburn and the West Buttress

From his vantage point atop McKinley in 1913, Hudson Stuck felt certain that the great peak would never be climbed by any route other than the Muldrow Glacier. Upon his return from McKinley, he reported:

> The south side has been tried again and again and no approach discovered, nor did it appear from the top that such approach exists. The west side is sheer precipice; the north side is covered with a great hanging glacier and is devoid of practicable slopes. . . . Only on the northeast [via the Muldrow] has the glacier cut so deeply into the mountain as to give access to the heights. . . . There is only one way up the mountain, and Lloyd and his companions [the Sourdoughs] discovered it.[1]

McKinley mountaineers continued to climb in Stuck's and the Sourdoughs' footsteps through the end of the 1940s. From 1932 to 1948, eight expeditions attempted to reach the mountain's top (five succeeded). And all traveled up the Muldrow Glacier.

Not until 1951 did a party attempt to challenge Stuck's views and what had become the conventional McKinley mountaineering wisdom. Leader of that expedition was a New Englander whose name has become intimately linked with the mountain: Bradford Washburn.

A highly successful mountaineer, photographer, author, lecturer, cartographer, explorer, and scientist, Washburn was for decades widely recognized as the world's leading authority on Mount McKinley. From his first photographic and aerial mapping flights over the peak in 1936 until his death at age ninety-six in January 2007, he devoted much of his life to its study and exploration.

Washburn spent more than 200 days on the mountain slopes, visited it in every month except February, and stood on its summit three times. In 1960, he produced his highly acclaimed Mount McKinley map, still considered a cartographic work of art. And his photographic record of the mountain will almost certainly never be matched.

Over the years, Washburn also acted as McKinley's visionary, recommending several new routes to the mountain's top. His remarkable vision was first demonstrated in 1947, when he publicly proposed a new path to the summit–which he called the West Buttress Route–in *The American Alpine Journal*, and predicted that it, not the Muldrow, would be the safest, easiest, and quickest way up to McKinley, if an expedition received aerial support.[2]

In 1950, when a group of Colorado mountaineers wrote to him and requested photographs of his proposed new route, Washburn

Courtesy of Bradford Washburn and the *Anchorage Times*

BRADFORD WASHBURN, WIDELY RECOGNIZED FOR DECADES AS THE WORLD'S LEADING AUTHORITY ON MOUNT MCKINLEY UNTIL HIS DEATH IN 2007, STANDS ON ITS SUMMIT IN 1947 WITH WIFE, BARBARA, THE FIRST WOMAN TO REACH THE MOUNTAIN'S TOP.

---

asked to join their expedition and was quickly added to the team roster. This would be his third attempt to reach McKinley's summit; he'd already stood on the continent's roof in 1942 and 1947, the second time with his wife, Barbara.

When Barbara Polk met Brad Washburn in 1939, her single mountaineering experience had been an ascent of New Hampshire's Mount Washington—by car.[3]

Thanks to the persistent efforts of a mail carrier who knew them both, Polk applied for, and got, a job as Washburn's secretary at what was then the Boston Museum of Natural History. Less than a year later, Brad and Barbara married. They spent their honeymoon making the first ascent of Mount Bertha, in Southeast Alaska.

Seven years after the Mount Bertha climb, Barbara was invited to join her husband on a McKinley expedition. The trip was to be sponsored by RKO Radio Pictures, which wanted to make a short mountaineering documentary to promote an upcoming, full-length feature film about climbing, entitled *The White Tower.*

According to an account of the climb by Nan Elliot in the *Anchorage Daily News*, "RKO was thrilled that Barbara had climbed in Alaska and very much wanted her in the movie. In the eyes of the movie moguls, the addition of a woman to the expedition, a rare event in those days, would add a touch of glamour."

Barbara knew such an opportunity might not come again. So in spite of some parental anxieties, she accepted the invitation and the Washburns left their three young children in the care of the four grandparents plus an experienced nurse.

Named "Operation White Tower," the expedition began its trip up the Muldrow Glacier on Easter Sunday, 1947. The thirteen-member party included two professional cameramen and two public relations people who wrote daily press releases for the wire services. Because Brad Washburn also planned to conduct some mapping surveys, the team carried an enormous amount of gear and moved slowly up the mountain.

As the only woman on the three-month trip, Barbara later recalled:

> What I loved most was the sociability, the comradeship with the guys. We had a very congenial group. It's not the getting to the top that was the fun part. Every night was like a little dinner party. We sat in the cook tent and had good conversations and told jokes. I got very close and bonded with those people.

At 15,000 feet, Barbara lived in an igloo for nine days with two other men, while sitting out a severe McKinley storm. Brad, meanwhile, was stuck near Denali Pass during the storm. "That was probably one of the most interesting parts of the trip," she admitted, "getting along with two strange fellows for nine days in a little igloo. The storm was so bad, they had to keep track of you if you went outside to the john, so you didn't get blown off the mountain."

After joining Brad at Denali Pass, Barbara made her historic ascent to McKinley's summit on June 6. The day was cold and windy, with a windchill factor of −60°F. As the team neared the South Peak's top, one of Barbara's rope partners suggested that she go first. Later she commented:

> I wasn't very impressed with myself. But he was. I knew if I made it, I'd be the first woman. I don't think any other woman had tried it. All I could think of at the top was that I've got to get down safely. I've got to get back to my kids. It's always coming down where the accidents happen. So I was very unemotional and undemonstrative. I was just saving every ounce of energy. But inside I kept saying to myself, "Look where you are. You'll never be here again. Try to take it all in."

The Washburns descended together in the late afternoon to high camp and celebrated that night with a victory dinner. The following day, under calm and sunny skies, they ascended the North Peak and enjoyed a picnic lunch in 0° weather. Despite her apprehensions, Barbara and the rest of the team descended safely. Although hundreds of other women have followed her to McKinley's summit, she remains the only woman to climb the South and North Peaks on successive days.

Back in Massachusetts, a few newspaper stories were written about the historic ascent, and the documentary eventually played in theaters. But "nobody got excited we'd climbed McKinley," Barbara said. "I just settled back into motherhood."

Despite the interest shown by the Colorado group and Washburn's recognized expertise, many members of the climbing community scoffed at Washburn's West Buttress vision and some colleagues urged him to forget such foolishness. "People said it was a ridiculous idea. They told me, 'You can't do it. . . it'll never be done,'" he recalls.[4] Washburn wasn't about to be discouraged, however. And in June 1951, he and seven teammates began a climb that would forever change the nature of McKinley mountaineering.

The expedition had three main purposes: to study the mountain's geology; do survey work for a large-scale map of McKinley and surrounding peaks; and, above all, test Washburn's theory that the West Buttress would offer a shorter, safer way to McKinley's summit than the Muldrow Glacier. To accomplish these goals, the team was split into two parties. Four members circled the mountain from the north. The remainder were flown in to the Alaska Range by Terris Moore, an experienced bush pilot and climber who was then president of the University of Alaska.

By dropping Washburn, Henry Buchtel, Jim Gale, and Bill Hackett at 7,700 feet on the previously unexplored Kahiltna Glacier, Moore made aviation history and gave the climbers a huge advantage over early twentieth-century explorers by eliminating an extremely long and difficult approach hike. Such air assistance is now standard operating procedure for Alaska Range expeditions, but then it was hardly a common practice. Only a few times before had airplanes been used to transport climbers and/or supplies into McKinley. And all previous landings had been made on the Muldrow Glacier.

From their drop-off point, the four climbers traveled up the Kahiltna's main branch toward 10,300-foot Kahiltna Pass, setting up base camp at 10,100 feet. The next morning, C-47s belonging to the Alaska Air Command made aerial drops of equipment, food, and fuel.

Within a half hour, more than a ton of supplies had been delivered "at our front doorstep from a warehouse 130 miles away," Washburn later reported in *National Geographic* magazine. He explained:

> In the old days it would have taken a 20-horse pack train and three wranglers weeks to move this load from Anchorage to the lower end of the Kahiltna Glacier, 44 miles below our camp. From there to where we sat, it would have been such a prodigious job of backpacking to move these same supplies that we shuddered even at the thought.[5]

Although aircraft dramatically changed the nature and scope of mountaineering expeditions, few climbers questioned the ethics of aerial support. Says Washburn:

> There was a little bit of controversy [surrounding the use of planes]. The purists will always have something to complain about. But it never became much of an issue and it didn't bother me at all. We'd used air support in expeditions to other mountains as far back as the 1930s. Really, it was nothing new.[6]

The four-member party stayed at Kahiltna Pass for several days, while doing survey work for Washburn's McKinley map. On the evening of June 30, the four who'd been mapping geology on the north side of the mountain (John Ambler, Melvin Griffiths, Jerry More, and Barry Bishop) arrived in camp. And two days later, Terris Moore again made aviation history by landing his plane just above 10,000 feet—at that time the highest airplane landing ever made in Alaska—to drop off mail, film, and other supplies.

With the party reunited, the expedition turned its attention toward the West Buttress Route. The climbers had chosen a path that they hoped would avoid huge crevasses and avalanches, the two major dangers faced by previous McKinley expeditions. On July 4, the team began its journey along that path loaded down with sixty- to ninety-pound packs.

That night, Griffiths, Bishop, and More returned to base camp, where they would spend a week doing further geologic mapping. The other five spent the evening at 13,200 feet, where they built an igloo and erected a snow wall around the team's cook tent. The site where they established camp would later be named "Windy Corner," for reasons that will soon become obvious.

After a peaceful night, the climbers woke up to find their igloo tunnel drifted over with snow. Outside the shelter a blizzard raged, complete with sixty-mile-an-hour winds, dense fog, and heavy snow. Washburn reported:

> It took an hour to excavate the half-buried cook tent, retighten the guy ropes, and get inside. As John Ambler crawled into the tent, his beard white with frost and icicles, he said with some disgust, 'This kind of climbing is about 90 percent trying to stay alive and warm, and only 10 percent climbing!'

The storm's intensity increased throughout the day. By evening, wind gusts approached eighty miles per hour, the temperature had dropped to 14°F, and snow fell so heavily that visibility was reduced to a few feet.

The storm died on July 6, and the climbers spent the next two days ferrying loads to 15,400 feet. From there, they had to scale an 800-foot wall that leads to the crest of a granite ridge (the West Buttress proper). The wall rose at an angle of fifty to sixty degrees and presented the route's most challenging stretch of technical snow and ice climbing.

To scale that steeply sloping face, the climbers chopped steps into "the most wretched snow imaginable. . . . On the surface there was a thin, breakable crust; under it a layer of granular snow about like buckshot; then another thin crust, then a few inches of powdery snow and finally a solid mass of hard blue ice, all sloping much more than the average roof."

Once above the headwall, the climbers followed a knife ridge of granite to a large, open bowl. On July 9, Washburn, Gale, and Hackett established the team's high camp, at 17,300 feet. And the following morning, under cloudless skies, they set off for the summit.

At 5:45 P.M., the three climbers reached the mountain's top and, as Washburn described it, gazed upon a "marvelous sight . . . a cloudless panorama stretching nearly 400 miles from horizon to horizon, 125,000 square miles of Alaska visible in a single sweeping glance."

On descending, Washburn, Gale, and Hackett passed their teammates, upward bound in two separate groups. All eight climbers eventually reached McKinley's summit.

Afterward Washburn reflected with understandable pride:

> McKinley had been climbed from the west [after a southerly approach by plane], safely and speedily, in only seven days from Kahiltna Pass. We had proved that airplanes, loaded or unloaded, could land and take off halfway up that side of the peak. . . . Our new route up McKinley's 'impregnable' western face . . . was proved to be an ideal avenue of approach for future scientific work atop the roof of North America.

The West Buttress also proved to be an ideal avenue for the climbing public. Washburn's vision, combined with the increased availability of bush pilots, mountain guides, and high-tech climbing equipment, eventually opened up the mountain to a new breed of McKinley mountaineer: the adventure traveler.

During the twentieth century's first six decades, only 213 people tried to climb McKinley. But over the next fifty-three years, from 1960 through 2012, more than 38,000 people made attempts on the peak, most of them since the mid-1990s. Interest in the mountain began growing dramatically in the mid-1970s, due largely to a loosening of National Park Service restrictions and the increased availability of professional guide services, and has shown no sign of letting up. The number of McKinley climbers rose steadily from the late 1970s through the 1980s, finally reaching more than 1,000 in 1989 (1,009 to be exact). Attempts dropped slightly the next two years, but since 1992 at least 1,000 climbers have annually walked McKinley's slopes, with an all-time high of 1,340 in 2005. Many of those are people with little or no high-altitude climbing experience, who rely on the expertise of professional guides. That dependence has grown substantially this century and especially since 2005; some years, guides and their clients have comprised nearly half of McKinley's mountaineers.

Whether guided or not, the large majority of those attempting to reach McKinley's summit since 1970 have followed the West Buttress Route. And the trend has been toward increased use of that route. In recent years, 80 to 90 percent (and sometimes more) of all McKinley mountaineers have followed the West Buttress. It's easy to understand why the West Buttress has become so popular. As Washburn predicted more than fifty years ago, it's the easiest, safest, and quickest way to McKinley's summit.

Because the route is less challenging technically, it has unfortunately earned a reputation in some climbing circles as a "walk-up." Such a description is dangerously misleading, however. It is also inaccurate. This is no place for the untrained or out-of-shape adventurer. The West Buttress can kill; more than fifty people—including some world-class mountaineers—have died along this route, in a variety of ways: crevasse falls, climbing falls, altitude sickness, avalanches, and exhaustion-hypothermia.

Back in the mid-1980s, I, like thousands of others, came under McKinley's spell. The more stories I heard about the mountain, both good and bad, the more compelling it became. Apparently, under the right conditions, it could be climbed by someone without years of mountaineering experience or a lot of technical expertise—someone like me, a writer who spends much of his time sitting in front of a computer terminal. During the summer of 1986, the dream began to crystallize. I set a goal: McKinley in 1987. Because of my limited background, I chose to follow the West Buttress Route and go with an Anchorage-based guide service, Genet Expeditions.

The following is an account of that 1987 expedition, with intermittent excerpts from my diary.[7] It offers the viewpoint of someone who is not a hard-core mountaineer and illustrates the dangers and difficulties of ascending McKinley's most popular climbing route. (For historic, descriptive, and poetic reasons, I, like Hudson Stuck, chose to use the mountain's Indian name, "Denali," in this account.)

I lay in my sleeping bag trying to nap, but sleep was impossible. The tent was too bright, too hot. And I had too much nervous energy; my mind was working overtime.

It was late afternoon on May 31, and just a few hours earlier I'd flown into the Alaska Range as part of an eight-climber Denali expedition. We'd been dropped off at the Kahiltna Glacier Base Camp, the official starting point for most teams traveling up the mountain. Located at 7,200 feet on the Kahiltna's Southeast Fork, the base camp is often populated by several dozen mountaineers either starting or ending their trek up Denali, during the main climbing season from late April through mid-July. It's served daily by Talkeetna's air-taxi services, weather permitting, and is overseen by a camp manager who's in radio contact with both the bush pilots and National Park Service rangers. The team included two guides and six climbers:

Chief guide Vern Tejas, thirty-four, moved to Alaska in 1973. A transplanted Texan who settled in Anchorage, he saw Denali his third day in the state and "immediately fell in love with the mountain." Vern made his first ascent of Denali in 1978 and has guided on the mountain since 1979. In twelve previous attempts, he'd reached the summit ten times, including an ascent of the Cassin Ridge, one of the peak's most technically difficult routes.

Assistant guide Dolly LaFever, forty-one, was a public-health nurse employed by the state of Alaska and stationed in Naknek. An endurance athlete who twice won the women's title in the 210-mile Iditaski wilderness race, Dolly had been on Denali two times before, reaching the summit once. This was her second trip as a Genet Expeditions guide.

Kelly and Linda Stowell moved to Alaska in 1982, settling in Eagle River. Kelly, twenty-eight, was an unemployed construction worker, while Linda, twenty-six, was a petroleum engineer with Standard Oil. Each had done some ice and rock climbing, but neither had any high-altitude mountaineering experience. They were married on May 15; Denali was their honeymoon trip.

Dave Smith, thirty-seven, of San Francisco, had quit his job as a business manager in August 1986 and spent the previous ten months as an adventure traveler. He'd already sailed and sea kayaked off the California coast, climbed the three highest peaks in Mexico, bicycled in Australia, and scuba dived in the Great Barrier Reef. To prepare for Denali, he'd taken a winter mountaineering course on Washington's Mount Rainier.

Petr Sovcov, thirty-nine, of Kirkland, Washington, had climbed with Genet Expeditions on both Denali and 22,834-foot Aconcagua in Argentina, the Western Hemisphere's highest peak. In 1986, he'd reached the 19,000-foot elevation on Denali before turning back. Making its summit had been his obsession for the past year.

Clint Whitney, fifty, of Fair Oaks, California, was the group's old man. A former marathon runner who was employed by the Environmental Protection Agency, he'd started rock climbing at age forty. He'd scaled Mount Whitney and Mount Shasta in California and the Matterhorn in Europe. Clint was climbing Denali because he "wanted to experience a big mountain." The book *Seven Summits* was his inspiration.[8]

I'd been planning the climb for more than a year. For months it had been a distant fantasy—something to dream about and work toward. To build up strength, I lifted weights. To improve my endurance and aerobic capacity, I ran several times each week, went on long hikes, and climbed nearby hills while wearing a heavy pack. Now, suddenly, the adventure had begun. Inside the tent, I wondered if I was prepared to take on the challenge.

Outside, the Kahiltna Glacier broiled in the summertime heat. Temperatures in the shade reached 50°F. In direct sunlight, the heat was almost unbearable. As Petr said, it was "like being in a frying pan." Members of the team quickly stripped down to their polypropylene underwear. We coated our faces with number 15 sunscreen, added noseguards to sunglasses, and put on baseball caps with bandannas attached to protect head and neck. At 7,200 feet, in May, under clear blue skies, the chief dangers were heatstroke and sunburn rather than hypothermia and frostbite.

Because of the heat, Vern decided we should move immediately to a night-shift operation. In June, the skies above Denali never get completely dark, so we would travel during the cool of evening and early morning and rest during the middle of the day. After setting up base camp and eating our first mountain meal—bagels and cream cheese, sausage, two candy bars, and gorp—we were ordered to our tents to get some rest. Sleep wouldn't come, so I listened to the sound of the mountains. All afternoon we were serenaded by the rumble of avalanches.

Bill Sherwonit

EMILIO GUNTHER OF CALIFORNIA CARRIES GEAR IN HIS PACK AND SLED WHILE HAULING SUPPLIES UP THE KAHILTNA GLACIER, ALONG MCKINLEY'S WEST BUTTRESS ROUTE.

The mountains were covered by several feet of new snow, deposited by a series of storms that had lasted more than two weeks and ended only a few days before our arrival. The arrival of clear, warm weather made the snowpack heavy and unstable, and the peaks responded by releasing their loads every ten or fifteen minutes.

The storms had also reduced mountaineering success in the Alaska Range to almost zero during that two-week period. May is usually one of the best months to climb Denali, but not in 1987. Of the first 209 climbers to attempt it, only 27 had reached the summit, a success rate of 14 percent. By comparison, the success rate for Denali climbers ranged from 43 to 79 percent in the previous ten years.

Vern had been among those to be turned back from the mountain in mid-May. His party had been hammered by high winds for five days at 17,200 feet before retreating. It was the first time since 1980 that he hadn't reached Denali's top. Although success rates were down, climbing numbers were up. By the end of May, more than 550 Denali mountaineers had registered with the Park Service. Like us, most of those climbers traveled along the West Buttress Route.

The first couple of days, the carries to Camp I, are a real grunt. Just plodding along, one foot in front of the other, getting used to the weight of pack and sled and the snowshoes on my feet. After the first carry, I had muscle aches from shoulders to feet. My hips were the worst, from pulling the sled that was harnessed (by cord) to my seat harness. The weight dragged my harness and put a real strain on my hips. It was agonizing, just constant pain. But I was "a real trooper" and carried on without complaint.

Our first night in the Alaska Range was grueling. The food-and-fuel carry to Camp I at 7,500 feet began just after midnight and lasted until 8:00 A.M. Although we gained only 300 vertical feet en route to the cache, we traveled about five miles up the Kahiltna Glacier, carrying forty-five- to fifty-pound packs and pulling plastic sleds with about the same amount of weight.

During the carry, a new storm moved into the range, bringing wet snow and near-whiteout conditions. We arrived back at base camp soggy and exhausted. While Vern started up the stoves to melt snow and cook breakfast, most members of the team crawled into the tents to escape the wetness and get into sleeping bags. Breakfast, thankfully, was served to us in bed.

We remained in the tents until early evening. Not much was said at dinner or while we broke down camp. Team members were subdued, a reaction to both the dreary weather and our first nighttime carry. The lone exception was Dave, who sang the praises of the Alaska Range and expressed his eagerness "to get further up the mountain."

We left base camp at 8:30, the evening of June 1. Despite continued stormy weather, everyone's spirits seemed to rise as we moved up the glacier. Our second carry seemed much easier than the first, perhaps because the loads were lighter. And we'd gotten some needed rest. (Most McKinley expeditions make double-carries between camps, to reduce the weight being hauled.)

We reached our cache at about three in the morning, then stamped out a platform for our three tents, built a snow wall for protection against winds, and ate breakfast. Wet and weary, we retired to our sleeping bags at 5:00 A.M. Snow was falling, visibility was less than one hundred feet, and the temperature was in the mid-20s.

Food—and the eating of it—is becoming a frequent topic. Vern is doing his best to stuff us. And some of us are getting stuffed far too quickly. For lunch today we had French toast with jelly and/or peanut butter. Our designated serving was four slices each. Linda and Dolly only wanted two each and I could manage only three. The last few bites I nearly gagged. Dave, meanwhile, is Mr. Appetite, eating anything and everything—and lots of it. "I brought my appetite with me," he boasted, while the rest of us struggled to get our food down.

Right from the start, Vern warned us he would be our "mother hen." One of his self-appointed tasks was to goad, cajole, tease, browbeat, or bribe us into eating as much food as we could stomach. Anything that we found distasteful became "summit food," the message being that we had to eat it if we planned to make it all the way to the mountaintop. If he left it up to us, we wouldn't take in enough to build our strength for the climb, because at high altitudes people lose their desire for food. Eating, as well as drinking and breathing, must become a deliberate act.

"On the mountain, you have to consciously make yourself eat, drink, and even breathe," Vern had warned us during a pretrip briefing in Talkeetna, where the team had gathered for its flight into the Alaska Range. "What comes naturally down here, you have to force yourself to do up there. If you don't, you'll never reach the summit."

It's critical to drink lots of fluids to prevent dehydration, which makes a climber more susceptible to frostbite, hypothermia, and altitude sickness. A minimum of four to five quarts of water a day is recommended. To make all that water more palatable, we had a variety of mixes to add to melted snow, including instant soup, spiced cider, hot cocoa, tea, and coffee. But drinking much coffee was not advised, since it's a diuretic [research has since shown the diuretic effect of coffee to be a small one, of much less concern]. Our favorite mix while moving between camps was Kool-Aid—grape, cherry, strawberry, and lemonade.

Eating properly is nearly as essential as drinking enough. Climbers burn enormous amounts of calories, through both physical activity and heat production. "Going hungry can lead to increased acidity of the blood, which aggravates both fatigue and hypothermia," according to mountaineer and author Glenn Randall in his *Mt. McKinley Climber's Handbook*.[9] And Vern wasn't about to let that happen. So he did everything but force food into us.

Sometime during the morning of June 2 the weather changed once more. I awoke at midday to discover a deep blue sky, devoid of clouds. Again we sweltered under the baking sun.

With a return of clear and calm weather, the Alaska Range came alive with mountaineers. Dozens of teams moved up and down the Kahiltna Glacier. Two hundred yards from camp a parade of thirty climbers marched slowly up Ski Hill, while a handful of skiers carved S-curves down the slope. Reports from those descending to base camp were encouraging: in recent days a high percentage of climbers had reached the summit.

The view was superb, made even more spectacular by memories of the previous night's whiteout. We were camped in a huge glacial bowl and surrounded by the Alaska Range's best-known giants: Denali, 17,400-foot Mount Foraker, and 14,573-foot Mount Hunter. We could also see some lesser known peaks whose names are intimately tied to Denali's mountaineering history. Mount Frances, a 10,450-foot peak, was named for Frances Randall, who earned the nickname "Guardian Angel of McKinley" while serving as the Kahiltna Glacier Base Camp manager from 1976 through 1983 (she died of cancer in 1984). And 9,200-foot Point Farine honors the memory of Jacques "Farine" Batkin, a French climber who died in a crevasse fall during the first winter ascent of Denali in 1967.

Best of all, we were treated to a panoramic view of the West Buttress Route, which allowed Vern to give us a visual tour of the path we'd be following over the next two and a half weeks. "It's nice to be able to see where you're going," he said. "Sometimes you don't see anything at all until you reach 14,000 feet [because of cloud cover]."

Late in the afternoon, we were joined by Emilio Gunther, a forty-seven-year-old climber from Southern California. He'd planned to ascend the West Rib, a more technical route, but had been bothered by knee problems while moving up the Kahiltna Glacier. The West Rib leader, also a Genet Expeditions guide, had recommended a shift to the West Buttress, and Emilio had agreed to the change. He'd already met three members of our group and was welcomed onto the team.

We made our first carry to 9,500 feet. Left camp at 11:00 P.M. *last night and returned about 4:00* A.M. *As we moved up Ski Hill, Denali's summit ridge was bathed in a golden alpenglow, created by the midnight sun, while a bright quarter-moon slowly sank behind Kahiltna Dome. Except for a solitary skier, our team was alone on the trail. The only sounds were the sleds dragging in the snow, our steady breathing, and the rush of an occasional gust of*

Bill Sherwonit

MEMBERS OF THE ENDORPHIN EXPEDITION TRAVEL UP THE KAHILTNA GLACIER IN EVENING, WHILE MOVING EQUIPMENT FROM 9,500 TO 11,000 FEET.

wind. I felt energized, exhilarated in the cold evening air. I found a rhythm, a steady pace that felt comfortable; the carry wasn't a struggle as it had been moving to Camp I. Just as we returned to camp, morning's arrival was signaled by pink, then orange, and finally yellow bands of light on Mount Foraker.

While the carry to Camp II at 9,500 feet proved to be enjoyable, the return trip to Camp I was pure fun. After we'd cached the food and fuel, Vern suggested we take a ride back down the Kahiltna Glacier on our orange plastic haul sleds. "It's the only way to go," he said with obvious glee. "It's the icing on the cake for the daredevils in the group."

After being convinced that crevasses wouldn't present a danger as long as the sledders stayed along the marked trail, five team members chose to take up the challenge: Vern, Kelly, Linda, Dave, and I. The rest hiked back. Roped up in two sledding teams, we cruised down three hills. Last and definitely best was Ski Hill, also known in some quarters as "Crash-and-Burn Hill," with an elevation drop of about 800 feet.

In predawn light, we slid down Ski Hill, sometimes in control, more often not, while reaching speeds later estimated at up to thirty miles an hour. We experienced a few spectacular wipeouts on the crusty snow, but all the sledders reached the bottom in good shape and loved every minute of it.

"C'mon, let's do it again," shouted Dave. "I'd compare sledding down the Kahiltna to scuba diving in the Great Barrier Reef."

"Yeah," Vern responded, "with fresh blood in the water."

That afternoon a strong, steady wind began blowing down the Kahiltna Glacier, ending three and a half days of calm weather. Petr greeted the wind's arrival with a smile and the comment, "Welcome to McKinley. The first three days have been a joke. Now things get serious. Now we get to see a little of what the mountain has to offer."

The wind wasn't particularly fierce, gusting only to twenty or twenty-five miles per hour. But it drove wet snow down the glacier, creating blizzard conditions. And it blew directly into our faces as we moved camp to 9,500 feet on the night of June 3.

The temperature was warm, close to freezing, as we labored up the glacier. But the combination of a driving wind and wet snow was chilling. When we took breaks for food and drink, the wind quickly cooled our bodies, serving as a warning that this was prime hypothermia weather. Vern set a slow, deliberate pace to prevent overheating and exhaustion.

While struggling up Ski Hill, Dave reminded anyone who wanted to listen, "Remember, you paid good money to suffer like this."

We reached Camp II at about 3:00 A.M. on June 4 and immediately began to set up a tent platform and protective snow wall. The work was tiring, especially after our five-hour march up into the storm, but it kept us warm until we could escape into the safety of our tents.

The Park Service requires all Denali expeditions to have an identifying title. Ours was "Endorphins," suggested by Dolly and enthusiastically seconded by Dave. The rest of the party had no better ideas at the time, so Endorphins—the name for naturally produced opiates that cause the phenomenon known as "runner's high"—won by default. Not coincidentally, both Dolly and Dave are runners. And the name was appropriate for another reason: as we worked our way up the mountain, we were getting naturally high on Denali.

Following our first carry to 11,000 feet, Kelly came up with a more suitable moniker for the group: "Nightcrawlers." As he observed, "We're the only climbers on the mountain who don't have tans. And we don't need sleeping bags because we do all our traveling at night and sleep during the heat of the day." As the name suggested, we'd been crawling up the mountain—at least in comparison to many Denali expeditions. But our slow pace was by design. Vern wanted to average about 1,000 feet of elevation gain per day. "We're not going to push it," he told us. "We're in no hurry. I want people to get properly acclimatized and I don't want people burning out."

Nearly everyone in the team appreciated Vern's philosophy. The exception was Dave, who complained on a few occasions, "We're going too slow. I want to get up there faster, to go for it."

During the night, a sparrow somehow got into one of the other tents; it was safely released by Dave. And this morning, Vern found a yellow warbler on one of the packs, its feet frozen to the metal frame. "It was trying like heck to take off, flapping its wings like it was going to fly off with the pack," Vern said. "So I blew on its feet and thawed them out enough to free it."

Other than humans, we saw only one form of animal life during our trek up the glacier: birds. From base camp to 9,500 feet, we spotted geese, ducks, warblers, finches, sparrows, and ravens. Unlike climbers, most of the birds don't hang out on the Kahiltna Glacier by choice. Kahiltna Pass is used as a major migration route by waterfowl and songbirds. Sometimes as they fly through the Alaska Range, the migratory birds are caught in storms; they become disoriented and/or stressed and end up spending unscheduled time in the mountains. Many of the weathered-in birds soon die from lack of food and water, or by freezing.

The exceptions are ravens, which seem to do quite well in this land of ice, snow, and rock. They've earned a reputation as master scavengers. The *Mt. McKinley Climber's Handbook* warns:

> Climbers ferrying loads on McKinley face one final and unexpected problem: ravens. These tough, intelligent and powerful birds can wreak havoc on a cache, consuming an amazing amount of food and scattering much of the rest. They go through sturdy nylon duffel bags like they were paper, plastic bags like they weren't there. Caches have been attacked all the way up to 16,400 feet.

Ravens supplement their diet by feeding on the bodies of songbirds that die before finding their way out of the range.

On June 5 we again shifted climbing gears. The nightcrawlers became day-trippers, in response to colder temperatures as we moved up the mountain. No longer was it too hot to travel during the day, and by the time we reached 14,000 feet, the nights would be bitterly cold.

The weather for our first afternoon carry was ideal: warm, but with a cooling breeze. Nearly everyone traveled in a single layer of polypropylene underwear. We arrived at 11,000 feet in late afternoon. After setting up Camp III, we spent a few hours practicing crevasse-rescue techniques.

That evening, we received a memorable visitor. A climber who introduced himself only as Harry staggered into camp, obviously exhausted and seeking shelter for the night. Harry said he'd climbed Denali as part of a two-person expedition from Holland, reaching the summit on June 3. While descending, the Dutch team met a German climber traveling alone. "The German asked if he could rope up with us, because of the crevasse danger," Harry explained. "But after some time, he decided to go on ahead unroped. My partner also went on ahead [unroped] without giving any kind of reason."

Unable to keep pace with the other two, Harry fell behind and was left on his own, without any shelter. He arrived at 11,000 feet just before midnight and several hours behind his partner, who had stopped near our camp for a short rest before heading farther down the glacier.

Harry was clearly in no condition to continue traveling alone, without a chance to recuperate. When informed that his partner had not waited, he said sadly, "It is not the custom in my country for a climber to leave his partner. It is not a good thing to do. This is not an alpine hike; it is serious business. I am rather ashamed to even say it happened."

Harry shared a hot meal with us and then was invited to share a tent with Dave and Clint. It turned out to be a long night for those two, because Harry was a world-class snorer. His nighttime rumblings echoed loudly through camp. Dave barely got any sleep, and by morning, he was ready to do bodily harm.

After breakfast, Harry continued on his solo descent. "At least now we know why his partner left him behind," Dave observed, with some sarcasm. "He probably didn't get any sleep at all when he was teamed up with Harry."

The weather at 11,000 feet was nasty as we broke camp on June 7. The wind blew twenty to twenty-five miles per hour, snow fell heavily, and visibility was less than a hundred feet. From this point on, we wore crampons instead of snowshoes, for easier travel on ice and hard-packed snow slopes.

Eight hundred feet higher, the weather became much worse than nasty: we ascended into a full-blown blizzard. The storm's sudden intensity made me think of Petr's earlier comment. Now things really get serious—and dangerous.

Standing on an exposed ridge, we were blasted by winds that gusted to fifty miles per hour. Wind-driven snow reduced visibility to a few feet and stung our faces. The air temperature was 20°F, but the windchill registered about −20°F. I could feel the cold cutting through my clothing.

My mind cried out, "Let's move, let's move!" but Vern called for an "eat-drink-and-be-merry" rest stop despite our exposure to the roaring wind and bitter cold. Although none of us had any appetite, his decision made sense. Conditions could be even worse up ahead; we needed food and water to guard against dehydration and exhaustion.

Pulling my water bottle out of my pack was an excruciating task. To work the zipper, I had to remove my overmitts and wool mittens, exposing my hands to the cold. They grew numb within a few seconds. Petr had a more serious problem. He'd underdressed, wearing only his long johns under his windpants, and his legs had become chilled. Petr had two choices: add a third layer, or wait and hope the weather improved. Rather than risk becoming hypothermic, he opted for a change of clothes.

Vern used two of our packs to set up a makeshift windblock. Then he and Dolly helped Petr strip down to his underwear, pull on a pair of pile pants, and finally put the windpants back on, all while being blasted by gale-force winds.

After ten or fifteen minutes–it seemed much longer–we resumed our trek to Camp IV at 14,200 feet, with the wind-driven snow now blowing directly into our faces. We hit a stretch of trail where drifts of soft, fresh powder one or two feet deep had been deposited by the wind, and the deep snow slowed our progress even more. We would move only a few steps before stopping briefly to rest.

My miseries were compounded by a lack of goggles. (A couple of experienced mountaineers, Vern included, had advised me I'd do fine without goggles; it turned out to be bad advice.) All I had to protect my eyes from glare and blowing snow were glacier sunglasses. They fogged up so badly I could barely see. And when I tried to wipe the glasses, snow caked on them, making things worse.

I struggled ahead, breathing hard and fast and fighting off panic. I felt completely at the mercy of the weather and Vern's guiding expertise. For the first time, I thought of death. Another group just ahead of us decided to turn back. As they passed by, Vern told the party's leader, "I don't blame you," but added, "We're going on." I wondered why. Later Vern explained:

> Our food and fuel was up ahead [we'd cached it at 13,500 feet the day before]. We had enough for one night if we'd gone back to 11,000, but what if the storm lasted several days? We had to continue. That's one of the chances you take. If things got too bad, I planned to dig in at 12,500 feet or Windy Corner [elevation about 13,200]. But there was never any question of going ahead.

Fortunately, the mountain gods took pity on us. The clouds broke, the snow stopped, and the wind eased up. The sun helped to warm the air, so the chill wasn't as biting. Trudging through the deep, soft snow remained hard work, an upward struggle in the truest sense. But the worst was past.

Storms aren't the only obstacle to face. We passed through several crevassed areas (moving camp from 11,000 to 14,200 feet). . . . The hazards are everywhere, it seems. Climbing this mountain is hard, painful, sometimes dangerous work. I struggle with my load, my shoulders ache. I wonder whether reaching the summit is worth the struggle and risk. The camaraderie, the scenery—which is so spectacular when the skies clear—and the challenge have made it worthwhile so far.

We reached Camp IV at about nine in the evening on June 7, just as a group of rescuers was bringing an injured climber down from the Messner Couloir, a 5,000-foot chute of snow and ice. Details of the fall were sketchy. Rumors were that the climber had broken ribs and perhaps a punctured lung. He was taken to the high-altitude Denali Medical Research Camp, located about 200 yards from our campsite, and within minutes was airlifted off the mountain by helicopter.

Later I learned that the injured climber was Tom "Bo" Bohanan, a mountaineer from Colorado. I'd met Bo in 1985. That year he'd reached 19,600 feet via the West Buttress. With Denali's summit only a mile away and 700 vertical feet above, Bo had to turn back, a victim of exhaustion and the extreme cold. He returned to Talkeetna with a nose blistered by frostbite and several frost-nipped fingers and toes.

At that time he'd admitted, "It was frustrating. You hear all those stories about fat executives and middle-aged housewives and it's like anybody can do it. But we saw how bad it can get. It was scary, and real sobering."

Now, two years later, Bo had made the summit by a much more difficult route. But while descending, he caught one of his crampons on a pack strap, lost his balance, and began tumbling out of control down the forty- to fifty-degree slope. He finally stopped rolling after a fall of about 1,500 feet–and less than fifty feet from the lip of a huge crevasse.

Bo proved lucky. His only injuries were a fractured hip and bruised ribs. He was also fortunate that the fall had been witnessed by two Swiss climbers who just happened to be watching his descent.

"Bo would've been dead if the Swiss hadn't seen it happen," later reported Dr. Howard Donner, a California physician who was participating in the Denali Medical Research Project. "He was unable to move and was dressed in lightweight clothing. He was already hypothermic when we got to him."

While watching the rescue operation, I began feeling lightheaded and dizzy. The altitude and strenuous climb from 11,000 to 14,200 feet had taken its toll. My head began to hurt–a dull, throbbing ache. It wasn't too serious, but definitely caught my attention. The next day, I discovered I wasn't the only one with these complaints. After spending our first night at 14,200, Petr said he had a minor headache, Vern woke up "with a hangover," and Dolly suffered from both a headache and nausea.

We'd been instructed to pay close attention to any headaches. They can be an early warning sign of mountain sickness, an illness caused by the body's failure to adjust to lower oxygen levels in the air at high altitudes. Mountain sickness can begin when a person ascends too fast. Unfortunately, there are no hard-and-fast rules for climbers to follow that will ensure proper acclimatization, because each individual adapts differently to high-altitude changes.

Vern's take-it-slow, don't-push-it approach to ascending the mountain was intended to minimize the risk of high-altitude sickness. Other preventive measures included the consumption of lots of liquid and the use of deep-breathing techniques, designed to increase the intake of whatever oxygen was available.

Despite such safeguards, I had a rather frightening taste of mountain sickness on June 9. Early in the afternoon, we began a carry to our next camp at 16,400 feet on the crest of the West Buttress ridge. To get there, we had to climb a snow-covered slope 2,000 feet high, using crampons and ice axes. The upper 1,000 feet crossed a steep wall of hard-packed, crusted snow and ice, at angles from forty-five to nearly sixty degrees. Across that section, a fixed-line rope had been bolted into the snow, thanks to the efforts of three Alaskan guide outfits that work on Denali.

While going from 14,200 feet to 16,400 on Tuesday, Vern keeps up his usual methodical pace. But about halfway up the slope, my right heel begins to burn, like a blister is forming. . . . The agony really starts on the fixed line. Placing the crampons and getting a foothold in the snow and ice with bunny boots [white, insulated, rubberized boots] is a painstaking and painful process. My heels begin to ache terribly, and each step becomes agonizing. My mind blanks out everything but moving the ice axe, my hold on the fixed line, and stepping up. It seems like the climb will never end. I'm roped up with Linda, who's in lead, and Dolly. Linda is also struggling.

Finally I reach the ridge. Everyone is standing around; they've been waiting ten to fifteen minutes. Once on top, I realize just how exhausted I am. My heels hurt horribly—more a deep ache than a burning pain. [Later I learned the pain was from tendons being stretched.] My mind is a little fuzzy, spacy. I'm not thinking clearly. I drop my pack to take some photos; the scenery is rejuvenating. There are several other parties around. I wonder if I look as burned out as I feel.

We still have to travel about 300 yards—and gain 200 vertical feet—to our cache at 16,400. Dolly and Linda have gone back to 14,200, so I'm now roped up with Emilio and Dave. It's a struggle, but I make it. Dave asks me if I'm doing all right, that I seem a little out of it. I say I'm tired, but doing OK when actually I have some doubts myself.

Starting back down, I know I'm not too sharp, so I try to concentrate harder. Going down the fixed line is OK to start, although I have some trouble tying into the line. About halfway down, I lose my balance and stumble. I get my ice axe into the snow and the line tightens before I fall far. Dave again asks if I'm all right; I say sure, but I'm feeling frustrated and embarrassed. I stumble once, twice while trying to regain a foothold. I walk a few more yards, then stumble again. I can't believe this is happening to me. I feel like an incompetent clown, putting on a show for all the people at 14,200.

Several more times, I fall, stumble, or lose my balance. I want to prove that I can handle this descent, but I'm failing. Will this be the end of the climb for me? Will Vern decide I've reached my limits after this debacle? Dave tries to be encouraging, telling me "You're doing fine, Bill." But I know better. As we approach the end of the fixed line, I see that the crampon on my left boot has been twisted; it's not sitting properly on the boot. That was one of the problems, a reason that my feet kept slipping out of footholds. I should have seen it earlier.

Finally we reach the end of the fixed rope. Vern calls for a rest break, and Dave helps me fix the crampon. I appreciate his help. Vern and Dave encourage me to eat and drink. We continue on and I handle the remainder of the route without problem. The snow is soft and deeper, making footholds easier. Once at camp, Clint, Petr, Vern, and Emilio offer encouragement. I feel sharper, more in control, more relaxed. Things are going to be OK.

The carry lasted ten and a half hours. When we returned to Camp IV at 11:30 P.M., the temperature was −15°F and skies were clear, giving us spectacular views of Hunter and Foraker bathed in alpenglow. Although tired, I felt clearheaded again.

While watching me struggle on the descent, Vern had become convinced that my exhaustion was complicated by altitude problems, that I'd been ataxic—suffering from a loss of coordination caused by a lack of oxygen. Afterward, he provided a combination pep talk/lecture:

> We all have days like that. I've seen people take some nasty spills coming down the fixed line. My second time down, I took a wicked somersault. Bunny boots are tough with crampons [most of the team was wearing double-plastic boots with supergaiters].
>
> Part of the problem may have been not eating and drinking enough. Hopefully, you learned a lesson. And it was a good one, because nobody got hurt. The only harm done was to your ego and pride.

Several other team members also had been showing signs of high-altitude illness. So before retiring for the night, Petr, Emilio, Dolly, Vern, and I took Diamox, a drug that's used both to prevent and treat mountain sickness. All of us felt considerably better in the morning; no headaches, nausea, or dizziness were reported. (Diamox is not a guarantee against mountain sickness, however, and may cause fatigue and other side effects.)

June 10 was beautiful, warm, and mostly sunny. It was good weather for traveling, but Vern declared a rest-and-recuperation day to allow us more opportunity to acclimate. Everyone seemed happy to take a break except for Clint. He was scheduled to meet his girlfriend, who was flying up from California on June 19, and was eager to keep moving. "I won't forgive you if it's storming tomorrow and we can't move," Clint told Vern, only half-kidding.

We used our day off to dry and air out clothing and sleeping bags, reorganize gear, update journals, play cards, relax, and talk. As usual, camp had an upbeat atmosphere. Team members got along remarkably well throughout the climb. There were no squabbles, no quarrels, no hard feelings. And when someone was feeling down or struggling, others would offer support, as several team members had done for me after the headwall episode.

Despite the day of rest, Linda never fully recovered from the first carry to Camp V. "I just wore out [going up the fixed line]," she said. "I was getting nauseated when I moved too fast. At the bottom I was taking two breaths for every step; at the top it was five." On June 11, as we began our second push to the top of the ridge, Linda traveled only a few hundred yards from camp before sitting down, exhausted. Too weak to continue, she headed back to 14,200, accompanied by her husband. Kelly wasn't having any physical problems, but decided to stay with his wife because, as he said, "we're a team."

My heels again ached badly as we climbed the fixed line, but it was something I just had to endure. And except for the heels, I felt good. Once above the headwall, I let loose with a cheer. The most difficult and painful climbing was now behind us.

We make two trips from 16,400 to 17,200, to carry all our fuel, food, and gear in a single day. My feet continue to ache on the steep stretches, but my stamina is good. Today it is Petr's turn to struggle. He must sit and rest several times. Vern tells Petr to drop his pack, but Petr refuses—a matter of pride. Much of the route is along the top of a ridgeline. In places it is very narrow, only a foot wide. Even roped up, a falling climber could get seriously hurt. Whoever calls this a walk-up is crazy. It demands endurance and snow-climbing skill with ice axe and crampons.

The trip is hard work, and there are too many things that can go wrong—storms, high winds, the extreme cold, crevasses, high-altitude sickness. I can see why the summit is so important to so many people. It makes the pain and risks worthwhile. As Petr said, "Once you're at the summit, you forget everything else."

I'd come to climb Denali for the adventure; it was to be a once-in-a-lifetime experience. Reaching the summit was my goal, but that wasn't crucial in determining the success or failure of my trip. Most important

BILL SHERWONIT

THE AUTHOR SITS OUTSIDE HIS TENT, WHICH IS PROTECTED BY A WALL OF SNOW BLOCKS, WHILE CAMPED AT 17,200 FEET ON MCKINLEY'S WEST BUTTRESS ROUTE.

---

was returning to base camp in good condition. I could appreciate the sentiments voiced by Mike Johnson, a climber we met as he was descending the mountain. Johnson had been turned back at 19,900 feet by high winds and whiteout. But as he told us, "It was a successful trip. We still have all our fingers and toes. We had a good trip."

Such an attitude was the exception, not the rule. Most climbers on Denali seemed obsessed with reaching the summit. Many would be willing to scrimp on safety for a shot at the top. Dr. Donner, whom I visited at the medical research camp, agreed: "People seem summit-crazed. I think it's a reflection of our Western culture. We're so goal oriented. It's the destination, not getting there, that's important."

At least two members of our party—Petr and Dave—had summit fever. Nothing less than the top would be acceptable. Petr's obsession was tied to his 1986 failed attempt (also with Genet

Expeditions) to climb Denali. On its first summit try, the team was turned back at 19,000 by a storm. The next day, the climbers tried again. But Petr stayed behind to rest, confident his teammates would again run into stormy weather. Conditions turned out to be ideal, however, and those who tried made it to the top. Petr was haunted by his decision to stay behind. This was his chance to exorcise the demons. "You can't just forget about it," he said. "I've been thinking about this for the whole year. You have to try again. You can't give up."

Emilio couldn't understand such thinking. "Too much emphasis is placed on reaching the summit," he said. "It's like you're defeated if you don't do it. But there's more to it than that. It's the whole experience of being on the mountain. The Natives had great respect for this mountain though they didn't try to climb it like the white man. That's big medicine up there, man. We have to give it respect too. There's too much talk about 'conquering' the mountain. You don't conquer the mountain. You climb it if it lets you."

The man in charge of our expedition was clearly summit oriented, as evidenced by his record: ten times reaching Denali's top in twelve previous tries. But his emphasis was placed on reaching it safely. "There's a real temptation to add another notch," Vern admitted before the climb. "But the safety of the clients is more important. That's my job."

Based on his considerable experience, Vern believed:

> The key in reaching the summit [via the West Buttress] is willpower. Willpower to eat when you're not hungry, drink when you're not thirsty and consciously breathe when your body isn't telling you that you need oxygen. If you do all those things—weather permitting—then you stand a good chance of reaching the summit.

Of course that's assuming a climber has properly trained for the mountain.

Through the first two weeks of our expedition, we'd been blessed with ideal weather, except for the one storm. We had ascended to 17,200 without any delays, and were now in position to take a shot at the summit.

June 13 at Camp VI was designated another rest day, though we probably couldn't have reached the summit even if we'd wanted. Winds gusting up to forty miles per hour rattled our tents, and the 2:00 P.M. windchill temperature was −45°F. Our tents protected us from the wind and were warmed by the sun. We spent most of the day in our sleeping bags, but in midafternoon left the warmth and security of our tents. With our snow saws, we cut blocks of snow, which were used to reinforce the walls surrounding our camp, and to build an igloo so Vern and Dolly could escape the wind while cooking our meals.

Our climbing party was awakened the next morning by the sounds of reveille, played by Vern on his harmonica. Unfortunately, his musical wake-up serenade was not a call to action. Our plans to attempt an assault on Denali's summit were postponed by "bad" weather. Gusting winds rushed through camp, and above us the mountain was wreathed in lenticular clouds, an indicator of high winds on the summit. "There's a climbing rule that says 'Don't go up when there's a lenticular,'" Vern said. "It's not a smart thing to do."

At 9:00 that morning, the temperature at 17,200 feet was −10°F, but winds of twenty miles per hour drove the windchill to −50°F. Up high, winds and temperature would have been much more severe. We watched and waited until midafternoon, hoping the winds would subside. With no change, Vern put the summit try on hold.

Petr, who woke up feeling nauseated and weak, was relieved to get the extra day's rest. But Clint was getting antsy. "I really hope it's nice tomorrow," he said. "I don't know if I can take another day of this lying around." And because of the weather, lying around in our tents is mostly what we did. Clint, Emilio, and I shared a tent. To pass the time, we read books, napped, wrote in our journals, and shared our perspectives of the climb.

"I keep asking myself why I did this," Clint said, adding with a grin, "I think it was a big mistake. It's been an ordeal; cold and miserable. In the future, I'll stick to two- and three-day trips. I'm not so sure about climbing any more of these big mountains. Maybe my criterion should be to not climb any mountain that has snow on it."

Emilio, also on his first major expedition, said, "This is a quantum leap above 'roughing it.' This is survival. It's quite a mountain. I wouldn't advise anyone to try it unless he has a lot of experience." While we passed time in our tent, Vern returned to 14,200 feet to check on Linda and Kelly, leaving Dolly in charge of the team. The doctors at the medical camp had diagnosed Linda's problem as simple exhaustion. It turned out that Kelly, who'd seemed to be in good shape, actually had more severe mountain sickness than his wife.

Sunny, blue skies, but again, strong winds. Perhaps stronger than Sunday. Large clouds of snow are being blown off Denali Pass (18,200 feet). The wind shook and rattled our tents all night long. People got out of their tents for breakfast, then retreated back inside. The wind-chill temperature is again down to 50 below. I'm reminded of a comment made by a French climber we met in Talkeetna: "Experience is not so important. More, it is the weather. The weather is everything." So maybe the mountain is giving us a lesson here. David and Petr are without doubt "summit crazed," and until recently Clint has talked a lot about "getting up there and bagging that peak." Yet the mountain has the final say. Unless conditions are right, it's not going to happen. I think that now, for me, Denali is more appealing than ever. There is certainly no conquest. You come, stay awhile, and if the mountain agrees, you're allowed into its most guarded, private reaches. . . . It is an alien world to us. And I don't think that those below will ever fully appreciate the mountain.

All members of our party were optimistic when we went to bed on June 15. The wind, after blowing continuously for three days, had died down. And the weather forecast was for light winds. But a new storm system moved in during the night. Again we were forced into a waiting game.

Vern, aware some members of the team were becoming impatient, stopped by our tent to deliver a hang-in-there pep talk during day three of our enforced layover. "The biggest challenge is sitting around, waiting for the storm to break," he said. "If you wait long enough, there's a good chance you'll outlast the weather and get a shot at the summit."

Clint wasn't convinced, however. "I'm not crazy about waiting six or seven days–or five, even–to get a chance at the summit. The summit doesn't mean that much to me." Vern calmly replied, "There are some people in the group who are willing to wait six or seven days. We've got to compromise. Now's the time we have to pull together. Keep your heads up, guys." Clint's growing impatience threatened to create a schism in camp, the first such instance on our trip.

Petr attributed much of our healthy group interaction to Vern's leadership. And Vern again demonstrated that leadership by arranging to have Clint descend with another climbing party. It was also a chance for Kelly and Linda to leave Camp IV at 14,200, where they'd been waiting the last five days. Though they'd hoped to remain together throughout the climb, the newlyweds agreed to part company for the remainder of the expedition. Linda headed down the mountain with Clint, while Kelly joined us at 17,200. Escorted by Vern, he reached high camp at 2:30 A.M. on June 17, after more than eight hours on the trail.

This evening we learned from another party that Denali Pass, normally a wind tunnel, was calm, sunny, and warm today, while our camp at 17,200 was blanketed in a whiteout. So go the fortunes of climbing. The mountain was out in all its splendor tonight, with clear skies and little wind. Very frustrating. I think we'll make a summit run Wednesday in just about any kind of weather.

June 17 started out just as the previous four days had: cold and windy. Early in the morning Vern discussed our situation with all of us. Several team members were clearly tired of waiting. Petr, who was having problems with the altitude, wanted to call it quits. Both he and Dolly had job commitments to consider. And Emilio had a flight departure to California scheduled for June 21. Time was running out.

Late in the afternoon, the wind died and the clouds broke. Suddenly, unexpectedly, it was sunny and calm. Vern decided we should take advantage of the break in the weather. There was no telling how long the "window" might last. At four o'clock he told the group, "Start getting your things together. We're going up."

Nighttime ascents of Denali are uncommon because of the extreme cold. Vern had led only one before; on that trip, a German climber had suffered frostbite on both feet and eventually lost several toes. And I was apprehensive about the prospect for another reason: Vern estimated a round-trip time of about twelve hours, eight up and four back down. I wondered how I would do, attempting the summit with no sleep.

By the time we had eaten a meal and packed our gear it was 5:30 P.M. Our decision to make an attempt had stirred lots of activity at neighboring camps. Another guided group started up the mountain just after us; they were making a carry to 18,000 feet, as part of a south-north traverse across the mountain. And a Swiss couple that had been waiting five days at 17,200 also decided to go for the top.

About a quarter mile from camp, before we'd gained any elevation, Kelly called it quits and returned to camp. He hadn't been able to adequately acclimatize after his ascent from 14,200 the previous evening and didn't have the endurance to continue. Like Kelly, my legs felt like lead weights as we started out. In my case, the leaden feeling was probably the result of four days of inactivity. But as we began to head up the ramplike trail to Denali Pass, my legs gradually lightened up. The pace was comfortable and I felt strong.

After traveling for about an hour and a half, we stopped to rest. I removed my glacier glasses because the light had become subdued. Or so I thought. Once moving again, I began to feel lightheaded and mentally weary. It may have been the lighting, which was brighter than I first judged it; certainly my eyes felt tired. Or maybe I was just feeling the altitude.

Gradually I began questioning the wisdom of continuing on. Here I was, feeling tired enough to sleep after only two hours of climbing and we had another ten hours to go. Through the night. . . . How important was the summit, anyway? Much of the pressure to reach the top came from outside. I had to prove myself. If my team was going to reach the summit, so was I. But the important thing was getting off the mountain safely.

By the time we reached 18,200-foot Denali Pass, the temperature had dropped several degrees and Petr was dragging. He was weak, tired, unable to continue. Once more turned back in a summit bid, he returned to 17,200, escorted by Dolly. I felt badly for Petr. We'd all been rooting hard for him to reach the summit.

That left four of us: Vern, Emilio, Dave, and me. I wasn't feeling great, but decided to carry on. The cold concerned me the most. Feeling chilled in the −20°F temperature, I put on all my cold-weather clothing, including my expedition-weight parka, although it was still early in the evening. I wondered how much colder it could get.

Though rest and nourishment were essential, I almost dreaded our eat-and-drink stops. My overmitts and woolen mittens made packing and unpacking food and water a miserable chore. Each time we ate or drank, I had to expose my hands to the cold and then struggle to rewarm them.

I tried putting my glacier glasses back on to protect my eyes, but they fogged up from my breathing. After several minutes spent trying to clear them, I decided to go without any eye protection. As Vern said, he'd never heard of anyone getting frostbitten eyes. The combination of my parka hood and balaclava (a knitted "helmet" that covers the head and face, with a small opening for the eyes and nose) left just a small slit across my eyes exposed to the cold.

As we continued on and up, the ice crunched beneath our crampons. I began having major breathing problems. No matter how deeply I breathed, I couldn't seem to get enough air—enough oxygen—into my lungs. I started dragging on the rope, slowing Vern's deliberate pace. And with about 1,000 vertical feet still to climb, my feet were painfully cold. During a rest break at The Archdeacon's Tower (elevation about 19,550 feet), I spent several minutes doing kick exercises to warm my toes, with only a little success.

Despite the physical problems, my determination had grown. Once above Denali Pass, the nature of our expedition had changed. The success of the team depended on the success of each individual. No longer was there an assistant guide to watch over an ailing climber. If one of us had been unable to continue, the entire party probably would have been forced to retreat; I was certain Vern wouldn't leave a member of the party behind. Knowing that, it became easier to put up with the pain. Each of us was working for the party as a whole.

Emilio had the same sort of feeling. "I felt like quitting," he later admitted. "There was one time I was hurting so bad, I just wanted to stop. But I knew if I stopped, we all stopped."

My body wanted to quit, but I wouldn't let it. . . . Somehow, I kept pushing on, trying to ignore the hurts. I was near my limits of endurance, close to exhaustion, just hanging on as best I could. One foot in front of the other. Block out everything else.

We left our packs at The Archdeacon's Tower and continued on across the Football Field, a shallow, windswept snow bowl about a quarter mile wide. Then, in what seemed like slow motion, we ascended the 800-foot-high snow and ice wall leading up to the summit ridge.

When we finally reached the ridge, it was covered with soft, fresh snow. There were no tracks. "Nobody's been up here for a week," said Vern, who broke trail, followed by me, then Emilio, and Dave.

As we neared the summit, I felt no elation or sense of victory, only relief that the ordeal was ending. But once on top, my relief was mixed with the deep satisfaction and joy that comes with a hard-earned achievement. Our stay was painfully short, no more than ten minutes. We let loose with a couple of "Yee-hahs!" and linked hands in tribute to the team's and each other's success. But it was very cold, −30°F. And while there wasn't much wind, even the gentle breeze that blew across the summit drove the windchill to −40°F or colder.

The time of our arrival at the top of North America was 3:54 A.M., June 18. I tried taking some summit photos to document our success, but my coordination was poor and my hands grew numb seconds after being removed from the mittens. I had trouble focusing and snapped only a couple of pictures, which was unfortunate because the sun had just risen above a layer of low-lying clouds, bathing Denali and surrounding peaks in a rosy glow.

Both Vern and Emilio were also suffering from the cold. They had extremely cold feet and Emilio was shivering badly; he was becoming hypothermic. Vern made Emilio do a set of jumping jacks to generate some body heat. Then we left the summit.

While heading down the mountain, we took great care to watch our steps. A large percentage of mountaineering accidents occur on the descent, when climbers all too often lose their edge, their concentration. We arrived safely back at Camp VI at 8 A.M., fourteen and a half hours after our start.

The remainder of the day, the team rested, except for Dolly. Forced to return to camp with Petr the previous night, she made a solo ascent to the summit while we slept. Dolly returned in the evening, reporting a glorious afternoon at the top of Denali.

Despite worries about my feet, the only damage to my skin was one frost-nip blister on my right hand, which I'd gotten from holding my camera bare-handed on the summit. Emilio wasn't so lucky. The tips of five toes and three fingers had turned bluish-black and had no feeling; they'd been frostbitten.[10]

By evening, large blisters had formed on Emilio's fingers and toes. Vern said that he would lose some skin but probably not any of his digits. Infection was the biggest danger; if the blisters broke, bacteria could enter the wounds.

We began our descent on June 19 under clear, calm skies. Still tired from the ascent, several of us stumbled during our march from 17,200 to 14,200. Again, being tied into roped teams saved us from any serious mishaps. Petr and Dolly, who were overdue at their jobs, traveled all the way to base camp in one very long day. The rest of us stopped at 11,000 feet. We planned on an easy downhill stroll to base camp on June 20, but the mountain changed those plans dramatically.

During the night, a storm moved in. We awoke to three feet of new snow, strong winds, and a visibility of about fifty feet. The trail was obliterated, so the route down-glacier was defined only by the wands that are placed every 200 feet, more or less, to mark the trail. But we all were anxious to leave, and Vern led us down the Kahiltna, confident that he could safely find his way to base camp even in the whiteout conditions.

Progress was slow as we traveled from wand to wand. All around was only flat, gray nothingness. Some stretches of the trail were marked poorly, or not at all. We zigzagged across the glacier, once more dependent on Vern's knowledge of the terrain, his judgment, and compass bearings.

Our group carried about two days' supply of food and fuel; if we'd been forced to bivouac, a storm lasting several days could have put us in a survival situation. And in such poor visibility, there was a much greater chance of stumbling into a crevasse. Frustrated, cold, and scared, I again questioned the wisdom of our decision to proceed. Maybe we should have stayed at 11,000 feet, where several other parties had also been camped.

Fortunately, we escaped such troubles. Several hours of back-and-forth wandering brought us to the bottom of Ski Hill (elevation about 7,700 feet), where the cloud ceiling began to lift and the snowfall ended. We were home free.

We reached base camp just before midnight. Our trek from 11,000 feet had taken nine hours; normally it's a five- or six-hour descent. Bush pilots had also been delayed by the storm and were working late, returning people to Talkeetna in the fading daylight. Emilio, limping badly because of his tender, blistered toes, was given a priority seat on one of the planes.

I caught the last flight of the evening, leaving the Alaska Range after twenty-one days on Denali. In the end, despite harsh conditions, the mountain had been kind to our group. Five of nine team members had reached the summit while following the West Buttress footsteps—and vision—of Bradford Washburn.

RENNY JACKSON

CLIMBERS REACH THE TOP OF A STEEP COULOIR WHILE ASCENDING THE CASSIN RIDGE, WHICH IS NAMED AFTER LEGENDARY ITALIAN MOUNTAINEER RICCARDO CASSIN.

Chapter Seven

Cassin's Conquest of the South Face, 1961

On the south side of McKinley rises a steep, 9,000-foot-high granite and ice spine that dissects McKinley's South Face and leads directly from the Kahiltna Glacier to the mountain's summit.

Though Bradford Washburn made no attempt to climb this precipitous route, he played a critical role in its first ascent. While conducting aerial photographic surveys of McKinley in the 1930s and 1940s, he became convinced that the mountain's "impossible" South Face could be climbed, just as he'd anticipated that the West Buttress would, with air support, prove to be the safest and easiest route up McKinley.

Years later, in the 1956-57 issue of *The Mountain World*, Washburn proposed several new routes to McKinley's summit, including one that he described as "probably the most difficult and dramatic of all . . . the great central bulge on the fabulous 10,000-foot South Face of the mountain. . . . This route may be classed as unequivocally excellent climbing from start to finish." That bulge, he emphasized, "presents an almost unbroken succession of precipitous pitches of granite and ice . . . with only two or three short stretches where the climber can catch his breath and relax at all."[1] Despite Washburn's inspired commentary, the South Face's great central bulge remained untested until 1961, when a climbing party representing the Italian Alpine Club paid a visit to the mountain.

The Italian expedition was organized by Carlo Mauri, a talented climber and guide who'd made the first ascent of Gasherbrum IV, a 26,000-foot Himalayan peak, in 1958. In planning for the trip to Alaska, Mauri recruited the legendary Riccardo Cassin to spearhead the most difficult and dangerous route yet attempted in Alaska. During the 1930s, Cassin had built a reputation as one of Europe's most brilliant alpinists, becoming the first climber to ascend three of the Alps' most difficult and dangerous north-face routes: the Grandes Jorasses, Piz Badile, and Cima Ovest di Lavaredo.

By 1961, Cassin was in his fifties, but he was still greatly respected for his toughness and mountaineering intelligence. As Italian climber Fosco Maraini put it, "There is something indestructible about this man; Paleolithic and Neanderthalish. Climbing with him you sense an inner force utterly alien to our complicated, mechanized, intellectualized world."[2]

Cassin was eventually named the expedition's leader.[3] Mauri, meanwhile, was forced to drop out after suffering a severe injury while skiing. Joining Cassin were five young Italians belonging to the elite Spider climbing club based in the town of Lecco: Giancarlo (Jack) Canali, Gigi Alippi, Romano Perego, Luigino Airoldi, and Annibale Zucchi. Of the six, only Cassin and Canali had high-altitude experience. The group also asked Bob Goodwin, a noted American mountaineer, to join them in Alaska.

While still in Italy the group contacted Washburn, who encouraged their attempt of the unclimbed South Face. En route to Alaska, Cassin stopped in Boston and spent several hours studying Washburn's extensive collection of McKinley maps and photos, which provided a clearer picture of the difficulties awaiting the team. After considerable discussion, Cassin agreed that the South Face's central bulge would present an extreme, yet perhaps achievable, challenge.

Cassin arrived in Anchorage on June 9 and made connections with Gianni Stocco and Armando Petrecca, Italian-Americans who'd settled in Alaska. While helping Cassin locate and organize the expedition's gear, they got caught up in the excitement of the climb. Promoting themselves as passionate and experienced climbers, the two men began lobbying for spots on the expedition. Cassin was hesitant to add two unknowns to the team. But because he hadn't heard from Goodwin as arranged, Cassin reluctantly agreed to take Stocco and Petrecca into the mountains. Once there, he could judge their abilities and commitment firsthand.

Climbers and gear were flown into the Kahiltna Glacier in mid-June by Don Sheldon, the first and most famous of a long line of "Denali Flyers" to be based in Talkeetna. Before dying from cancer in 1975, Sheldon flew climbers to and from the mountain for more than two decades, from the early 1950s to the mid-1970s. During that period, he offered aerial support to numerous McKinley expeditions and participated in several rescue operations. Arguably, he knew the mountain better than any bush pilot past or present. Sheldon, as much as anyone, helped open McKinley to the mountaineering masses and laid the groundwork for the air-taxi industry now based in Talkeetna.

In his book *Fifty Years of Alpinism*, Cassin reported that "the spot where Sheldon left us was not quite where we had calculated from the topographic map, for we could not land at the right place because of the snow conditions." But other accounts of the climb indicate that Cassin chose an incorrect landing spot, against Sheldon's advice. According to Chris Jones's account in *Climbing in North America*:

> As [the team] flew into the mountain, Cassin carefully pinpointed the landing zone. Sheldon carefully told him it was the wrong place. Cassin insisted. Climbers and gear were dropped off [at 7,700 feet] and Sheldon flew away. A couple days later he returned to check on their progress. Much to Sheldon's delight, Cassin meekly asked if he would ferry them to the proper landing place [at an elevation of 9,500 feet].[4]

(Both drop-off sites were located within a portion of Mount McKinley–now Denali–National Park that the federal government has since made off-limits to aircraft landings. Expeditions to McKinley's southern routes now typically begin at the Kahiltna Glacier Base Camp, located on the glacier's Southeast Fork, at an elevation of about 7,200 feet.)

By late June, finally joined by Goodwin, who'd been on another Alaska Range expedition, the team had established a base camp at 11,300 feet on the Kahiltna's East Fork. And Cassin had determined that his two other late additions, Stocco and Petrecca, were totally unprepared for such a hazardous undertaking. "Bluntly I tried to convince them to withdraw because they were unprepared physically, technically, and psychologically. It would have been an unforgivable weakness on my part to take them with us."

It took a few days, but Stocco and Petrecca eventually got the message, both from Cassin and the environment. They left the team on July 4, one day before the team began its ascent, which had been delayed by several days of stormy weather.

The Italians followed classic European expedition tactics. An advance rope team of three climbers explored the route, finding a

RENNY JACKSON

CLIMBERS SIT ON A NARROW LEDGE ABOVE A COULOIR ON THE CASSIN RIDGE.

path up the sheer granite and ice spine and putting in a fixed line; a second team of three followed behind, transporting food and equipment up the mountain. Putting in a route over such steep terrain was difficult, dangerous, and often exhausting work that demanded the lead climbers' full concentration. Cautiously seeking out both hand (or ice axe) and foot placements on near-vertical slopes and securing their ropes with bolts or ice screws, their progress was, at times, excruciatingly slow. So periodically, roles would be switched: lead climbers would become equipment packers, and vice versa. A series of camps was established along the route, but during the first two weeks of the ascent all expedition members returned frequently to base camp for welcome rests and easier acclimatization to the high altitudes.

The group's first major obstacle was a steep couloir. Operating in shifts, the climbing teams struggled to find the path of least resistance through a complex series of sixty-five-degree ice-coated walls, overhanging rock faces, and granite spires—a long and exhausting struggle made even more difficult by steady snowfall. Their ascent was stalled on several occasions, when the climbers encountered unscalable barriers that forced them to retreat and seek out alternate routes through the near-vertical ice and rock maze. Already, Cassin noted, the central ridge "was presenting all the uncertainty and difficulty I had foreseen."

Ice, rock, and snow were not the only challenges to be faced. On the night of July 9, a violent wind began battering the team's base camp. The next morning, three team members resumed their reconnaissance of the route despite the gales. By late afternoon on July 10, the wind had grown so strong that it whipped the base camp's tents into a flapping frenzy that sounded like machine-gun fire. Once, when leaving his tent to check one of the others, Cassin was nearly flattened by a gust.

Gradually, the wind died down. But as it did, a heavy snow again began falling. Cassin grew worried about his teammates still on the ridge, but his fears were alleviated at 9:30 P.M., when they appeared in camp "completely encrusted in ice."

The lead climbers attempted to set up the team's first ridgeline camp on July 11, but thick fog and newly deposited knee-deep snow forced a retreat. They succeeded a day later, establishing Camp I on a tiny snow shelf at 13,400 feet. By July 15, they'd also put in camps at 14,200 and 17,000 feet; finally the team had worked its way past the most difficult and dangerous sections of rock and ice. (About this time, Goodwin was forced to leave the team because of a work commitment. It had been understood that he'd only remain with the expedition for a few days because of limited vacation time.)

With their high camp now in place, the Italians prepared to enter what Cassin called "the most committing phase of the expedition, that preceding the final attack." The climbers wouldn't return to base camp until either they'd reached the summit or been forced to give up their attempt. Early on July 19, the team began its summit push, roped into two groups of three.

"Our plan," Cassin later wrote, "was to attempt to reach the summit and then go back without stopping to Camp III. I was aware of the risks but, because of the bad weather, could see no other way. Each of us knew the strains, sacrifices, and commitments we were to take on this decisive day. The boys were truly magnificent in their complete dedication to the ascent, though a certain nervous tension showed on their faces."

While making their final approach, up steep ice and snow couloirs and a granite tower, the climbers were buffeted by a steady, fierce wind that penetrated their clothes. Complicating matters further were the high altitude, variable snow and ice conditions, and the temperature, which had dropped to about −35°F. Any movement was exhausting.

The six Italians reached McKinley's top at about 11:00 P.M., after seventeen hours on the trail. During their ascent, the climbers had barely eaten; their one meal for the day consisted of canned fruit.

With numbed, stiffened hands, they opened their packs and pulled out flags representing the United States, Alaska, Italy, the town of Lecco, and the Italian Alpine Club. At the summit they also left a small statue of St. Nicholas, patron of Lecco, and a crucifix.

Cassin tried to take some photos, but the darkness and cold made it nearly impossible. Talk was equally difficult, so the team celebrated its success in silence, with a short embrace. "As always, not one of us is in the proper mental state to feel the joy of our conquest," Cassin wrote. "The difficulties are not over until everyone has descended to safety." And in fact things got worse instead of better for the Italians during their descent.

Canali, whose feet had started to freeze on the ascent, became nauseated shortly after leaving the summit. (Despite Sheldon and Washburn's warnings about McKinley's extreme cold, the Italians had worn single leather boots with no insulation.) He seemed to recover, but just as the team prepared to descend a steep gully, Cassin heard "a sudden, sinister rustle." Turning, he spotted Canali tumbling down the icy slope. Cassin, who was tied onto the same rope as Canali, instinctively fell to the ground, jammed his ice axe into the snow and stopped his teammate's out-of-control slide. Though he wasn't injured during the short fall, Canali began vomiting heavily.

Plagued by frostbitten feet and altitude sickness, Canali had difficulty keeping his balance and fell several more times during the descent to 17,000 feet. Expecting such difficulties, Cassin had taken over as the rope's anchor-man and managed to stop each of the falls.

The severe weather also complicated matters. Though the wind had died down, it was now snowing heavily. Only through "a tremendous effort" did the six climbers reach Camp III at 6:00 A.M. on July 20; they'd been climbing twenty-three hours with little rest or food.

Once inside their tents, the climbers immediately began melting snow for drinks and a hot meal. Cassin, meanwhile, massaged Canali's frostbitten feet, already swollen and blue in color. "We all did our best to cheer him up," he wrote. "I tried to hide my fears so as not to upset the boys, but in Gigi's eyes I seemed to see the same anxious questions that nagged inside me. With Jack in this condition how were we to reach Base Camp? And what if he went on getting worse? Outside it snowed incessantly."

Though Canali's frostbite was the most serious, he wasn't the only climber suffering frozen extremities. Both Perego and Airoldi had slightly frostbitten hands. Adding to the climbers' discomfort were the overcrowded conditions. They were crammed into a pair of tents barely big enough for two people under normal circumstances.

Acting as both team leader and doctor, Cassin felt the strain of responsibility. Afraid that Canali might need help during the night, he had difficulty falling asleep. And though his feet were very cold, he lay as still as possible, not wishing to disturb his exhausted partners; as a result, he ended up suffering minor frostbite to his big toes.

High winds, cold temperatures, and heavy snow kept the climbers pinned in their tents for more than a day. Not until 11:00 A.M. on July 21 did Cassin feel it was safe to resume the descent.

Canali was unable to fit his swollen feet into his boots, and so Alippi offered him the use of his reindeer boots. It was a most generous offer, since Alippi was left with nothing more than four pairs of socks and a pair of soft inner boot linings to cover his own feet. With that footwear, Alippi was unable to use his crampons, so the descent became slippery torture for him.

The climbers again roped into two teams: Cassin, Canali, and Zucchi on one rope; Airoldi, Alippi, and Perego on the other. While descending a hanging glacier above Camp II, the inevitable happened. Alippi lost his footing and began hurtling down the ice. Perego's attempt to stop the fall failed, but Cassin miraculously managed to catch their rope and hold them.

Upon completing their exhausting descent to Camp II, the rope team of Airoldi, Alippi, and Perego chose to spend the night at that spot and get some much-needed rest. But Cassin, fearing that "a long halt might let Jack's condition become so much worse he could no longer stand," insisted that he, Canali, and Zucchi continue moving.

Through thickening fog and growing darkness the trio worked their way to Camp I, where they spent a cheerless night. Cassin's admiration for his partners is obvious in his account of the climb: "Annibale's stamina seemed inexhaustible, and Jack, despite his condition, was a real prodigy of moral and physical strength."

Cassin, Canali, and Zucchi completed their remarkable journey on July 22. Descending via the fixed lines that Cassin called the expedition's salvation, they were bombarded by numerous avalanches. Most of the slides were small, but near the bottom of the lowest couloir, Cassin was buried by a large avalanche that pinned him against the icy slope for what seemed like an eternity. Fortunately, he instinctively held on to the fixed rope. Though stunned by the slide, he escaped without injury.

Upon reaching base camp, the three ropemates filled themselves with food and drink. And once again Cassin massaged Canali's frozen feet. Though exhausted, the climbers got little sleep. Canali was kept awake by his frostbitten feet, and the others were kept awake by his moaning.

July 23 brought an end to seventy-five hours of continuous snowfall. With the sunny skies, however, came dozens of avalanches. Huge, heavy snow slides accompanied by blocks of ice and rock poured down the mountain. Those safe in base camp couldn't help but worry about their companions up on the ridge. But late that night Airoldi, Alippi, and Perego arrived in camp, ending the suspense and concern. "After days of tension," Cassin wrote, "we finally entered a state of grace, really a total relaxation of our nerves, which allowed us to savour to the full the joy of our success."

On the evening of July 24, the Italians improvised a sled and hauled Canali to the site on the Kahiltna Glacier where Sheldon and his airplane already waited. All team members were reunited in Anchorage a few days later. Airoldi, Perego, and Cassin were each treated for frostbite; Canali, though requiring extensive treatment and rehabilitation, eventually recovered fully from his frostbite as well.

The Italians returned as heroes. Among the congratulations was a telegram from President John F. Kennedy, praising the team for its "outstanding accomplishment under the most hazardous of conditions." Perhaps a greater accolade, however, was Washburn's observation in 1961 that Cassin and his five teammates had pulled off what up to that time was "without question the greatest climb in North American mountaineering history."[5]

Though Cassin labeled his team's route the South Buttress, it was later renamed in his honor. Now known as the Cassin Ridge, the South Face's "central bulge" is widely revered as one of McKinley's classic alpine challenges.

George Wichman

MEMBERS OF THE 1967 WINTER EXPEDITION: FROM LEFT, SHIRO NISHIMAE, ART DAVIDSON, JACQUES BATKIN, GEORGE WICHMAN, DAVE JOHNSTON, GREGG BLOMBERG, JOHN EDWARDS, AND RAY GENET.

Chapter Eight

The First Winter Ascent, 1967

By the mid-1960s, nearly all of McKinley's secrets had been revealed—at least from a mountaineering standpoint. Because of improved access, equipment, and techniques, each of its major faces and ridges had been ascended, including those once considered impossible (the one notable exception being the East Face, which remains unclimbed as of 2012).

No longer was North America's highest peak a mysterious place to climb. Except in winter.

From 1913 through 1966, more than 200 climbers reached the top of North America. But all of those ascents were made between early May and early August, when daylight hours are long and temperatures are relatively mild. No expedition had come close to attaining McKinley's summit in winter. In fact, none had ever tried. And, by all accounts, no one had even seriously considered the idea. "There was no doubt [a winter ascent] could be done by the right group," said Bradford Washburn. "But no one was interested in trying. It's a brutal place to be in winter."[1] Then came Art Davidson and Shiro Nishimae.

Davidson, a native of Colorado, had been introduced to climbing in high school. The introduction was not entirely a happy one; he recalls, "My first reaction was 'if I live through this, I'll never do it again.'" But the initial trauma gave way to exhilaration, and Davidson ended up getting hooked on the sport.[2]

Mountaineering soon became the focal point of his life—both the challenges of steep rock and the opportunity to explore new landscapes. In 1964, Davidson's wanderlust and love of mountains brought him to Alaska. It was there that his climbing career reached its zenith. During a seventeen-month period from April 1966 to August 1967, he participated in six major expeditions. All were successful. According to author David Roberts, who went on several expeditions with Davidson:

> [Davidson] was at home in his beloved mountains as few climbers I have ever known learned how to be, and his appetite was boundless. . . . I wonder if any other mountaineer has accomplished the like. . . . In Alaska, where more expeditions fail than succeed and where many pack it in and go home before they even get started, Art's confidence and energy seemed to set an impossible standard.[3]

Not long after his arrival in Alaska, Davidson began to feel McKinley's magnetism. During the summer of 1965, he joined the Osaka Alpine Club, which put in a new route along the mountain's South Buttress. Three of the Japanese climbers reached McKinley's summit, including the expedition's twenty-nine-year-old leader, Shiro Nishimae, described by Davidson as "a superb climber and a man of great wisdom who taught me much of what I know about high-altitude climbing."

In his mountaineering classic *Minus 148°: The Winter Ascent of Mt. McKinley*, Davidson explains that it was Nishimae who first suggested the possibility of a winter expedition:

> While Shiro and I watched huge cornices soften and crumble in the July sun, we tried to picture the winter storms that packed snow onto these massive ice formations overhanging the ridges. When we shed our shirts as we carried loads on the glacier, we wondered what the temperatures would drop to in February. It might remain below minus 30 degrees Fahrenheit for weeks. At these temperatures, with hundred-mile-per-hour winds, could a person survive, let alone climb? We shuddered to imagine McKinley's most eerie winter aspect–the darkness.[4]

Such imaginings infected the two climbers with a desire–a fever–to visit this still-unknown season of McKinley. And so, at age twenty-two, Davidson began preparing for the challenge he'd dreamed of since his childhood days in Colorado: a journey into unexplored territory.

Because no one had ever scaled the mountain's slopes in winter, no one knew what weather extremes might be encountered. From the readings obtained on minimum-temperature thermometers that some expeditions had left on the mountain, temperatures of −60°F, or colder, could be anticipated. Previous summer expeditions had experienced hurricane-force winds gusting to more than one hundred miles per hour. At least one experienced McKinley mountaineer predicted a winter expedition would face the most severe conditions ever experienced by humans.

As Washburn noted, not many right-thinking people would choose to expose their bodies to such brutal conditions. So, not surprisingly, Davidson had trouble finding other qualified mountaineers interested in participating in such a harrowing journey.

Several months of intense recruiting failed to produce any firm commitments. By July of 1966, Davidson had all but conceded that his winter dreams had collapsed. But just when things looked hopeless, a team began to take shape. By September, Davidson and Nishimae had been joined by four other climbers: Dave Johnston and Dr. George Wichman of Anchorage; Gregg Blomberg of Denver; and John Edwards, a native New Zealander who was then living in Ohio.

Although they were the expedition's catalysts, Davidson and Nishimae chose not to lead the McKinley team. Instead they sought "someone with a strong personality, who could gather the right people around him and fuse them into a close-knit group that could work smoothly under the most miserable circumstances." They picked Blomberg, who'd taught mountaineering for several years and led the successful ascent of a new route on Canada's Mount Logan. As head of Colorado Mountain Industries, Blomberg was also known for being a perfectionist in the manufacture and use of climbing equipment.

Wichman, a thirty-nine-year-old orthopedic surgeon, signed on as the team doctor. His twenty years of climbing experience included an unsuccessful attempt to reach McKinley's summit in April 1965.

Edwards, thirty-five, was a biologist who had climbed in New Zealand, England, the Alps, and America's Grand Tetons. According to Davidson, "He was fabled to be amiable, boisterous, occasionally mischievous, and at the same time a thoroughly levelheaded and thoughtful fellow. My first meeting with John reaffirmed the legend."

Another "rare, almost mythical creature" was Johnston, a twenty-four-year-old self-described climbing bum with a degree in forestry, whose mountaineering fanaticism had taken him to ranges scattered throughout North, Central, and South America.

His climbing experience included a traverse of Mount McKinley and a couple of first ascents on Mount Hunter, a 14,570-foot neighbor of McKinley.

The six climbers considered their Winter 1967 Mount McKinley Expedition to be complete. But in mid-December, Davidson began receiving long-distance phone calls from a man with a thick Swiss accent. That man was Ray Genet, destined to become a McKinley legend.

Genet wanted himself and a Frenchman named Jacques "Farine" Batkin included on the team. There was no question of Batkin's qualifications. One of the most powerful climbers in Europe, he had pioneered several difficult winter ascents of steep ice and rock walls in the Alps. Three years earlier, he'd participated in the first ascent of 12,240-foot Mount Huntington, a beautiful and extremely challenging peak located about eight miles north of McKinley.

Although short, the Frenchman had a powerful build, with enormous shoulders and a barrel-shaped chest. Years spent carrying flour sacks had developed his physique and also resulted in his nickname, Farine. Davidson had no doubts: "Farine appeared perfect for McKinley in the winter."

Genet was a different story. He had minimal climbing experience. His most noteworthy ascent was on a rounded 4,500-foot peak. Though he exuded enthusiasm and determination, the Swiss adventurer seemed to be trying to prove something to the team—and, perhaps, to himself. In the end, however, Genet's charm, friendliness, and unbridled enthusiasm won out. "Before we realized it," Davidson noted, "Genet was part of the expedition."

It was during the distribution of personal gear that Genet earned his famous nickname. In putting together his climbing outfit, he chose only bright-orange clothing. And to identify his equipment, Genet painted a skull and crossbones on each item. That insignia, combined with his black, bushy beard and robust laughter, prompted teammates to name him "Pirate."

The eight-member party flew into the Alaska Range in late January. Bush pilot Don Sheldon dropped the climbers on the Kahiltna Glacier's Southeast Fork at an elevation of about 7,000 feet. The team had chosen to follow the West Buttress, a route that is relatively protected from avalanches and not technically demanding. It offered a speedy descent, if necessary.

The first day in the range, two incidents occurred that foreshadowed later tragedy. Blomberg and Johnston were the first two climbers flown in by Sheldon. After being set down, they roped up together and began scouting the route for crevasses. Upon returning to the drop-off site several hours later, they were greeted by Batkin, who was filled with excitement and was running around unroped.

The two Americans were shocked by Farine's apparent carelessness. The US climbing community generally considers unroped glacier travel to be unsafe because of the dangers posed by crevasses. But foreign climbers, particularly Europeans and Japanese, often accept the risks of climbing unroped on McKinley and other Alaskan peaks.

Despite their concern, Blomberg and Johnston let the incident pass without comment. "Since Farine spoke no English and they spoke no French, they figured it would be nearly impossible to caution him without insulting him," Davidson later explained. "After all, Farine had more experience on glaciers than either of them had. . . . Farine was safe. The route was now clearly marked with willow wands. What did it matter?"

That night, while ferrying loads along a marked and presumably safe path from the landing site to the team's first camp about one mile up the glacier, Genet fell into a crevasse. He, too, was unroped. Fortunately, the crevasse was partly filled with snow and

Pirate landed unhurt after a twenty-foot tumble. Afterward, he tried to laugh off the incident. Nishimae and Davidson, who'd been following Genet on the trail, were upset both by Pirate's nonchalance and the team's decision to move gear across the glacier in darkness rather than spend the first night at the landing site. "We were all safe," Davidson wrote. "Nevertheless, I was still troubled by the near-accident and by what I thought was impatience."

On their second day in the mountains, the climbers ferried several hundred pounds of supplies to a temporary cache located about two and a half miles up the glacier, then returned to camp. The following morning, they prepared to move camp, hoping to establish a new one at about 7,800 feet, near the base of a hill that rises to 10,300-foot Kahiltna Pass. The route had been scouted and marked during the previous day's carry and no crevasses were exposed; it appeared safe. So the climbers again traveled unroped.

While filming his surroundings at about 2:00 P.M., Davidson noticed three of his teammates standing together a half mile ahead. Figuring they must be at the new campsite, he began his final approach. But after several steps, he plunged through the wind-hardened snow.

He'd fallen, waist-deep, into a hidden crevasse, and was supported precariously by a snow bridge. Below him, the crevasse dropped sixty to eighty feet. If the snow bridge collapsed, he'd be dead.

Some of the snow gave way, and Davidson sank up to his shoulders. Fighting panic and weakening muscles, Davidson inched his way out of the icy trap and up onto stable snow. "I rolled away from the crevasse and stood up on shaking legs," he recounted. "My lungs heaved wildly to catch their breath. I was shivering. My head was roaring. I wasn't going to fall on those rocks. . . . It was all over."

Looking back at his route, Davidson saw that he'd wandered off the marked trail while filming. The hole marking his fall was the only sign of the crevasse, which was perhaps part of a network of crevasses. Unfortunately, Davidson had no bamboo wands with him to stake out the danger area. He worried about Johnston, Batkin, and Blomberg, who were somewhere behind him on the trail, but told himself that they would stay on the marked path and thus avoid the weakened snow bridge through which he'd plunged.

Of one thing Davidson was certain: no matter how benign it appeared, the glacier most definitely was not safe. When everyone had gathered at the new campsite, he would warn them of the hidden crevasses and insist that team members rope themselves together to minimize the risks of glacier travel.

Upon joining Edwards, Wichman, and Genet, Davidson told them of his struggles. Soon, they noticed two figures, about a half-mile below. While awaiting the arrival of those two teammates, the climbers resumed building a tent platform. After a short while, they again looked down-glacier. Where there'd been two people, now they could see only one. Fearing the worst, they made their way quickly down the glacier.

Batkin, who'd been following Johnston up the glacier, had fallen into the same crevasse that nearly engulfed Davidson less than an hour earlier. Noticing his hole only thirty feet away, Davidson cursed himself for not having waited at the crevasse to warn the others.

Johnston descended into the crevasse and found the Frenchman, lying unconscious, on an ice shelf fifty feet below the glacier's surface. Joined by Blomberg, the climbers slowly and with great difficulty hauled their teammate out onto the snow. Farine's face was caked with blood and his eyes were open, staring blankly. There was no sign of a pulse, but Wichman massaged Farine's heart and applied pressure to his chest, while Davidson and then Johnston tried mouth-to-mouth resuscitation.

"George knew how to make a decisive check," Davidson wrote. "He shined a flashlight into Farine's eyes. There was no

George Wichman

MEMBERS OF THE 1967 WINTER EXPEDITION HAUL JACQUES "FARINE" BATKIN'S BODY DOWN THE KAHILTNA GLACIER TO AN APPROPRIATE PICKUP SITE.

contraction of the pupil. When he took the flashlight away, the pupil remained the same size. 'He is dead,' George sighed." Still, Davidson and Johnston refused to give up. For several minutes more they pushed on Batkin's chest and breathed air into his lungs. But the body remained motionless. Lifeless.

It was now getting dark. Davidson read a prayer. The team then left Batkin's body by the crevasse, tied into a rope, and headed for camp. Along the way, they met Nishimae, who'd been searching for an airdrop left by Sheldon. No one spoke, as each team member blamed himself for the tragedy.

Davidson recalled, at that point:

> I was too numb to feel the horror. Rather, I felt guilty. Though I didn't want to admit it to myself, I knew I should have stayed by the crevasse when I fell—to warn the others. At least I should have marked the hole

with something. If I hadn't been in shock, if I hadn't been so anxious to leave the place where I had fallen, Farine would still be alive.

Later that evening, crowded inside a tent, the climbers debated the pros and cons of continuing. Blomberg called the expedition a failure and proposed it be discontinued. His joy and enthusiasm for the winter ascent had vanished with Batkin's death. Davidson, Johnston, and Genet declared their desire to go on. Others were undecided. Finally, agreeing they were too deeply in shock to think clearly, the team members decided to wait a day or two before making any decision.

The men avoided talking about Farine. Explained Davidson, "To remove ourselves from the immediacy of our horror we abstracted it, spoke of it in general terms." But try as they might, they couldn't help but replay the horror of Batkin's death in their minds. No one slept easily that night. Inside his sleeping bag, Davidson stared at the dark for hours. Blomberg, feeling isolated and burdened by the responsibility that comes with leadership, wept silently. And Johnston wrote in his journal:

> It's real. It's like an underwater nightmare that never really happened. In retrospect, only this exists: my love for Farine.
>
> He seemed to have a special, glowing smile for me; the kind you get from your partner after a tough lead. It was a smile you felt; one I could feel and return, and know he felt the return. His love for climbing was written all over his face.
>
> I remember his freedom, like an untethered bird, as he wandered uncapped, and unmitted, and unroped about the glacier. His deep pleasure and peace of mind were written in his eyes when he wandered this way. He was happy and content with so little.

The next morning a storm moved in from the south, forcing the team to move camp away from a nearby slope that might avalanche if there were a heavy snowfall. The climbers retreated down-glacier, past Batkin's body, which they marked with a wand for later recovery. Fearing that their tents might be ripped apart by extreme winds, they roped up in teams of two or three and searched for snow they could cut into blocks, to build an igloo. (Not only are igloos and snow caves more wind resistant, they are also quieter, an important consideration when trying to sleep during a roaring storm, and much warmer in extreme cold than tents, because of snow's insulating qualities.)

In subzero temperatures and thick, blowing snow that chilled the climbers and reduced visibility to a few feet, they built their shelter at 7,500 feet. The harsh, stormy conditions in which they worked helped them to forget, if only temporarily, Batkin's tragic death and pulled the expedition members together because they had to work as a team.

The following day, the storm eased up enough to permit travel. While most of the team hauled Batkin's now-frozen corpse to an appropriate pickup spot, Nishimae and Genet hurried back to the original landing site, where a radio had been cached; they planned to call Sheldon, to ask him to fly the body back to town. The radio failed to work, however, leaving the climbers with no way to contact civilization and no way to call for help if they needed it.

The climbers knew they had to deal with Batkin's body and explain his death to the public before resuming their climb toward McKinley's summit. The team stamped a "LAND" message in the snow, and while awaiting some contact with the outside world, they resumed ferrying loads up the glacier.

On February 4, four days after Batkin's death, a pilot flying through the Alaska Range noticed the message. Upon landing, pilot Jim Cassidy was told of the tragedy. He in turn notified Sheldon. Less than two hours later, Batkin's body had been loaded into Sheldon's plane and Genet was heading for Anchorage with a press release written by Blomberg, explaining the circumstances of Batkin's death. The final two sentences read, "Jacques Batkin died in the pursuit of a winter ascent, in which he truly believed. We will continue the attempt with his spirit and presence very much in mind."

The decision had been made. The climbers would continue their march toward McKinley's summit.

Among the letters sent out on Sheldon's flight was a note from Blomberg to his wife in Colorado. He wrote, "[Farine's] death is a terrible thing, but should it alter our purpose? I don't know. I know many people will condemn us for going on. I know many mountaineers will condemn with good reason this avoidable accident, but I can't really see how our quitting now would help. . . . I don't know if I want to go for the summit myself, but I must support those who do. . . ."

The next day, as the team was carrying loads up the glacier, yet another member of the team fell into a crevasse. This time it was Edwards. Fortunately, the climbers were now traveling in roped teams, and Blomberg managed to stop the fall, but not until Edwards had plunged forty-five feet.

Though not severely injured, Edwards was unable to climb out of the crevasse. The team rigged up a pulley system designed to haul him out, but the rescue rope began cutting into the snow at the crevasse's edge. Complicating matters even more, Edwards had retied the climbing rope across his chest; as he was pulled upward, the rope began to constrict his breathing. Screaming that he felt faint, Edwards became incoherent. Then there was silence below.

With Edwards's life now clearly endangered, Nishimae rappelled down into the crevasse, rearranged the ropes, and began pushing from below. With Nishimae's help, the team pulled their injured, exhausted, and nearly unconscious teammate up onto the glacier's surface. He'd been stuck in the crevasse for more than three hours.

Despite bruised ribs, a sore arm, and an aching back, Edwards felt understandable relief after his rescue. But his climbing partners were troubled; they knew they had nearly lost him.

The climbers spent a somber evening in their shelter. No one felt much like talking. Davidson said:

> I felt lonely and discouraged by the apparent ineptness of our expedition. After one week we had succeeded in losing one man; another was off trying to explain that death to the outside. John and I had both nearly disappeared into crevasses. The expedition was bogged down by something. . . . It seemed we were struggling in a sort of quicksand; all our efforts were getting us no further up the mountain, only deeper into the vicious tangle of our frustrations.

Following a fitful night, the climbers awoke on February 6 to another blizzard. The day's agenda was simple: rest and try to recuperate from the traumas of recent days. The next day brought improved weather conditions, so team members resumed shuttling gear from their landing-site supply cache to the igloo. To do so, they had to cross the crevasse field where Edwards had fallen. Still shaken by that incident, they moved extremely slowly, and cautiously probed the snow before each step. Using that method, several other crevasses were discovered and safely avoided.

By the morning of February 8, Davidson and Johnston were anxious to move camp from their "Kahiltna Hilton"–the igloo at 7,500 feet–up to 10,200 feet. Nishimae, however, convinced his teammates they should be patient and wait another day or two for Genet's return. So the climbers continued shuttling supplies to be used in the highest camps. Ultimately, they hoped to have at least ten days' worth of food and fuel at the high camp at 17,200 feet.

The climbers didn't have to wait long for their missing partner. Genet returned on February 9, bringing a stack of mail, some fried chicken, several cans of beer, a new radio, and news clippings about Batkin's death. Genet's arrival seemed to revive the team's sagging spirits. "With Pirate back, we felt fresher; it seemed we were making a new start," Davidson said. "Our revived enthusiasm, combined with an airdrop at 10,200 feet that Sheldon made for us, helped us move camp quickly."

Thirty-six hours after Genet's return, the team settled into a small complex of igloos built just below Kahiltna Pass. That "iglooplex," as it was christened by Edwards, included two eight-by-eight-foot shelters for sleeping, a connecting chamber in which food and equipment was stored, plus a large dining area, in which all seven climbers could sit comfortably.

Daily temperatures at 10,200 feet averaged about −20°F, about 15° colder than at 7,500. The increased cold affected nearly everything the climbers did. While lacing boots or tying into the rope, they had to pause more often to warm their hands. At night in the iglooplex's dining room, they often took turns marching in place to keep their feet from becoming numb. It took longer to melt ice and snow into water, and hot drinks turned cold in a matter of seconds. Lunch snacks had to be carried close to their bodies to thaw out their rock-hard consistency. At the slightest sign of a breeze, face masks were put on, to guard against frostbitten noses.

Several days of clear weather enabled the team to transport supplies to 13,200-foot Windy Corner. The next campsite would be in a glacial bowl at 14,400 feet. At these higher elevations, snowshoes were replaced by crampons. And while carrying their forty- to sixty-pound loads, the climbers increasingly felt the effects of altitude. They had to breathe harder, rest more often, and step more slowly.

On February 14, the climbers bade farewell to their iglooplex. Upon reaching a supply cache at 12,500 feet late in the afternoon, they decided to spend the night at that site. That night the temperature sank to −42°F, which the team took as reason for celebration. "We shouted and began singing nonsense songs at the top of our voices," Davidson recalled. "Minus 42 degrees–what an event to celebrate on St. Valentine's Day. Our elation ran unchecked. . . . This is what we had come on McKinley to find. We were getting into the cold temperatures at last."

The team finished its move to 14,400 feet on February 15. Temperatures approaching −40°F, combined with a slight breeze, brought the windchill temperature to −50°F. In such conditions, the climbers had to avoid breathing too deeply, because they felt a burning sensation in their lungs whenever they drew in too much of the extremely dry, cold air. Once beyond Windy Corner, the climbers only had to negotiate a gently rising slope, about one-and-a-half miles long, to reach their next campsite. Despite the gentle grade, Edwards struggled; he was still weakened and bothered by a sore back from his crevasse fall. Only a few hundred yards from the team's destination, he shed his pack and fell in a heap on top of it. According to Davidson, Edwards suggested, "Maybe I could rest . . . for a while . . . leave my pack here . . . then make it."

Davidson recalled, "The tight expression on John's face spoke of his weariness. . . . It seemed unfair that what most of us would remember as a pleasant afternoon was an ordeal for John." Edwards's teammates agreed he should stay and rest. An hour or so later, Nishimae and Davidson returned and accompanied him the remaining distance.

At 14,400 feet, camp was established below the ice wall leading to the West Buttress ridgeline, in a location protected from avalanches. The team hoped to build two snow shelters before dark, but only one was completed because they had trouble finding snow of the right consistency for snow blocks. While the men worked on their igloos, high clouds moved in from the south, and the temperature rose to a relatively balmy −20°F; both were signs of an approaching storm.

The blizzard arrived the next morning, as the team was completing its second igloo. For the next three days, snow fell so heavily that visibility was reduced to fifty feet or less. Though unable to start up the ice wall, the climbers continued ferrying loads from below. Davidson found the challenges of working in the storm "a relief from the more intangible troubles we'd been batting our heads against down below . . . the strain of the hidden crevasses, the accident and even the uncertainty of whether we'd go on."

Despite the stormy weather, members of the expedition became increasingly excited about achieving the summit, which finally seemed within reach. The enforced rest also helped Edwards acclimatize to the altitude and regain some of his strength. He talked hopefully of making a summit attempt. On February 19, the sky cleared enough to permit an ascent of the steep ice face leading to the West Buttress ridge. The group cached a load of supplies at 16,200 feet, where the thermometer registered −32°F, then returned to the camp at 14,400 feet.

The next morning, stormy weather again socked in the mountain and the climbers were forced to hole up inside their snow shelter for two days. Pirate had brought along a line-of-sight CB radio, and on the evening of February 21, he called Anchorage and got a weather report: several days of clear weather were predicted.

February 22 dawned clear and calm. Taking immediate advantage of the weather, Blomberg, Genet, Edwards, and Wichman ferried gear to the team's high camp at 17,200 feet. Because they didn't plan to descend until a summit bid had been made, the foursome carried food, gas, two small stoves, snow shovels, an ice saw, a four-person tent, more than a hundred wands, extra sweaters, and their sleeping bags.

Davidson, Johnston, and Nishimae stayed behind to get additional supplies from the 12,500-foot cache. The extra provisions might be needed at high camp if the team were forced to wait out a prolonged storm. "There was no immediate danger in splitting the party," Davidson wrote. "Still, none of us would feel completely at ease until our two groups, without communication between each other, were again one group."

The team members reunited at 17,200 feet on February 23. Although they had endured short spells of bitterly cold weather and were stalled by several blizzards during their first three weeks on the mountain, the climbers had been lucky to miss the brutal, extended windstorms that frequently batter McKinley in winter. And now, finally, they were in an excellent position to try for the mountain's top. Despite that fact, it soon became apparent that Blomberg, Edwards, and Wichman were feeling down. All three had experienced great difficulty in their ascent to high camp and they now talked pessimistically of the team's summit chances. According to Davidson, "Their drawn features made them appear like invalids recuperating from a prolonged illness."

Exhaustion and discouragement weren't Blomberg's only difficulties, however. His big toe was slightly purplish. Clearly, it was frostbitten. Fortunately, only the skin was affected. Wichman said that if Blomberg drank large amounts of fluid and didn't lace his boots too tightly, the damaged tissue wouldn't prevent him from making a summit attempt.

The constant subzero cold had begun to take a toll, and the worst was almost certainly ahead. Blomberg's toe had been frostbitten in −20°F to −40°F weather. But at high camp and above, on McKinley's uppermost slopes, even harsher conditions could be expected. That night, as the temperature at 17,200 feet fell to −50°F, Davidson couldn't help but wonder if Blomberg's frostbite was only the beginning of physical problems among the team. If so, who'd be next?

His question was answered the following morning, though altitude, not cold, turned out to be the cause of the next problem.

Leaving the team's snow cave to urinate, Davidson became dizzy. Then his head began to ache and waves of nausea swept through his body.

He was suffering from altitude sickness, caused by insufficient oxygen in the blood. The only sure remedy was to descend; at the 14,400-foot camp Davidson would have a much better chance of recuperating. He later recalled:

> Dejected, my head throbbing, I rested while the others hurriedly broke camp. I hated to think that I wouldn't be able to try for the summit myself. And, as my fears raced on, I pictured myself having to be airlifted off the mountain by helicopter. The worst torment was that the others were being forced to descend because of my sickness, my weakness.

Blomberg decided that four people would be sufficient to help Davidson descend. The two climbers to stay at the high camp were Genet and Wichman. If conditions permitted, they at least would have a shot at the summit.

The change in altitude worked wonders for Davidson. Only twenty-four hours after becoming ill, he seemed cured. His head no longer hurt, the nausea and dizziness were gone, and his muscles no longer ached. In short, "it seemed that I'd been given a new body during the night," Davidson recalled. "I became restless for action. No one was more surprised than myself that I seemed to have recovered from my bout of mountain sickness."

Despite that unexpectedly sudden recovery, the group took a rest day, to ensure that everyone would be acclimatized before reascending.

On February 26, the five climbers at 14,400 began their return trip to 17,200 feet. Davidson, Johnston, and Nishimae got a late start, however, and it was already dark when they finally reached the top of the ice wall. Davidson chose to bivouac alone at 16,500 feet, where he watched the full moon rise over the glaciers and peaks of the Alaska Range, while Johnston and Nishimae continued on to the high camp.

The next morning dawned clear but breezy. Figuring it was too windy for a summit try, Davidson felt no urgency for an early start. But upon reaching a high point near the end of the ridge, he noticed "two black specks" on the ice wall leading to 18,200-foot Denali Pass. "I realized the wind had died down," he wrote. "The specks moved. The others must be trying for the summit, I thought. I had been left behind."

Davidson felt an urge to rush ahead, but realized that would only result in exhaustion and diminish his chances of reaching the summit. A decision had to be made: should he stay in camp or continue on alone, despite the dangers of traveling solo? After a short inner debate, Davidson chose to follow his teammates. As he continued up the slope, his compulsive drive to stand on McKinley's summit gradually lessened, replaced by a lighter sense of well-being. He would simply go as high as he could, without taking unnecessary risks.

Above Denali Pass, Davidson climbed into clouds. Visibility was poor, but he could follow his teammates' trail. About an hour beyond the pass, he spotted several figures descending through the whiteness. The climbers reported that they'd been forced to turn back at 19,000 feet because dense clouds hid the route.

As the team resumed its descent, the men noticed that the clouds were thinning. The sky had opened and the route to the summit was clear. But going back up was out of the question. It would take at least an hour, probably more, to even regain the lost ground. Night was approaching and no one was prepared to bivouac.

"We had to continue down," Davidson wrote. "If they had only waited above 19,000 feet for another fifteen minutes, everyone, except perhaps myself, would probably have reached the summit."

Once back at the snow cave, the climbers considered the question of food. If the entire team remained at 17,200 feet, there would be enough for three more days. If only three people remained, the food could be stretched to perhaps a week. But that meant the others would have to descend to 14,400 feet and, in all likelihood, give up any chance of reaching the summit. "Far into the night we tried to decide who, if anyone, should go down," Davidson wrote. But no decisions were made.

The team awoke to clear but cold and windy weather on February 28. The temperature outside the snow cave was −43°F. A summit try seemed impossible. Davidson explained:

> The weather we feared most was the violent wind, which can rise within an hour's time from a gentle breeze. . . . We were especially cautious about venturing out from this high camp because only a thousand feet above, and right on our route, was Denali Pass, the most notorious wind slot on the mountain. Up high in winter even a 50-mph wind could destroy a climbing party, because at −50°F a 50-mph wind creates an equivalent windchill temperature well below −100°. None of us had ever experienced conditions like that, but we expected that if the wind caught us above this camp there could be no retreat except to dig under the ice and sit it out.

But after breakfast, the wind began to die. Wichman and Edwards were too exhausted to make another attempt, but the others began readying their gear. By 10:00 A.M., everyone was ready to go except for Blomberg. Nishimae volunteered to wait for the expedition leader, so Davidson, Johnston, and Genet roped together and headed toward Denali Pass.

At the pass, Johnston cached food and sleeping bags where they wouldn't be blown away. Then he, Genet, and Davidson waited for their teammates, still a quarter mile below.

But by the time the second two reached Denali Pass, both had lost their drive. Nishimae seemed very tired, while Blomberg admitted, "I feel strong enough, but my heart's not in it today." Davidson, Genet, and Johnston took turns trying to convince their partners to continue, but without success. Nishimae and Blomberg wished the others good luck, and then returned to camp.

That decision made, the team of three resumed its ascent. Slowly, patiently, they moved upward. Far below, against the mountain's base, clouds began to gather, but there was no reason for alarm; McKinley's upper reaches were still clear.

Of greater concern was evening's all-too-rapid approach. The climbers soon realized they wouldn't make the summit before sunset. A decision had to be made: climb after dark, or retreat to camp. They continued to climb.

Plodding ahead, the trio passed The Archdeacon's Tower (a granite spire named to honor Hudson Stuck) at 19,550 feet, then climbed a small rise. From the top of that crest, only a broad snow bowl commonly known as the Football Field separated them from an icy wall leading to the summit ridge. "Suddenly nothing was hidden!" Davidson would write. "Our remaining uncertainty vanished! We were going to reach the summit! For the first time in all the years I had been climbing, tears rolled down my cheeks as I looked toward the summit of a mountain."

They easily crossed the plateau, but once on the ice wall, their pace slowed to a crawl. They took four or five breaths between every step and every fifteen steps rested a half minute. After what seemed an eternity, they reached the final ridge. Twilight was already giving way to darkness.

Carefully working their way along the ridge crest, the men noticed a strong breeze coming up the south face. Finally they came to an aluminum pole, sticking out of the ice. A moment passed before they realized the pole marked McKinley's summit. Davidson, Johnston, and Genet grabbed each other in a three-way hug, shouted, and slapped each other's shoulders in celebration. They'd made it; the first men to stand on North America's top in winter.

Ironically, darkness hid the surrounding mountain wilderness. All that could be seen were some faint greenish lights to the south—the lights of Anchorage. There were no lights above; a high layer of clouds had apparently moved in after sunset.

While taking note of the high overcast, the climbers also felt the cold. Though it was only a few minutes after seven, the temperature had fallen to −58°F. Meanwhile the wind had continued to pick up. Johnston estimated it was blowing twenty miles per hour across the summit, producing a windchill of nearly −130F.

After leaving several mementoes, including Farine Batkin's hat, which Johnston had carried since their teammate died, the climbers began descending. Because of the darkness, they had a difficult time retracing their path.

Upon reaching their parachute-covered supply cache at Denali Pass (where they'd left three sleeping bags plus some food and fuel), the three discussed whether to continue their descent or sleep until dawn. Davidson recalled:

> Dave wanted to go on. Pirate, fully bushed by this time, said he would just as soon rest the few hours until it would be light. I argued that we shouldn't risk the steep ice in the dark while we were so tired. Dave insisted we get it all over with, but in the end I persuaded him that it would be safest to spend the night at the pass.

Covered by the parachute, Davidson, Johnston, and Genet spent the night huddled among a jumble of rocks. The next morning, March 1, they were awakened by a vicious wind. The parachute was being whipped wildly and made loud cracking noises like a rifle or bullwhip. They tried to anchor the chute, but each time, the wind tore it away. After an hour of struggling with the canopy, Johnston, taking his sleeping bag, left the others and sought relief from the wind on the opposite side of the rocks.

Without Johnston's help, Genet and Davidson could not hold the parachute down. Genet tried, but in the −40°F air nearly froze his hands doing so. After a brief struggle, Pirate let go and the wind immediately tore it away. It snagged on a rock, then was gone.

Now the climbers, protected only by their clothing and sleeping bags, were exposed to the full force of the wind. "It was as if gravity had shifted," Davidson wrote, "and instead of holding us down, was pulling us across the landscape."

Genet and Davidson wedged themselves between the rocks and huddled together. But exposed to the gale, and windchill temperatures below −100°F, they couldn't relax. Whenever they tried, the wind began pushing them down the gently sloping ice. Genet seemed to be losing his will to live, sinking into apathy. Davidson knew he had to find a more protected site. Perhaps Johnston had found a safe spot. He went looking.

Davidson crawled to the crest of a small rise and spotted Johnston crouched on the ice fifteen feet away, his back to the wind. Working his way over, Davidson got caught by a blast of wind. The sock he'd been wearing on his left hand was blown away. With his one protected hand, he grabbed onto a rock, but "the wind flung and tossed [his] body as though it were weightless" and his arm began to cramp from the strain. If Davidson lost his grip, he'd be blown across the ice. He had no choice but to grab for the rock with his bare left hand even if that meant freezing it. Finally he lunged. And piercing cold sliced through his hand.

Davidson pulled himself up to the rock, then pushed off toward Johnston, who had chopped a small ledge in the ice. Safely in the arms of his partner, Davidson lay there wheezing and shaking, trying to catch his breath.

"Man," said Johnston, "we've got to dig in."

Down below at the high camp, the others had started off on their own summit attempt, but it soon became obvious the winds were too severe. Wichman and Edwards retreated, while Blomberg and Nishimae continued ascending toward Denali Pass, hoping to meet Davidson, Johnston, and Genet. "When we approached the pass it was evident why [they] hadn't descended," Blomberg wrote in his diary. "The wind was howling like crazy. I tried to lead up to the pass, but was turned back by the wind."

Nishimae climbed high enough to see one sleeping bag among the rocks, flapping in the wind. Then he too was pushed back. Seeing only the one bag, Nishimae was certain his teammates were dead. But fearing that such bad news might cause Blomberg to "lose his mind," the Japanese climber reported seeing three. Only later, upon reaching camp, did Nishimae share the truth. The climbers at 17,200 feet hoped that their teammates were on the leeward side of the rocks, protected by the parachute and perhaps sharing a sleeping bag. The lone bag spotted by Nishimae almost certainly contained Genet; Davidson and Johnston were on the opposite side of the rocks, huddled in their bags beyond Nishimae's view. The most frustrating part, Blomberg wrote, was that, "If we could have reached them—they were less than a hundred feet away—we could have told them the wind wasn't so bad on this side of the pass. We could have told them to make a try."

Because the Denali Pass cache included only some lunch food, one stove filled with gas, and a cooking pot, Blomberg feared the trio above could last no more than a few days even if sheltered from the wind. Still, he hoped for the best: "On the bright side, they are the strongest of us. . . . They're all tough as nails. With a tiny break in the wind, they can't help but make it."

Up at the pass, Johnston had almost single-handedly created the shelter that he and his partners needed to survive. For more than an hour, while battered by winds exceeding one hundred miles per hour, he dug into the ice with his axe and shovel and gradually hollowed out a small cave. Just before completing it, Johnston collapsed from exhaustion. But Pirate had miraculously fought back from the edge of unconsciousness, and despite his frozen hands and feet, which were already beginning to swell with frostbite blisters, he finished the job. Recovering from his exhaustion, Johnston then helped Davidson into the cave.

Once inside, Johnston also took responsibility for cooking, because his hands were the only ones capable of working the stove. The climbers' new home was extremely small. At the wide end, there was barely enough room for all their shoulders. And it was too short for them to stretch out completely. At the foot end, the floor-to-ceiling distance was one and a half feet; at the larger end, there was barely enough room to lie on one's side. Despite the cramped quarters, it kept them safe from the wind. And as Davidson noted, "That was all that mattered, for the moment."

The three survivors estimated the wind speeds at the pass to be at least 130 miles per hour. Combined with the −30° to −45°F temperatures outside the cave, the windchill temperature would have been somewhere off the bottom of the chart, which ends at −148°F. One hundred and forty-eight degrees below zero.

Yet the worst was over, or so they assumed. They hoped that the wind would slack off by morning and they'd rejoin their teammates at 17,200 feet. But the wind didn't slacken on March 2. In fact, its fury seemed to increase. Late in the day, it occasionally hit with enough force to shake the cave's roof, causing ice crystals to fall from the ceiling.

There was little talking inside the snow cave, as the climbers retreated inside themselves. The only thing that aroused their interest was their one meal of the day, which stretched from late after noon until after dark because of the difficulty in preparing it. The meal consisted of a gorp stew, a few pieces of canned ham, several slices of cheese and salami, and three pieces of hard candy. Johnston had found the ham, as well as some cans of bacon and of peas, hidden in the rocks at Denali Pass; they'd been left by some previous party. If the climbers had to remain holed up for several days, that extra food could prove to be a lifesaver.

By the end of the day on March 2, the wind had blown nonstop for thirty-six hours. And it showed no signs of letting up. While lying in the darkness, both Genet and Davidson were worried about their frozen extremities. The longer they were forced to wait, the worse their frostbite would become. Frostbite wasn't the only worry. Fuel was running low, and food supplies, even though supplemented by the canned goods, were small.

On March 3, with the wind still blowing hard and steady, Johnston made a horrible discovery. The cans of bacon and peas had been punctured; the extra food they'd been counting on was rotten. Davidson wrote:

> Immediately we were angry for being so cruelly cheated, but only after several minutes did we realize how the spoiled food had transformed our trial with hunger into a confrontation with starvation. We had almost nothing left to eat. . . . The combined calorie count of our remaining food was probably adequate for one person for one day.

An already desperate situation got even worse when the stove failed to light. Not enough fuel remained for it to build up the pressure needed to vaporize. The only hope was a gallon of gas that Johnston had cached at Denali Pass three summers before. He'd spotted the bottle earlier in the climb but there was no guarantee it still held usable fuel. Though hungry and thirsty, no one volunteered to go out into the wind. Instead they prayed the wind would end and tried to imagine what their teammates might be doing below.

The group at 17,200 feet had decided to send two climbers down to base camp (7,500 feet) to attempt a call out on the radio cached there. Despite severe winds, Blomberg and Edwards descended to the 14,400-foot camp on March 3, where they took shelter in the igloos. In his diary, Blomberg admitted, "Shiro and the others are more optimistic about the chances of those up at the pass than I am. . . . Every minute they wait, they become weaker and have less resolve to make a run for it."

Pain had become a natural state of being for Johnston, Davidson, and Genet by March 4. Mouths were drying up from dehydration, and lips were cracking. Muscles ached and it became very painful to shift positions or stretch, yet the ice made backs and legs sore when they remained still for very long. Their sleeping bags had iced up, losing loft and insulating ability and making the climbers more susceptible to the cold penetrating their cave.

Sometime during the middle of the day, Johnston rationed out the day's meal: a fig bar and two hard candies per person. Outside, the wind continued to roar. There'd be no escape before dark; the climbers would be imprisoned in their cave at least one more night. Without fuel, they wouldn't survive. Someone had to go for the gas, and right away.

Without a word, Pirate volunteered. He got out of his sleeping bag and, wearing booties offered by Davidson (Genet's own boots wouldn't fit over his swollen, frostbitten feet), went out into the wind, which had become more erratic. Strong gusts were interrupted now and then by short lulls.

Ten, then fifteen minutes passed. Still no Pirate. Just when Davidson and Johnston were ready to give up hope, their teammate returned with the fuel. "Bad!" Genet gasped. "I couldn't stand up, even in the lulls. Something's wrong with my balance. I crawled all the way, clawing into the ice with two ice axes."

They got the stove going, and were able to melt snow for drinking water. After thirty-six hours without liquid, the men "drank and drank and always waited for yet another canful," to fill the needs of their badly dehydrated bodies.

Down at 14,400 feet, the wind had died. But Edwards and Blomberg were forced to spend the day holed up in the igloo because of whiteout conditions. Wrote Blomberg, "The waiting is more terrible than moving. But to move now might mean the complete destruction of the party."

By March 5, those below Denali Pass were becoming resigned to the worst. "The time has become more or less critical and we just don't have the slightest hope. We don't discuss it," Wichman wrote in his journal at 17,200 feet. Then he and Nishimae began descending. Meanwhile at 14,400, Blomberg noted, "Roaring still over Denali Pass and hope gives out for the three above."

Up at the pass, the lulls between wind gusts steadily increased in number and length. The storm seemed to be coming to a gradual end. If the climbers had been stronger, they might have attempted to go down. "Unfortunately," Davidson observed, "we had become so weak that the wind would have to be completely gone before we could descend with any confidence." Yet the idea of spending another night in the cave was dreadful, because by morning their food supplies would be gone.

To make things worse, the pack that had been used to block the cave entrance was blown away during the night. A steady draft began circulating −35°F air through the shelter, making the cold penetrate their bodies.

The winds surging through Denali Pass continued to die as morning gave way to afternoon. Gusts were less frequent and carried less force. And the evening of March 5, they stopped. Davidson, who'd been dozing, said "[I] woke in the dark to a strange sound. I was startled. To ears that had become unaccustomed to quietness, the silence sounded nearly as loud as the wind's roar had that first morning."

Shortly after, Johnston began cooking a farewell dinner. He passed around the can of hot water and divided the remaining four slices of cheese. With renewed hope the three men ate their meager rations, then drifted asleep, confident they'd be leaving in the morning.

On March 6, Wichman and Nishimae resumed their descent, reaching the iglooplex at 10,200 feet "in a condition of despair." Of their teammates' fate at Denali Pass, Wichman wrote, "The more we think about it the more agonizing it becomes, so in conversation with one another we try to avoid the sentiments of death."

Edwards and Blomberg, meanwhile, had descended to base camp, where they called Anchorage. They learned that a rescue effort was being mounted. Climbers had arrived from as far as Seattle to help save the stranded expedition members. They were awaiting a break in the weather that would enable them to fly to the mountain.

Unaware of any rescue plans, Johnston, Davidson, and Genet began preparing to save themselves. Spirits were high. After surviving the storm, the climbers felt there was nothing they couldn't do. That enthusiasm was short-lived. Johnston, the first to leave the cave, ended it with a single word. Whiteout.

"We had never considered the possibility of a whiteout," Davidson recalled. "Blinded by the whiteout, we might wander about the ice forever, or rather, until we collapsed, or walked off an edge, or fell into a crevasse."

The climbers could see only twenty to thirty feet in any direction. But that wasn't the only problem they faced. After several days in the cramped cave, their bodies were stiff, achy, and weak. All had trouble keeping their balance.

No one wished to reenter the cave. Waiting another night in the cave without any food would be suicide. Johnston suggested that they wait to see if the whiteout would clear. Davidson agreed. Genet, the weakest of the three at that point, was silent.

The climbers grew tired of waiting and began to search among the rocks for a cache of food. They found nothing. Staring at the scattered remains of a large supply cache his teammates had already checked, Davidson recalled some advice given him by Nishimae: "When there is only one way to survive in the mountains, you must check every possibility to the very end in order to find the one that works." The already scavenged cache was such a possibility: perhaps some food remained hidden at the bottom. Davidson attacked it with his ice axe, beating and tearing at the frozen debris. Though his frostbitten hands throbbed with pain, only one thing mattered: he had to check every last inch of rubble. He chopped at the ice until he collapsed, exhausted and gasping for breath. Soon he was again flailing at the ice with his axe.

Eventually Davidson reached an unopened box that contained clothes and several white cloth bags. Within the bags were dried potatoes. Continuing to search, Davidson found a box of raisins (packaged in a wrapper at least fifteen years old) and even an unopened, unpunctured can of ham. Once more the team had dodged disaster.

After enlarging the cave for one final night's lodging, Johnston made hot drinks and cooked up a potato-raisin-ham stew. "Life seemed easy again," Davidson wrote. "Our cave was more comfortable and we had the security of knowing there would be something to eat the next day." If need be, they could now hold out several more days, but they prayed it wouldn't be necessary.

The next morning was again marked by calm. And, just as

important, the whiteout had dissipated. After eating, drinking, and enduring the painful process of putting on boots, the climbers left their cave and practiced walking on their aching, frozen, swollen feet.

On their descent, Johnston took the back of the rope, since his were the only hands not frozen. If necessary, he could provide an anchor. Yet in reality the rope was nothing more than what Davidson described as psychological protection. If one member slipped, all three would be pulled off the slope.

Going down to 17,200 feet, they had to traverse a slope of thirty to forty degrees. Normally, it wouldn't have been much of a challenge. But supported by aching, weakened, stiffened legs and frostbitten feet, each step was near the limits of their abilities.

As they inched their way down the ice wall below Denali Pass, one of Genet's crampons loosened. Despite the difficulty of maneuvering half-frozen fingers, Pirate, with Davidson's help, managed to reattach the crampon to his boot while maintaining his balance on the icy thirty-degree slope.

Upon reaching high camp, the trio found the snow cave empty except for some delicacies that their teammates had left in one corner: sausage, coconut balls made by Blomberg's wife, and fruitcake baked by Davidson's grandmother.

Back outside the cave, the climbers were spotted by a four-engine plane circling high overhead. Moments later, Sheldon showed up in his Cessna 180. He brought the plane in low and dropped a package. Inside were some smashed oranges and a radio. Probably damaged by the fall, the radio didn't work.

After eating at 17,200 feet, the climbers resumed their descent. Near the bottom of the ice wall that connects the West Buttress ridge with the 14,000-foot basin, they entered a thick cloud. Sky and glacier became a single wall of grayness. Despite a visibility of less than twenty feet, they somehow found the igloos. They hoped to find their companions, but like the snow cave above, the igloos were deserted except for food left by the others. Though they feasted that night on mashed potatoes, rice, jello, gorp, and freeze-dried meat, Davidson, Johnston, and Genet couldn't help wondering what had happened to their teammates.

"There wasn't even a note," Davidson commented. "Were we alone on the mountain? Where were they? None of us felt like voicing our disappointment that the others were gone, that they must have given up on us."

March 8 dawned calm, clear, and bright. Standing in the sun, Davidson couldn't remember ever feeling so at peace within. That peace was soon shattered, however, as a jet roared overhead. Soon the jet was joined by the four-engine plane seen from high camp a day earlier.

The presence of the aircraft stimulated the climbers' desire to reach the Kahiltna Glacier, where they could be picked up by Sheldon. Unaware that a rescue mission was in progress and not expecting special assistance, they were surprised and a bit annoyed when the plane circling above began dropping packages attached to parachutes. The first two drops landed in crevasses; the third was retrieved by Pirate. It was, as they had guessed, another radio.

Talking with the pilot, the threesome was happy to learn that Blomberg and Edwards were safe at 7,500 feet, and that Blomberg had insisted on remaining at McKinley until all team members were accounted for. So they hadn't been abandoned after all. While Wichman and Nishimae hadn't yet been spotted, they were thought to be at the iglooplex. The pilot asked the trio if they wished to be picked up by one of two helicopters already on their way from Talkeetna. The second helicopter would retrieve Blomberg and Edwards from base camp and drop off a search-and-rescue team to locate Wichman and Nishimae.

The suggestion of rescue created mixed feelings; Johnston, Davidson, and Genet felt both irritated and thankful. After all they'd been through, the three men felt the rescue operation was unnecessary. They could descend under their own power. They didn't like the idea of being responsible for such a big commotion. Still, it was reassuring to know that others had been concerned enough to risk their own safety to help save the missing climbers. And there was the frostbite to consider. The three were descending on half-frozen feet. Each step brought excruciating pain.

Late in the afternoon, after debating for more than an hour the pros and cons of being rescued, the climbers finally notified the airplane pilot that they would accept a ride. The pilot, in turn, relayed their message to the helicopter crew waiting lower on the Kahiltna Glacier. It was a wise decision. Another storm front was moving in from the northwest. Winds of more than a hundred miles per hour were expected within twenty-four hours. Already a deep, distant roar could be heard; McKinley was stirring again. The climbers began wondering which would arrive first at Windy Corner where they waited, the wind or the helicopter.

A gentle breeze had grown into a steady wind by the time the helicopter set down at Windy Corner. The climbers jumped in, leaving their rope behind. Seeing it lying on the ice, Davidson felt a twinge of regret:

> It seemed unfair that the rope which had tied the three of us together over so much ice had to remain on the mountain. Only now that we were leaving did we begin to fully realize how isolated we had been and how closely the three of us had been bound together; it would never be that way again.

Davidson, Johnston, and Genet were reunited with Edwards and Blomberg in Talkeetna, where a huge crowd of media, friends, and just-plain-curious people had gathered to greet the five climbers. Nishimae and Wichman later joined their teammates in Anchorage.

After the expedition, all team members except Nishimae, who returned to Japan, went to Fairbanks for some postclimb medical (or physical) testing. The scientists conducting the tests "just shook their heads in disbelief at the human wrecks the mountain had sent back to them," Davidson wrote. "They described us in clinical terms such as 'obtundation,' which denotes dullness or depression."

During their five weeks on the mountain, the three who'd reached the summit had lost an average of thirty-five pounds each. Five of the seven surviving climbers suffered some degree of frostbite. Edwards's ear and Blomberg's big toe healed within six weeks, but the others required more lengthy rehabilitation.

Johnston's frozen feet required forty-five days of hospital treatment. He was bedridden for another sixteen days and eventually lost some toes. Davidson was restricted to a wheelchair for eight weeks while recovering from frostbite and spent six weeks after that on crutches; he too had parts of some toes removed. Although Genet froze both his hands and feet, he was released from the hospital after three weeks.

For periods ranging from a few hours to several days, all expedition members experienced a sense of isolation and unreality that is normally associated with severe psychosis.

The team later learned that its estimates of the extremes of the incredible storm they had experienced were conservative. According to Davidson, the US Air Force's Aerospace and Recovery Center determined that winds on McKinley's upper slopes had exceeded 150 miles per hour, with temperatures of −50°F. So the resulting windchill temperature during those life-threatening days at Denali Pass was, in fact, considerably colder even than −148°F.

Since that first winter ascent in 1967, eight other expeditions have successfully climbed McKinley in winter through the spring of 2012. In all, sixteen people reached the mountain's summit, including four solo climbers. And six mountaineers had died trying. One of the more amazing winter ascents was pulled off by Russians Artur Testov and Vladimir Ananich, who reached the summit in the dead of winter: January 16, 1998. The Russians were fortunate to climb in one of the mildest winters ever recorded on McKinley; due to El Niño's impact, temperatures on the lower mountain were similar to those more typical of May and June. Others have attempted December-January depth-of-winter ascents, including solo climbers, but as of this writing, all have so far been turned back.

Stories of several solo attempts–and two dramatic successes–are described in Chapters 10 and 11, and a listing of all successful winter expedition parties through spring 2012 (the most recent in 1998) is provided at the back of the book.

HOWARD SNYDER, THE HALL OF THE MOUNTAIN KING, CHARLES SCRIBNER'S SONS

PAUL SCHLICHTER, A MEMBER OF THE 1967 WILCOX EXPEDITION, HOLDS A FLARE WHILE ON MCKINLEY'S SUMMIT, PRIOR TO THE FIERCE STORM THAT CLAIMED SEVEN LIVES.

Chapter Nine

The Wilcox Expedition Disaster, 1967

The year 1967 was one of unprecedented tragedy, as well as triumph, on Mount McKinley. The remarkable success and survival story of Ray Genet, Art Davidson, and Dave Johnston was followed, less than five months later, by the worst mountaineering disaster in Alaska's history.

In late July, seven climbers belonging to the twelve-member Joseph F. Wilcox Mount McKinley Expedition died on the mountain's upper slopes during a severe windstorm. Details of the tragedy are sketchy, since the expedition's five survivors were lower on McKinley when their teammates died. A search-and-rescue team sent to look for the missing climbers found only two tents—one shredded by wind, the other intact but filled with snow—a few scattered pieces of gear, and three frozen bodies.

Not surprisingly, the severity and mysterious nature of the disaster prompted considerable second-guessing and analysis within the mountaineering community. It also inspired three books. The first, written by team member Howard Snyder in 1973, was titled *The Hall of the Mountain King*.[1] That was followed eight years later by *White Winds*, written by expedition leader Joe Wilcox.[2] More than a quarter century later, in 2008, a third book was published, written by an author who reexamined the episode, James Tabor: *Forever on the Mountain: The Truth Behind One of Mountaineering's Most Controversial and Mysterious Disasters*. This chapter will focus on events as presented by Snyder and Wilcox.

Both of their books provide detailed accounts of the Wilcox expedition and document events leading up to the tragedy, and they attempt to answer the question "Why?" But they offer quite different perspectives. Snyder claims that insufficient mountaineering experience and inadequate leadership contributed greatly to the seven deaths. Wilcox rebuts many of Snyder's claims and comments: rather than place blame on human error or individual weaknesses, he attempts to show that the seven men died because they were unlucky enough to get caught, with almost no forewarning, in the most severe and prolonged high-altitude windstorm ever encountered by climbers on McKinley or perhaps anywhere on earth.

The differences in perspective are due, at least in part, to Wilcox and Snyder's roles in the expedition. Snyder had originally intended to lead his own McKinley party, composed of four Colorado residents who knew each other well and had climbed together previously. But a day before the group's departure to Alaska, one of the team members broke his hand in an automobile accident and had to drop out. National Park Service regulations in 1967 required that McKinley parties include at least four people.

Now down to three, the Colorado climbers had two choices: postpone their trip indefinitely, or join forces with another team. Only one other party was planning to be on the mountain at the same time as the Colorado climbers: Wilcox's.

Unlike Snyder's small, tightly knit trio, Wilcox's nine-member team included only one person with whom he'd ever climbed. Several of the climbers were complete strangers to each other, having been recruited by letter or phone. No one in this "mail-order" expedition had ascended a peak higher than 14,410-foot Mount Rainier (two of the Coloradans had climbed higher than 18,000 feet), and four of the nine had little mountaineering experience. In planning his expedition, Wilcox decided those four would act as support climbers; they'd conduct some scientific studies on the Muldrow Glacier and ascend no higher than 11,000 feet.

Though members of both groups had misgivings about a merger, the two teams joined into one expedition, with Wilcox as the leader. From the start it was an unhappy alliance. Wilcox questioned the Colorado climbers' commitment to the team as a whole, after observing that they isolated themselves while in camp and made no attempts to interact socially with the others. Snyder, meanwhile, complained that he and his partners were too often left out of any decision making.

Despite their unresolved internal tensions, the climbers began their trek at Wonder Lake on McKinley's north side and proceeded up the Muldrow Glacier Route rather smoothly, albeit slowly. (While bush pilot services and glacier landings have greatly improved access to McKinley's western and southern climbing routes, the Muldrow Glacier Route has, with a few exceptions, remained a long-distance walk-in since it was first explored by the Sourdoughs in 1910. Mountaineering-related plane landings were made on the Muldrow in 1932 and again during the 1940s. But in the early 1950s, the National Park Service enacted regulations that prohibited aircraft from landing on the glacier, which is located within park boundaries. Since then, Wonder Lake Campground has served as the primary starting point for teams ascending McKinley via the Muldrow Glacier. Located at the end of Denali Park Road at an elevation of 2,100 feet, Wonder Lake is about thirty-seven trail miles and 18,220 vertical feet from the mountain's summit.) On July 14, twenty-seven days later, the expedition established its high camp at 17,900 feet, just below Denali Pass. Along the way, Wilcox revised his plan of keeping four climbers at 11,000 feet. All twelve team members would be given an opportunity to reach the summit, if possible.

The team awoke the next day to high winds and snow. But by midmorning the sky had begun to clear and the air grew calm. Eight of the expedition's twelve members were at 17,900 feet, in position to make a summit attempt (the remaining four were ascending from 15,000 feet). But only Wilcox and the three Colorado climbers chose to try. The others decided to spend the day in camp.

"I found it hard to believe that they didn't want to go on to the summit today," Snyder commented in his account, "since by now the sky was a bright blue and the wind had dropped to about five mph." Emphasizing his own eagerness to get started, he further noted that park rangers had warned the team that July 15 "would be our last day of good weather for a time, with a storm due to move in tomorrow, July 16. It is essential to both safety and success on Mount McKinley that a good day never be wasted, especially high on the mountain."

Wilcox, too, was at first surprised by the decision of Jerry Clark, Dennis Luchterhand, Hank Janes, and Mark McLaughlin to stay in camp during a near-perfect summit day. But later he reasoned that they simply had preferred to wait for their friends who were still below.

Snyder, Wilcox, Jerry Lewis, and Paul Schlichter left high camp at 12:03 P.M. As the afternoon passed, the weather grew even more beautiful. Under crystal-clear skies, the team ascended through air that was both calm and warm—so warm that Snyder and Schlichter shed their windjackets and down vests and climbed in shirtsleeves.

At 6:29, the four men stepped onto the summit plateau and celebrated their ascent with a can of soda pop and a chunk of chocolate. No longer was the air calm. Or warm. The thermometer read 6°F, but a wind gusting to twenty-five miles per hour drove the windchill temperature as low as −30°F.

After an hour and a half on the mountain's top, Wilcox and the Coloradans returned to high camp. They arrived just before 10 P.M.—and just ahead of John Russell, Walter Taylor, Steve Taylor (not related), and Ansel Schiff, who'd spent ten hours ascending from 15,000 feet. All twelve climbers were now at 17,900.

Late that night, a storm moved in. Winds gusting to seventy or eighty miles per hour, combined with fog and snow, limited visibility to a few yards and kept the climbers holed up in their tents for more than twenty-four hours. Some team members who had not yet reached McKinley's summit talked of possibly abandoning any further attempts and heading down the mountain at the earliest possible chance.

The storm began to break up by midmorning on July 17, and the four who'd already stood on the mountain's top prepared to descend to 15,000 feet. Schiff, one of the expedition's least experienced climbers, also chose to go down. Everyone else opted to stay at 17,900 feet, hopeful the weather would improve enough for another summit try.

The group of five began their descent at noon. According to Snyder's account, Schiff, Wilcox, and Lewis were suffering from exhaustion and altitude sickness. Their weak condition demanded a slow pace and numerous rest stops, during which "they would collapse to the ground."

Two of the seven who remained at high camp also showed signs of altitude sickness. Both John Russell and Steve Taylor felt weak and nauseated, and Russell had vomited several times in the last two days.

More than an hour after leaving 17,900 feet, Snyder glanced back up the mountain and was surprised to see people still in the high camp. The afternoon had brought ideal summit weather: cloudless skies, brilliant sunshine, and no wind. Why were the climbers above so slow in taking advantage of the beautiful conditions? Puzzled, Snyder turned away from his teammates above. He would never see them again.

The Colorado climbers, Wilcox, and Schiff reached the 15,000-foot level at three o'clock and set up camp. There was little for them to do now but wait for the others. Throughout the afternoon and evening the sky overhead remained clear, the air calm. But a dense blanket of fog gradually formed around the mountain's upper slopes, obscuring McKinley's summit.

At eight that evening, as previously scheduled, the expedition's two groups made radio contact with Park Service staff at Eielson Visitor Center, located along the park road and used as a communication and resource center. (Though the Wilcox Expedition carried two-way radios in 1967, such equipment wasn't required by the Park Service until the following year.) Wilcox and Jerry Clark, the summit team's designated leader, were unable to hear each other, so their messages were relayed through Eielson. Clark informed park staff that his party consisted of six climbers—one person, Steve Taylor, had chosen to stay at high camp—and asked if there were a large cornice on the summit. Wilcox answered yes over the radio despite the protests of Snyder, who insisted the summit was not corniced and argued that an affirmative response would mislead Clark's group.

After being informed of Wilcox's "Roger," Clark told Eielson staff that he expected the team to reach the top in forty-five minutes to an hour. Instead, the party became lost.

In a follow-up 9:30 P.M. radio call to Eielson, Clark admitted his confusion. He said the route was poorly marked with wands; apparently many had been blown away during the July 16 storm. With visibility reduced to about 400 feet by the heavy fog and without the benefit of trail markers, the climbers couldn't be certain of their location. They were, Clark said, "just floundering around." His report was cut short by cold-weakened batteries, which made further transmission impossible.

Clark called Eielson again at 10:45, but his radio went dead before any message could be sent. Without communication, unsure of their location, and unable to find any trail markers in the fog and late-evening twilight, the climbers had to make a choice: camp out in the open, without the benefit of tents and stoves, or return to camp.

A descent to 17,900 feet would almost certainly mean the end of any summit hopes; the climbers, many of them already approaching exhaustion, would be too weak, too burned out, to make a second attempt. And a late-night descent along a poorly marked trail in whiteout conditions presented its own hazards. So the team chose to bivouac on the upper mountain. Whether or not the climbers dug snow caves is unclear; if not, they had only sleeping bags to protect them from the bitterly cold night air.

July 18 dawned bright and clear. The fog had dissipated, enabling the summit team to relocate the route to McKinley's top. By midmorning a cloud cap had once again formed on the upper mountain, but the climbers were now back on track, certain of their course. Slowly, painfully, they worked their way upward through a thickening veil of white.

At 11:30 A.M., Clark called Eielson with news that his group had reached the summit. He briefly mentioned the bivouac and noted the team would stay on top only five to ten minutes more because of the cold, then handed the radio to Mark McLaughlin, who asked that a message stating he was "A-okay" be sent to his parents. In response to a question from Eielson, McLaughlin reported that the view from McKinley's summit consisted of "four other guys at the moment. That's all. It's completely whited out." Accompanying Clark and McLaughlin to the top were Hank Janes, Dennis Luchterhand, and Walt Taylor.

Eielson's radio operator asked what had happened to the party's "seventh man," failing to note that the presence of five climbers on the summit left two people, not one, unaccounted for. McLaughlin replied that Steve Taylor remained at 17,900 feet because he hadn't felt well. But no mention was made of John Russell, who'd started for the summit with Clark's group. We can only guess that Russell had been too ill or weak to make the top. If unable to continue, he most likely stayed at the bivouac site or returned to high camp.

After a few minutes of conversation, the radio began to lose power. Before signing off, McLaughlin said the party would make its next call at 8:00 P.M. As the five men began their descent, a heavy snow started falling, accompanied by strong winds.

Back at 15,000 feet, Snyder, Wilcox, and company assumed that Clark's group had reached McKinley's summit the previous night and expected their teammates to arrive in camp sometime that afternoon or evening. It was only during their evening conversation with Eielson that they learned of the team's overnight bivouac and delay in reaching the mountaintop. Clark, meanwhile, failed to make radio contact with the visitor center as scheduled. But neither Wilcox nor Snyder was concerned, figuring that members of the summit team had been too tired or busy to remember the call.

The snow and windstorm that began on July 18 continued the next day. During a brief midmorning break in the weather, Wilcox observed lenticular clouds over McKinley's north and south peaks. The remainder of the day, blowing snow and dense clouds restricted visibility to a few hundred feet or less.

Travel in such conditions would have been extremely difficult, particularly for climbers recovering from a summit ascent. It made sense that Clark's group would remain at high camp, rather than risk descending. The climbers at 15,000 feet waited patiently for the usual evening radio transmission, at which time they could learn more about the status of their teammates higher on the mountain.

At 8:00 P.M., Wilcox talked briefly with Eielson. Then he and the others at 15,000 feet began waiting for word from the high camp. For the second straight night, there was only silence from above. Wilcox was worried:

> A sinking emptiness gripped my emotions. We had never missed radio contact on successive days. If Unit One [Clark's group] did not call, they could not call. . . . Either the radio was not functional or else no hand was capable of pressing its transmitter key. . . . The situation had all the aspects of an emerging emergency. There were no options to consider; our only course of action was to climb back immediately to the high camp to investigate.

Although it wasn't completely dark, Snyder refused to make a nighttime journey up the glacier through heavy snow and high winds. Reluctantly, Wilcox agreed to wait until morning.

Carrying sleeping bags, extra clothing, four gallons of fuel, and a stove, Wilcox, Snyder, and Schlichter headed for high camp at 6:30 the morning of July 20. Schiff and Lewis, still not completely recovered from their altitude sickness, remained behind. A thick cloud mass hung over the mountain at 16,000 feet, but only a light snow was falling and the wind had dropped to about twenty miles per hour.

Shortly after the trio's departure, however, the wind began to pick up. Soon it was blowing forty to fifty miles per hour, creating a ground blizzard and whipping snow harshly into their faces. Staying on the snow-drifted trail was nearly impossible; many of the wands marking it had been blown away or buried. Whenever the climbers stepped off the path, they sank up to their knees–or deeper–in soft powder, adding to the struggle.

The wind continued to grow stronger and the cloud ceiling dropped, creating a whiteout. The three men were forced to stand still for several minutes at a time, straining to see wands marking the path. Gale-force winds knocked them to their knees and obliterated their tracks within minutes.

Progress was terribly slow. The climbers knew their chances of reaching high camp in such weather were almost nil; meanwhile their own camp had disappeared into milky whiteness. Wilcox began wondering if they'd be able to find their way back. As the leader, it was his decision to proceed or retreat. He continued on, knowing seven teammates at 17,900 feet might be in desperate need of help.

At 9:00 A.M., Wilcox stopped and called over the radio for an updated weather forecast, but Eielson had none. In two and a half hours of travel over gentle terrain, the climbers had gone less than one mile. Already they were nearly drained of all energy. For the last several hundred yards, there had been no wands to guide the way. Continuing would be foolish, if not suicidal. Wilcox cached the fuel, then the three men returned to camp, hoping for the best, but fearing the worst.

That afternoon the sky cleared for about three hours, though the wind didn't let up. The climbers at 15,000 feet could see

McKinley's summit, but unfortunately they weren't in line-of-sight with the high camp. Both Wilcox and Snyder spent much of the afternoon scanning the slope above, looking for some sign of their teammates. Wilcox later recalled:

> I was almost sure that we would see seven men descending at any minute. Even a very conservative leader would take advantage of such a weather break. . . . I considered starting back up, but didn't as the weather began to deteriorate again. What could be keeping the upper party?

And Snyder noted, "We could not climb uphill in the face of the wind, but I had thought that perhaps with clear skies and the wind at their backs, Clark's team could descend. But we had seen nothing."

When no radio contact was made with the high camp the evening of July 20, Wilcox asked that Don Sheldon do an aircraft overflight. But any such flight would have to wait indefinitely. The storm that had battered McKinley almost continuously since noon on July 18 grew even worse on the twenty-first. Snyder estimated the wind speed at 15,000 feet to be at least sixty miles per hour, with gusts to one hundred. The men found it nearly impossible to stand, or even breathe, outside the tents. Up high, the wind was probably much stronger.

Snow driven by the hurricane-force blasts threatened to collapse Schiff and Wilcox's tent, and they were forced to take turns shoveling snow away from the shelter. On one of his shifts, Wilcox stood up and was lifted off his feet by a gust of wind:

> My feet left the ground and I was airborne. Reacting quickly, I grabbed a tent guy line as I sailed by. It held. I located the shovel and crawled back to the drifted side of the tent. . . . During the strong

> gusts I could only hug the surface, unable to shovel or even breathe. . . . The snow was drifting faster than I could shovel and the tent was going under.

Wilcox and Schiff had no choice but to move in with the Colorado climbers. Five men were now squeezed into a tent made for three.

The extreme gales blew all night and into the morning. By mid-morning on July 22, the sky had cleared but the wind wouldn't let up. The climbers at 15,000 feet remained huddled in their sleeping bags. They hesitated to light the stove within the crowded tent, and starting it outside was impossible, so nearly a full day had passed since they'd prepared a warm meal or melted snow for water.

The group was running low on food, fuel, and morale. And at least two of the men–Lewis and Schiff–were very weak. According to Snyder's account, Wilcox too was "as weak as a rag doll," an observation that Wilcox later disputed.

Whatever his physical condition, Wilcox continued to hope that he, Snyder, and Schlichter might try again to reach high camp. That hope faded, however, during a radio conversation with Eielson on July 22. When park ranger Wayne Merry asked if anyone in the group felt strong enough to return to high camp, both Snyder and Schlichter shook their heads "No." In frustration, Wilcox answered, "Not more than one of us would feel like going up."

The tension and distance between Snyder and Wilcox at this point of the climb was great. Of Wilcox's reply to Merry, Snyder thought, "He was implying that he was willing and able to make the ascent. Willing he may have been, but able he most certainly was not." And yet Wilcox recalled:

> Hope sank into the pit of my stomach and surfaced as anger. "Here are two men in fairly good physical condition calmly turning their

backs on the lives of others," I thought. Biting my lip, I fought an impulse to broadcast my emotions over the radio.

Later that night, in another radio conversation with park personnel, Snyder defended his position: "We have three pretty sick people up here. This is why we could not go up. We have to get these people down." Wilcox, however, considered Snyder's reason to be a poor excuse. Or, even worse, a blatant lie. He insisted that only Lewis needed to descend as soon as possible; the rest were more storm-weary than ill. The problem was mental, not physical. Wilcox later wrote:

> I was astounded by Howard's desperation to justify the desertion of the high party. He had fumbled with the radio and battery pack in the cold for more than four minutes, critically draining our weak batteries to tell Eielson something that was not only incorrect but impertinent to the rescue operation. . . . Lewis and Schiff were weak. I wondered who the third sick man was supposed to be.

While Snyder and Schlichter prepared for a morning descent, Wilcox considered the possibility of remaining alone at 15,000 feet and conducting a solo climb to high camp. The decision was ultimately not his to make, however. On the morning of July 23, Wilcox woke up with numb hands, which he could use only with great difficulty and considerable pain. As the expedition leader sat dejectedly in the middle of the tent, teammates began packing his gear. Finally, Wilcox admitted defeat and unhappily "joined the deserters" whom Snyder was leading off the mountain.

As they did when descending from 17,900 feet, each of the five men hooked into a 270-foot rope (actually two ropes tied together), with Snyder and Schlichter—the two healthiest climbers—on the ends. As the roped team traversed the Harper Glacier, the group got its first look at high camp in several days. They could see no tents. No people. No sign of life.

Heading down Karstens Ridge, the climbers met a Mountaineering Club of Alaska (MCA) expedition, led by Bill Babcock of Anchorage. The Alaskans escorted Wilcox's party to their camp at 12,100 feet and provided them with food, hot drinks, and medical care.

Wilcox and Schiff's physical condition had improved dramatically as the team moved to lower elevations, and even Lewis, the sickest member of the group, showed signs of recovery from his high-altitude illness. A medical check by MCA team member Dr. Grace Jansen-Hoeman revealed that Lewis's feet had suffered minor frostbite. Wilcox's hands, meanwhile, were nearly back to normal. As he'd suspected, they weren't frostbitten; the numbness had been a temporary condition. (Several of Wilcox's toes had been frozen, but he didn't discover the frostbite until lower on the mountain.)

From 12,100 feet, the team made another call to Eielson. Radio-operator Gordon Haber asked Wilcox if he wanted to request an all-out rescue for the upper camp. Wilcox responded "No," adding that he might call for such an effort pending the results of an overflight of the high camp by Sheldon, whenever weather permitted.

Once again, the perspectives provided by Snyder and Wilcox's accounts differ dramatically. According to Snyder, Wilcox "still could not bring himself to believe that Clark's team was in mortal danger, just as he had been unable to realize that he, Schiff, and Lewis were dangerously ill [at 15,000 feet]." Only after lengthy discussions with Babcock did Wilcox finally understand a full-scale rescue was necessary. At one point Babcock told Snyder, "Wilcox sounds looney."

Wilcox, meanwhile, wondered:

> Weren't we already in a rescue? Our backup, the Alaska Rescue Group, had already been notified. . . . Airplanes had not been able to fly near the mountain in over a week without risking having their wings ripped off in the turbulence. Even if they could, the mountain was not about to be stormed by paratroopers and helicopter landings would be unlikely at extreme elevations. The MCA party was not only the best positioned and acclimated, but the only feasible rescue team unless another was higher. And this possibility was being checked out. I could not see how more could be accomplished by calling an all-out rescue. Perhaps a hundred people would mill around Wonder Lake for a week drinking tea and scratching their heads.

Though initially shocked that no full-scale rescue had been requested, Babcock agreed not much would happen that wasn't already being done. The MCA leader did explain, however, that any demand for an all-out rescue might facilitate high-altitude reconnaissance flights and, perhaps, Air Force assistance.

"I pondered his thoughts," Wilcox recounted. "Finally I decided that, if necessary to increase the tempo of the support operations, I would give the go-ahead on a rescue." That evening, Wilcox radioed the Park Service and requested that rescue operations immediately follow an overflight of the high camp, if necessary. If that meant calling for an all-out rescue, he was making that request.

On the morning of July 24, five members of the MCA party prepared for their search-and-rescue ascent to 17,900 feet. Dr. Jansen-Hoeman, who'd been suffering migraine headaches, felt she would be a liability in a rescue effort, so she descended with Wilcox's expedition.

The split that had been forming for several days now became final. The six climbers separated into two rope teams: the Colorado trio on one; Wilcox, Schiff, and Jansen-Hoeman on the other. They headed down the mountain as two groups operating independently of one another.

In deep snow, with poor visibility and winds gusting to thirty-five miles per hour, the teams made their final descent. In one exhausting twenty-five-hour push, the Colorado climbers descended 8,000 feet and hiked fifteen miles before finally setting up camp and getting a full night's sleep. Wilcox's rope team took a four-hour rest stop while descending the Muldrow Glacier but caught the Colorado crew and passed its camp late on July 25.

Though they'd safely reached the tundra lowlands, the climbers faced one final obstacle the next day. Before ending their journey at the Wonder Lake Campground, they had to cross Clearwater Creek and the glacially fed McKinley River, now at flood stage following several days of heavy rain.

Wilcox's team was the first to reach Clearwater Creek. While trying to find a route across the flooded stream, Wilcox was swept off his feet and barely made it to the opposite bank before collapsing. Rather than have the others risk crossing, Wilcox told Schiff and Jansen-Hoeman that he would continue on alone and arrange to have a helicopter sent back for the others. (The expedition radio had been left on the mountain, with the MCA party.)

Wilcox's greatest challenge still lay ahead. Upon reaching the McKinley River, he discovered:

> [The river was a] blackish, mile-wide devastating force, gouging the earth with abandon. . . . The sight exceeded my wildest imagination, sending waves of overt fear through me. . . . I was up against the wall. I had endured all that the mountain could give me, only to be decisively defeated so close to civilization, almost within sight of the road.

It didn't appear possible that even a strong, rested man could cross this wildly raging torrent of ice-cold water. Yet what choice was there? Tired, aching, wet, and chilled from his crossing of Clearwater Creek, Wilcox felt himself becoming hypothermic. Figuring it was better to die trying than to sit and wait "like some sick dog," he waded into the river's bitterly cold water.

Fifty yards from shore, the river swept Wilcox away. Unable to touch bottom, he struggled to keep his head above water while being pulled downstream by the current. Kicking, stroking, he frantically tried to push himself across the channel as the distant shoreline rushed by. Gradually the struggles diminished, as first his feet, then his entire body began to go numb in the glacial runoff. He tried to swim but his legs and arms refused to respond.

The end was near, Wilcox knew it. Then, miraculously, the river dropped him on a gravel bar. He lay there for several minutes, coughing and vomiting. His arms and legs were bruised and scraped and several of his knuckles were badly cut, but he was alive.

Calling on his remaining strength, Wilcox crossed one final channel, which fortunately was shallow enough that he didn't have to swim. Then he numbly hiked to Wonder Lake Campground and got a ride to the ranger station. There he arranged for a helicopter to pick up the remaining five climbers at Clearwater Creek. By evening all were delivered to Wonder Lake Ranger Station, where they were treated to milk, cookies, cold showers, and warm beds.

Wilcox and the Colorado climbers parted company on July 27. Not surprisingly, it was a strained goodbye. Four of the expedition members left the park and traveled to Anchorage: Lewis by plane (he was flown back for medical treatment), Snyder and Schlichter by truck, and Schiff by train. Only Wilcox chose to remain at McKinley.

Before leaving, Snyder, Schlichter, and Schiff stopped at park headquarters and talked with superintendent George Hall and chief ranger Arthur Hayes. Hall suggested that perhaps the seven missing climbers had mistakenly descended the West Buttress side of

Denali Pass and were safely sheltered in snow caves somewhere on the mountain's southern side. He further commented, "We've checked over their application forms. They've got some experienced men, including a couple with rescue experience. We don't see how anything too serious could have happened to a party that large."

The climbers were shocked and outraged by such an attitude. "What do you mean, nothing could have happened to them?" Schiff exploded. "They haven't been heard from in ten days!" Hall wasn't the only one to hold on to such hopes, as unrealistic or naive as they may have been. Back at Wonder Lake, Wilcox continued to believe his teammates might somehow still be alive. "I could not bring myself to assume that they had perished," he admitted.

But Wilcox and park officials were forced to face the tragic truth on July 28, when members of the MCA expedition finally reached high camp.

At 17,200 feet the Alaskans found an ice axe lying on the snow near the climbing route. Six hundred vertical feet higher they discovered a bamboo pole, decorated with neoprene streamers, stuck deep in the snow and tilted uphill. Russell had carried that ten-foot pole, planning to use it as his summit flag. A blue sleeping bag encased in a red shell was wrapped around the pole's bottom. Inside the bag were a pair of down booties and wool socks.

A few hundred yards upslope was the Wilcox party's high camp at 17,900 feet. There the MCA climbers found two tents. One was still intact, but nearly buried and filled by drifting snow. No climbers or sleeping bags were found inside. The other tent had been shredded by high winds. Inside was a partly decomposed body, in a crouched or sitting position. The dead man was frozen to the tent fabric and the tent's center pole. It appeared he'd been trying to steady the pole when he died. One of the hands was gloveless; both the exposed hand and the man's face were blue-green in color, swollen, cracked, and covered with frostbite blisters.

The tent fabric had apparently radiated some heat since the climber's death, causing the body to partially thaw and begin to decay. The smell of decomposition was overwhelming, which kept the searchers from making too close an inspection. No positive identification was made but Wilcox initially assumed the body was Steve Taylor's, since he'd remained at high camp while the others climbed to the summit. Much later he concluded the body may have been Russell's.

The MCA team also found enough food to last one person ten days, but no fuel. And no sign of the other six climbers.

It wasn't long before more victims were located, however. On July 29, with aerial spotting help from Sheldon, the Alaskans found two more bodies at an elevation of about 19,000 feet. The bodies were located on a steep, crevassed slope about 300 to 400 feet apart and on a line between high camp and The Archdeacon's Tower. Both bodies were in sitting positions with one leg extended, as though the men had been bracing themselves against the wind. One was partially wrapped in a sleeping bag, but no ropes, ice axes, or packs were found near them. Based on clothing and sleeping bag descriptions, the victims were tentatively identified as Walt Taylor and Dennis Luchterhand.

The MCA team failed to find any more bodies or gear before descending McKinley on July 30, and an August expedition organized by well-known Alaskan mountaineer Vin Hoeman (Grace Jansen-Hoeman's husband) was unsuccessful in its attempt to uncover additional evidence that might help solve the mystery of the missing climbers.

In their post-expedition analyses, Snyder and Wilcox agreed that the seven men who died were victims of tragically bad luck. If Clark's party had made its summit attempt one day or even a few hours earlier, or if the storm had begun a few hours later, it's likely no lives would have been lost. But their versions of what might have happened on McKinley's upper slopes the night of July 17 and in succeeding days differ considerably.

In Snyder's reconstruction of the seven climbers' final hours, he supposes that Clark's group didn't get any higher than The Archdeacon's Tower on July 17. Unable to communicate with Eielson because of weak radio batteries and lost in a whiteout, the summit team chose to bivouac at 19,550 feet rather than return to high camp. The six climbers each carried a sleeping bag, but unfortunately hadn't brought a tent, shovel, or stove. Already weakened by the day's ascent, they were forced to spend a bitterly cold night in the open, without any hot drinks to provide warmth or prevent dehydration.

By morning the fog had dissipated, enabling the climbers to regain their bearings and locate the route to McKinley's summit. The group resumed its ascent minus Russell, who was too weak to continue. Now consisting of five men, the team climbed the headwall leading to the summit ridge. Clouds again began to build around the upper mountain. But this section of the trail was better marked and easier to follow. Despite poor visibility, the five men reached the mountain's top sometime after 11. They spent no more than fifteen or twenty minutes on the summit, surrounded only by whiteness.

After reporting their success to Eielson the climbers descended into a growing storm. Winds of at least thirty to forty miles per hour now whipped the upper mountain, driving sheets of snow into their faces and dropping visibility to a few yards.

Upon reaching The Archdeacon's Tower, the group rejoined Russell, assuming he hadn't already started back to camp. Rather than follow the normal route to Denali Pass, the climbers descended a steep slope toward camp, either because they were lost or because they wanted to avoid the wind-blasted ridge leading to the pass. At an elevation of about 19,400 feet, the slope became much too difficult to negotiate in such high winds, especially with several of the men near exhaustion. The group stopped to rest and consider its alternatives.

Retreat was cut off, that much seemed clear. Not even the strongest climbers felt capable of fighting their way through such a fierce, blinding blizzard. They had no choice but to bivouac one more night in subzero temperatures, hoping the storm would ease up by morning.

Already dehydrated and chilled, they attempted to dig a cave or trench with their ice axes but had little success finding shelter from the wind. Once more they slipped into their sleeping bags, perhaps huddling together for warmth. As the climbers shivered in the cold, wind-blown snow began drifting over the bags.

The storm that began at midday on July 18 continued without letup into the next day. Every member of the summit team now suffered from frostbite and hypothermia. All day long and through the night, the storm raged; high winds and zero visibility made travel impossible.

On the morning of July 20, the wind continued to howl. But the snowfall ended and the sky began to clear. The tents at 17,900 were visible. Desperately needing water and the protection of a shelter, the men had little choice but to try reaching camp. It was the only remaining hope.

Luchterhand and Walt Taylor got out of their sleeping bags and tried to rouse their teammates. Some may have been incapable of responding. Unroped, those able to walk resumed their descent, heading directly for high camp. The already steep slope became steeper and was split with crevasses. Perhaps one or more of the men fell into a crevasse, but at least two were able to avoid the chasms. One reached 18,800 feet, the other 19,100 feet, before the mountain was again enveloped in clouds. The men sat down to rest, hoping the sky would again clear. They never stood again.

And Steve Taylor? Without a radio, unable to communicate with either the summit team or his teammates at 15,000 feet, he spent his final days alone at high camp. Expecting Clark's group to return the night of July 17, Taylor grew worried when the team failed to show. Sometime between July 18 and 20, he probably tried descending to 15,000 feet, but was forced to return to 17,900 by high winds and blinding snow. Hurricane-force gales shook the tent violently and pulled at the seams. To keep the tent from collapsing, Taylor gripped the center pole, trying to keep it upright. Eventually the weakened seams began ripping apart. The tent burst. Yet even while sinking into unconsciousness, Taylor continued holding the pole in a death grip.

Wilcox, in his version of the tragedy, assumes that Clark's summit party brought shovels and a stove in addition to sleeping bags. When it became clear that they wouldn't reach the summit on July 17, the climbers debated the pros and cons of camping out versus descending. Knowing that previous expeditions had camped overnight on or near McKinley's summit and realizing they probably wouldn't get another chance at reaching the top, the six men chose ambition over caution and spent the night in snow caves.

The morning of July 18 brought clear skies and the hoped-for opportunity to reach the summit. As his teammates prepared for the final assault, Russell made a difficult decision: still bothered by altitude sickness and unable to keep himself properly hydrated, he would have to descend or risk freezing his fingers and toes, which already were numb. Not wanting any of the others to forfeit a summit chance, Russell abruptly grabbed his bamboo pole, put on his pack, and departed for 17,900 alone.

By late morning, the remaining five had reached McKinley's top. After a short time on the summit, they descended into high winds and heavy snow. Once again, visibility dropped to almost nothing and gales battered the climbers' bodies. Unable to see more than a few feet in any direction, they decided it would be foolish to try reaching camp and instead retreated to the snow caves built the previous night.

In their shelters, the climbers considered their options. Following the normal ridgeline route to Denali Pass was out of the question; that would directly expose them to the full force of the wind, now blowing at one hundred miles per hour or more. Waiting out the storm also seemed undesirable because some members of the group were showing signs of altitude sickness and needed to descend. A third alternative was to follow a compass bearing from The Archdeacon's Tower to high camp, but that was an uncharted course with unknown hazards. Finally, after much debate, the climbers decided to split the group. The two strongest men would begin a compass-guided descent to camp and mark their path with wands. The others would follow four hours later, assuming the first two hadn't returned.

The two climbers began their trek through the fierce storm, carefully working their way down the steep, crevassed slope. Finally they came to a thirty-foot-high cliff. Cautiously the men tried to find a detour around the cliff, but couldn't. Frustrated and tired, they returned to the caves with the bad news. The summit team used the last of its fuel to melt snow for drinks and attempted, without success, to contact Eielson. Then the five climbers once again crawled into their sleeping bags. They now had little choice but to wait out the storm.

Meanwhile, at high camp, Russell had joined Steve Taylor. Together they spent a restless night, waiting impatiently for the return of their teammates. On the morning of July 19, the two agreed that Russell should descend at least partway to 15,000 feet and try to signal the lower camp with smoke flares. The attempt failed. Before returning to 17,900 feet, Russell drove his bamboo pole into the snow, hoping the lower camp would be able to see it and recognize it as a signal for help.

Later in the day, Russell decided to check out Denali Pass; perhaps the summit team had been able to descend at least that far. Already weakened by illness, he struggled to 18,200 feet but found no sign of the group. By the time he rejoined Taylor at high camp, Russell had become hypothermic and had frostbitten his hands. He desperately needed to descend, but the storm had gotten worse and travel was impossible.

Up in the snow caves, Clark's party spent all of July 19 huddled in sleeping bags, trying to conserve energy but gradually weakening. With the fuel used up there was no way to replenish fluids. Morale deteriorated and fear began to set in.

July 20 brought a break in the storm and hope to the climbers stuck high on the mountain. Clark, Walt Taylor, Luchterhand, Janes, and McLaughlin left their caves. Roped together, they headed down the steep slope leading directly to high camp, hopeful they could avoid crevasses and somehow circumvent the thirty-foot cliff that had stopped them two days earlier.

But dense clouds and blowing snow soon engulfed the mountain once again. Winds blowing 100 to 150 miles per hour tore at the five men and forced them to crawl on hands and knees. Movement either upslope or downslope became impossible, so they dug two shallow snow caves. Their bodies now dehydrated and numbed by the cold, the men began to lose feeling in their toes and fingers. Frostbite was setting in. A day had passed since they'd last had a drink and their food was nearly gone as well. Outside the caves, screaming gales swept the climbers' gear down the mountain. Packs, shovels, ice axes, ropes—all were blown away.

By July 21, winds had begun eroding one of the caves. Luchterhand and Walt Taylor knew their chances of reaching high camp were almost nil. But with their shelter being destroyed and no tools to make repairs, they had little choice but to try. After explaining their decision to the others, the two men headed into the storm. Soon they became separated. Pounded by the winds, first one man, then the other stopped to rest. And moved no more.

In the other snow cave, Clark, McLaughlin, and Janes's numbed and dehydrated bodies moved ever more slowly. Their senses dulled, and their will to live drained by the cold, they silently and peacefully slipped into unconsciousness while drifting snow turned their shelter into a snowy grave.

At high camp, Steve Taylor and Russell were also fighting a losing battle with the storm. For more than a day, they took turns clutching the tent's center pole, struggling to keep it upright. Russell was responsible for holding the pole in the early hours of July 21. But by morning he was dead, a victim of exhaustion-hypothermia. Upon discovering his partner's death, Taylor was overcome with shock and fear. No longer could he stay in the tent; he would have to try descending alone.

Taylor grabbed his sleeping bag and ice axe and headed for the low camp. He stopped to rest at Russell's bamboo pole and wrapped the sleeping bag around the pole's base, probably to keep it from blowing away. When he resumed his journey, Taylor left the bag behind. It had become too much trouble to carry.

Stumbling down the mountain, Taylor hardly noticed when he dropped his ice axe. Beaten by the wind, his energy reserves drained, he fell, got up, then fell again. Sometime around midmorning, he collapsed one last time. Windblown snow gradually covered the lifeless form, burying it forever.

No disaster analysis would be complete without some final reflections. In concluding his "true story of a tragic climb," *The Hall of the Mountain King*, Snyder offered several thoughts on the circumstances and actions that contributed to his teammates' deaths. His commentary included the following observations:[3]

- Wilcox, the expedition leader, didn't know the members of his team well enough. Steve Taylor was the only one he'd met, or climbed with, before the expedition was put together
- Neither Wilcox nor any of the eight climbers he recruited had any high-altitude experience and none had extensive winter training in cold weather or high winds.
- At least two members of the expedition, Schiff and Steve Taylor, had so little experience they shouldn't have even been on the mountain.
- Some team members were lulled into a false sense of security by the expedition's large size and abundance of food, fuel, and gear; they fell prey to the adage that "there's safety in numbers." According to Snyder, several expressed the opinion that a large, well-equipped team could handle any situation. The abundance of gear also led some of the climbers to treat equipment carelessly and, on some occasions, abusively.
- At several of the camps, including the two highest, tents were pitched at right angles to the prevailing wind, thus making them more susceptible to drifting and collapse. At both 15,000 and 17,900 feet, it would probably have been wise to build igloos or snow caves rather than depend on tents.
- Extra radio batteries were cached at 12,000 feet and therefore were unavailable when needed high on the mountain. As a consequence, messages could not be transmitted at critical times.
- The Park Service didn't have the ability to provide frequent and local weather forecasts. Most of those given were for Anchorage, not the Alaska Range, based on National Weather Service reports. The second summit team had no idea a severe storm was approaching.
- An insufficient number of wands was brought to high camp for the first summit attempt, so the route was only poorly marked by Wilcox and the Colorado trio. If more wands had been

available and the trail marked more clearly by the first party, Clark's group may have reached the summit on July 17 and thus descended to camp before the storm arrived.

- Good weather experienced earlier in the climb, combined with the first summit team's relatively easy ascent on July 15, may have lulled the second group into complacency. Clark's group let three hours of ideal climbing weather slip by before leaving camp on July 17. And the party included at least two climbers who'd been suffering altitude sickness, which no doubt slowed the pace. If the party had started three hours earlier, it probably would have reached the summit without having to bivouac overnight through the storm.

Wilcox disagreed with nearly all of Snyder's criticisms and comments. He also expressed amazement that anyone could possibly take Snyder's account seriously since, according to Wilcox, it contained so many errors of fact and reasoning, and he publicly wondered why Snyder would "vigorously and exhaustively distort events and facts in an attempt to discredit the organization, leadership, and personnel of the Wilcox group."

Wilcox's account of the expedition, *White Winds*, was written to set the record straight, from his perspective. Wilcox also produced a hundred-page booklet, *A Reader's Guide to The Hall of the Mountain King*, which contains item-by-item rebuttals of Snyder's facts, figures, and comments.[4]

While a thorough examination of Wilcox's rebuttals is hardly possible here (interested persons are advised to read both accounts and make their own judgments), his responses to several of the chief criticisms made by Snyder or other mountaineers are worthy of mention:[5]

- Though the expedition may have been one of the oddest assortments of climbers ever assembled (with the Colorado group constituting an "awkward appendage"), the team's makeup resulted in very little friction throughout most of the trip. The principal clash of personalties–between Wilcox and Snyder–took place at 15,000 feet, while the upper party's fate was still in doubt.

- The leader of the second summit team, Jerry Clark, had previously climbed with everyone in that group and was close friends with each. Therefore, Wilcox argued, "more favorable cohesion within a group would be unrealistic to expect."
- Every expedition member had some previous cold-weather and high-wind climbing experience. As evidence, Wilcox presented detailed climbing resumes.
- Neither of the men Snyder describes as the team's two weakest climbers participated in the second summit attempt. Ansel Schiff descended to 15,000 feet while Steve Taylor remained at high camp. The men who accompanied Clark were among the expedition's most experienced climbers and compared well with participants in other McKinley expeditions.
- At least one veteran mountaineer was highly critical of the decision to leave Steve Taylor alone at 17,900 feet, calling such an action "unforgivable." In response, Wilcox noted that he was philosophically opposed to leaving a lone man in camp, particularly if ill. However, he explained," To leave a man with Steve Taylor at high camp would virtually forfeit that man's chances of reaching the summit: a goal for which each person had invested a great deal of time, money and energy; a goal for which each man had already endured a great deal of danger and adversity; a goal which, at the time, seemed only a gentle stroll away. The mild danger of leaving a lone man in camp for a few hours was greatly overshadowed. Steve likely realized the imposition and probably insisted that he be left alone."
- It's unlikely that fresh batteries, and thus improved radio communications, would have aided any rescue of the climbers.

Better radio contact would certainly have enabled Clark's party to notify the Park Service of its need for help. But white out conditions and hurricane-force winds would probably have made it impossible for rescuers to reach the climbers in time to save them.

- Although in retrospect Clark's group took insufficient food, fuel, and gear to the summit, the team was, in fact, much better prepared than most summit parties. In addition to the warm clothing, full water bottles, and extra food that most teams take to McKinley's top, Clark's group also brought sleeping bags, shovel, snow saw, radio, and probably a stove. (Despite Wilcox's conviction that the team carried a shovel, saw, and stove, there's no proof they had such items.)
- The second team did not let three hours of "perfect weather" slip by on July 17. In fact, they probably waited until they were certain the weather was appropriate for a summit try. Some delay in starting may have been caused by the climbers' careful preparations for an attempt, their efforts to find three quarts of fuel that had been buried by snowfall, or a desire to make Steve Taylor as comfortable as possible for his stay in high camp alone.
- Rather than believing there was safety in numbers, members of the Wilcox group were skeptical about the creation of a large group such as that formed by the merger of two expeditions.
- Snyder's criticism that snow caves should have been dug at 15,000 and 17,900 feet was a valid one. One built at high camp might have saved the lives of Steve Taylor and/or Russell. Yet according to Wilcox, at no time during the expedition did Snyder suggest that snow caves be dug.

Wilcox also seconded Snyder's observations regarding Park Service weather reporting and emphasized that the expedition was unable to get regular and reliable weather information throughout its climb. If Clark's group had realized that a major storm was approaching, it's likely the team would have retreated rather than spend a night camping on the mountain's upper slopes. (It should be noted, however, that radio operators based at Eielson were completely dependent on National Weather Service reports they received, when relaying weather forecasts to the Wilcox party. In 1967, park rangers had no direct communications link-up with the Weather Service as they do today, so the information was usually secondhand and not always timely. As Snyder commented, even the available forecasts were of limited value, because they applied to the Anchorage area, not to the Alaska Range. And because McKinley often generates its own weather patterns, much of what happens on the mountain could never be forecast. Ultimately, climbers must themselves monitor weather patterns, rather than rely on outside sources.)

In addition to his commentary on weather reports, Wilcox directed some blame at the Park Service and other rescue groups, accusing them of dragging their feet even after it became clear the climbers were in considerable danger. Yet he recognized that members of his own expedition were in the best position to help the upper group and failed to do so. And he admitted that even a prompt response would probably have failed to save the members of Clark's party, because of the storm's severity.

Wilcox seemed most tormented by the lower party's inability, or unwillingness, to make a second rescue attempt, after being turned back on July 20:

> It was my feeling then and now that we were morally committed to the upper party and that we were obliged to make the return climb. It has been said by some that the 15,000-foot party made a gallant effort to aid the upper group, that we were nearing our physical and emotional limits, and we had done all that could reasonably be expected; logic justified our descent. The sober reality, however, is that we were not in a "reasonable"

situation. Fate had come to claim the lives of our companions. Extraordinary needs require extraordinary efforts.

In Wilcox's words, the five survivors became deserters. Rather than exert that extraordinary effort, they left their comrades behind. That, more than any error or inadequacy, was in his mind the expedition's great failure.

Wilcox may accuse himself and Snyder of acting cowardly or self-servingly when their teammates were in trouble, but no one can be blamed for the climbers' deaths. The seven who died chose ambition over caution. They took a risk that many climbers have taken and were unlucky enough to get caught by a severe summer storm.

In *White Winds*, Wilcox presents a detailed, thoroughly researched analysis of the storm that struck McKinley in mid-July 1967. Based on a review of National Weather Service data for the period 1946 to 1979, and with the assistance of a professional meteorologist, Wilcox concludes that the storm that killed his teammates "was in a class by itself. . . . For a full eight and a half days, the winds probably averaged 80 to 110 miles per hour with peak gusts well above 150 miles per hour. . . . The most profound characteristic of the storm was that winds were extreme day after day after day." Not even the 1967 winter storm that trapped Genet, Davidson, and Johnston for several days was so severe, he argues.

Many other mountaineers familiar with McKinley's weather dispute Wilcox's claims, among them Bradford Washburn, who conducted a critique of the disaster in September 1967. More recently, Washburn explained:

What happened was very tragic, there's no question of that. But to say the [July 1967] storm was "in a class by itself" is absolutely nonsense. The storm that killed those climbers was a typical McKinley summer storm, a southwester. If [members of the Wilcox expedition]

> had known more about mountaineering, they'd have seen all the portents of the storm developing. When you see high cirrus clouds coming in from the west, or a milky mist developing on the summit, there's bad weather ahead; you don't climb to the summit.
>
> A summer storm on McKinley is nothing to worry about, if you take the proper precautions. The temperature goes up, not down, during a storm and often in summer it will rise above zero. People who don't run into a storm sometime during a McKinley expedition are very lucky. When Barbara and I were on the mountain in May of 1947, we had to hole up for nine straight days. The winter storms are the ones to worry about; then you have the combination of extreme wind and extreme cold. There's absolutely no comparison.[6]

Though this issue may be debated endlessly, Wilcox was convinced that Clark's summit party encountered the most severe, high-altitude windstorm in McKinley's mountaineering history. In fact, he concluded, "it may well be that Clark's group was caught in the most severe, high altitude windstorm in the entire history of mountaineering."

Tabor's 2008 book, *Forever on the Mountain*, attempts to take an in-depth look at the events that led to the Wilcox disaster, based on his interviews with three of the survivors and others involved in the tragedy and rescue attempt, as well as research of National Park Service archival material. Tabor has admitted that "some conjecture was inescapable" and that he was forced to deduce "most-probable scenarios as I worked my own way to them through thickets of theory and conjecture." Some have praised his approach, others have disparaged it. Ultimately the book's "truth" largely remains speculation. There is no way to know the circumstances of the climbers' deaths nor whether an earlier rescue effort could have saved them.

Naomi Uemura, Courtesy of Kimiko Uemura and the *Anchorage Times*

JAPANESE EXPLORER NAOMI UEMURA SITS BESIDE HIS CLIMBING GEAR WHILE MAKING THE FIRST SOLO ASCENT OF MCKINLEY IN AUGUST 1970.

CHAPTER TEN

WINTER SOLO ASCENTS: WATERMAN, UEMURA, AND JOHNSTON

ONE OF MOUNTAINEERING'S extreme challenges is to solo: to climb alone, without the security and support–both physical and emotional–of teammates.

Both the risks and potential rewards of climbing are significantly increased when soloing. As Anchorage mountaineer Steve Davis has put it, "There is no room for error."[1] The simplest mistakes, the slightest injuries can prove fatal when there's no one else around to lend aid.

But as Davis points out, that's part of the appeal:

> Because you cannot make an error, everything else in the world has to be blocked out. You become totally focused on what you're doing and forget about other concerns. Your whole world is maybe six feet

> of snow or ice or rock. It's a small vacation from all the problems of day-to-day life. And it's an incredible adrenaline rush. You can be physically exhausted yet mentally refreshed.

There are other reasons mountaineers climb alone. Some desire the public acclaim that comes with a significant solo ascent. Others wish to avoid the restrictions and potential conflicts that are part of working with a team. Some seek solitude and the sense of freedom that comes with traveling alone. Or the opportunity to test themselves, to discover their limits. Whatever the prime motivation or degree of success, a soloist has the satisfaction of saying "I did this on my own."

As proof of their success, soloists sometimes leave an object at the summit—a flag, note, or other memento—or, more commonly, they'll take a photographic self-portrait while on the mountain's top. But as Davis explains:

> Within the mountaineering community, a climber's word is usually sufficient. Basically we're operating on an honor system. The only exceptions are when the objective is one that's highly coveted, or when there have been numerous failed attempts in the past, or when a climber is unknown, is a controversial figure, or is considered to be of questionable character.[2]

The first climber to go one-on-one with McKinley was Japanese adventurer Naomi Uemura, who took up the challenge in August 1970. Then twenty-nine, Uemura had already proven himself to be one of the world's outstanding mountaineers. He'd soloed more than a half-dozen great peaks, including Mount Kilimanjaro in Africa, Aconcagua (the Western Hemisphere's tallest peak) in Argentina, and Mount Blanc and the Matterhorn in Europe. He also had ascended Mount Everest with a Japanese expedition.

Just as important as Uemura's skills was his timing. From the mid-1940s through 1969, the National Park Service had not allowed solo attempts on McKinley, as part of its strict regulation of climbing activities. According to National Park Service files, a would-be soloist was refused permission to climb the mountain in 1946, because of the extreme hazards.[3] (Traveling alone, a mountaineer would be less likely to survive mountain sickness, hypothermia, or injury due to crevasse falls, avalanches, or other climbing accidents.)

Six years later, the Park Service enacted a regulation that specifically prohibited solo climbs of McKinley. And by the mid-1950s, the agency had established an entire set of restrictions intended to deny "foolhardy or ill-advised people" from attempting the mountain. To prove they were healthy, well-conditioned, and experienced mountaineers, all prospective climbers had to answer government questionnaires and submit doctor's certificates of well-being. Before any expedition, a team's food and equipment were subject to inspection. Parties had to include at least four expedition members. And expedition leaders were required to submit an expedition itinerary and arrange for a standby rescue party. If park officials felt the applicants didn't meet government standards, they would deny individuals or entire expeditions the opportunity to climb McKinley.

But in 1970, the Park Service loosened its restrictions. Mountaineers were still required to register with park rangers before climbs, but no longer did they need government approval to climb.

In his reply to Uemura's application, the park superintendent noted, "You have a great deal of climbing experience and I'm sure you realize the risks involved in climbing a [mountain] such as McKinley alone. We cannot authorize you to do so." But neither could they stop him.

Traveling light and fast—his pack weighed only fifty-five pounds—and subsisting on a diet of salmon, salmon eggs, and bread, Uemura left his Kahiltna Glacier base camp and ascended the West Buttress to the summit in eight days, about two to three times faster than the average expedition on that route. On August 26, he stood alone atop McKinley, and several days later he returned to Anchorage with photographic proof of his triumph.

In the three decades since Uemura's climbing coup, dozens of people have climbed or at least attempted to climb McKinley solo. A few have chosen technically difficult routes; especially notable was Charlie Porter's first solo ascent of the Cassin Ridge in 1976, recognized as a spectacular effort within the mountaineering community. But most have chosen to follow in Uemura's footsteps by taking the West Buttress approach. Among those to do so was Italian Miri Ercolani, who on July 21, 1982, became the first woman to solo McKinley (though her ascent wasn't officially recognized until the 1990s). She was followed, in June 1990, by Alaska's Norma Jean Saunders, the first American woman to reach the mountain's top while climbing alone.

McKinley rangers noted a steadily growing interest in solo ascents during the mid- to late 1980s, a trend they considered disturbing. According to Bob Seibert, then Denali National Park's chief mountaineering ranger:

> It's not something we recommend. If climbers want to solo, we make sure they understand the risks and try to convince them to travel with someone else, at least on the lower glaciers because of the risk of crevasse falls. Unfortunately, many of the climbers [intending to solo] have little or no Alaska Range experience. It's clear they haven't given any thought to their safety or the dangers. Once we talk to them and explain the situation, many will team up. Not only are solo climbers putting themselves at risk; if something happens, rescuers will be put at risk also.[4]

The risks of traveling alone–or unroped, even if with partners–on McKinley's glaciers are well-documented. Since 1932, when Theodore Koven and Alan Carpé were killed on the Muldrow Glacier, at least ten climbers have died in crevasse falls. Several others whose bodies were never found may have experienced similar fates.

Especially frustrating to park rangers are those mountaineers who insist on soloing the West Buttress during McKinley's peak climbing season in May and June. The idea of "climbing alone" on a route occupied by hundreds of other people is somewhat absurd; in such a setting it's difficult, if not impossible, to be completely independent. Furthermore, the presence of other climbers may, in fact, lead to careless risk taking. Soloists, especially those who are inexperienced or overconfident, may be lulled into a false sense of security when traveling a heavily populated route like the West Buttress in summer.

(Uemura made his 1970 solo climb in August, well after the end of McKinley's traditional climbing season, which runs from April through early July. Only one other group was on the mountain. According to newspaper reports of the ascent, a four-member team led by guide Ray Genet followed two days behind Uemura as a "silent back-up for the lone climber."[5])

In winter, of course, it's easy to find solitude on McKinley–to be utterly and completely alone with no room for error. Winter provides an unforgiving test of a soloist. And during the 1980s, several adventurers took that test, with varying degrees of success. One was thwarted by frostbite, others by inexperience. Two returned in triumph. And two didn't return at all. The ascents of Vern Tejas and Dave Staeheli are now considered among the greatest mountaineering feats in Alaska history. But just as intriguing, if not more so, are the tragic and mysterious deaths of John Waterman and Naomi Uemura.

In this chapter and the next are the stories of five who truly went one-on-one with McKinley.

John Mallon Waterman died in April 1981. How he died no one knows, because his body was never found, despite extensive searches. Waterman (not to be confused with Jonathan Waterman, contemporary mountaineer/author) was last seen walking up the Northwest Fork of the Ruth Glacier toward McKinley. He'd told friends he was going to attempt to climb the mountain's East Buttress. But those who knew Waterman best say he was intentionally walking to his death.

Waterman was a brilliant climber, by many accounts, and a tormented, emotionally unstable person. In 1978, he completed an incredible 145-day solo climb of Mount Hunter, a 14,570-foot neighbor of McKinley. Other mountaineers were both awed and shocked by the marathon masterpiece. In 1983, Glenn Randall called it "the most difficult and dangerous solo ascent ever made in the Alaska Range." Others used terms like "crazy," "bizarre," "amazing." Certainly, as Anchorage mountaineering guide Gary Bocarde once commented, "It's something you have to put into a separate category, all its own."[6]

But Waterman's climbing brilliance was all too often overshadowed by a darker, more erratic side. In a newspaper article headlined "Over the Edge," Randall wrote:

> As respect for [Waterman's] ability grew, so too did the stories about his raging bursts of anger, his foolhardy behavior in the mountains and his eccentric personality. Clearly, Waterman was driven—to spectacular accomplishments and, eventually, to madness. He so craved life on the brink that he was almost willing to die for it. In his twenty-ninth year, he apparently did.[7]

Born on the East Coast, Waterman was introduced to rock climbing at age thirteen by his father, and within a short time he became obsessed with mastering the sport. Less than four years later, he joined a McKinley expedition and reached the summit, becoming one of the youngest climbers ever to do so.

During the early to mid-1970s, Waterman climbed extensively within the Alaska Range, as well as in Scotland, England, Turkey, and the Alps. He gave himself totally to mountaineering, but in doing so discovered the mountains couldn't fill a growing emptiness. Instead of peace, he felt turmoil. Something was lacking; exactly what, he didn't know. In an interview with Glenn Randall, Waterman's father Guy said:

> John realized his life was missing something by being so single-minded. . . . Life was not easy for him. I think he felt he had difficulty dealing with people. He felt that he had never learned to deal with girls in high school because he was always climbing. He took a couple stabs at college, but never really got interested in anything the way he did in climbing.

Not only did mountaineering fail to fill Waterman's inner void; it created new pains, new losses. In his book *Breaking Point*, Randall reveals that "all of his close friends, those who had taught him to climb and accompanied him on his greatest adventures, had died, often in senseless accidents."[8]

As the toll rose—eight of his closest friends died in the mountains—Waterman became increasingly intrigued with his own death. He told close friends he expected to die in the mountains. That fatalism, says Randall, was in conflict with Waterman's "powerful desire to triumph in a way the world would notice." Nowhere was that conflict more apparent than on his solo ascent of Mount Hunter in 1978.

Twice before, Waterman had attempted to reach Hunter's summit, while climbing with others. Twice he'd failed. But those failures only made him more determined to succeed. Thus began his self-described "vendetta with Mount Hunter."[9]

Waterman decided that merely reaching Hunter's summit was no longer sufficient revenge for his earlier failures: he would conquer the mountain in grand style or, perhaps, die trying. And so he chose to solo the previously unclimbed Southeast Spur, a route that Randall calls "among the most difficult climbs in North America. . . . Even to experienced climbers, this is a nightmare, a bad trip. . . . [The Spur] is steep—unrelentingly so—with trouble at every turn."

In retrospect, Randall suggests:

> [Waterman] had been convinced he was a dead man when he flew out of Talkeetna, that he would never make it to the far side of the climb. Or perhaps not entirely convinced. Still, he knew the odds. In a strange way, that had been part of the lure of this adventure, for if he died at age twenty-five in a hopeless yet magnificent struggle with the mountain he conceived to be invincible, perhaps both the mountain and John Waterman would become a legend.

Instead of dying a tragic, heroic death, Waterman triumphed in a way that amazed the climbing world. On July 26, after almost eighteen weeks alone, he reached Hunter's summit via the Southeast Spur. It would take him another six weeks to descend the mountain. But no hero's welcome awaited in Talkeetna. Even worse, he was broke. He borrowed twenty dollars from Cliff Hudson, the pilot who'd flown him out of the Alaska Range, and went to Fairbanks, where he got a job washing dishes. Waterman later confided, "To me that was really the ultimate in what was wrong about society. After this horrible climb—or actually, this superb climb—my only societal reward was to be washing dishes, at the very bottom of society."[10]

His behavior grew more and more unconventional. As a music student at the University of Alaska Fairbanks, he sometimes ran around campus outfitted in a black cape and played a cheap guitar held together by masking tape. Later he ran for a school board seat on a platform advocating liberalized drug use and sexual freedom for students. After his defeat, Waterman set his goals even higher: president of the United States.

"My party was the Feed the Starving Party," he later explained. "My essential campaign priority was to ensure that nobody starved to death on the Earth. I thought feeding the starving people of the world would be the most dramatic and difficult thing I could do."

To help publicize his campaign, Waterman challenged President Reagan to a debate. And he decided to make the first winter solo ascent of McKinley on a diet of flour, sugar, margarine, milk, and baking soda, to demonstrate that people could survive on very little.

Waterman trained for the McKinley climb by running on icy roads in his crampons and lying naked in a bathtub of ice water. He then flew in to the Alaska Range on December 20, 1979. Even at an elevation of 7,000 feet, the temperature was −15°F. It would get much colder at higher elevations.

Prepared for an odyssey of fifty to one hundred days, Waterman brought 500 pounds of food, fuel, and gear. But from the start, he was beset with problems. His sleeping bag was too tight and didn't provide enough warmth. And the inside of the tent kept icing up, and showered him with ice crystals whenever he bumped its sides.

But deeper fears were also playing on his mind. When Cliff Hudson's son Jay flew in to the Alaska Range on January 1 to drop off additional supplies, Waterman quickly made his decision. "Take me home," he said. "I don't want to die."

Back in town, Waterman touched on his fear when he told a reporter, "You can't stress enough how terrible it is. It's just a good way to freeze to death in great solitude. . . . My equipment wasn't really going to keep me alive and that certainly was a factor in my decision. The mountain defeated me but he didn't eat me alive."[11] Yet he also expressed great embarrassment at the perceived failure and insisted the mountain had beaten him only temporarily.

Within two months, Waterman was back in Talkeetna, planning for a second attempt. Just as he was making final preparations, disaster struck. The cabin where he was staying was engulfed by fire. His tent, sleeping bag, climbing files, journals, and poetry were destroyed. According to Randall, Waterman went berserk. He stormed into Hudson's office and called state troopers, demanding a ride to the Alaska Psychiatric Institute in Anchorage. The troopers refused, saying Waterman didn't sound crazy. He shouted back, "What do I have to do, kill a kid?"

The next morning, Waterman flew into Anchorage with another Talkeetna pilot, Jim Okonek, and checked into the hospital. Within a few days, he became convinced that doctors were conspiring against him, and that they intended to lock him up as a dissident. After two weeks, he was released.

The following winter, tormented by his newest obsession—McKinley in winter—Waterman began yet another incredible journey. Once again he set out alone. But this time he started from the shores of Cook Inlet, near Anchorage and more than one hundred miles from the mountain.

Art Davidson reflects in *Minus 148°*:

> The dimensions of this venture are hard to grasp. In part, it was a throwback to the days of a Jim Bridger or Lewis and Clark when a toughened scout or trapper might find his way across hundreds of miles of frozen wilderness. But what kind of person would cap off such a trek by trying to climb North America's highest mountain, alone and in winter?[12]

NAOMI UEMURA, COURTESY OF KIMIKO UEMURA AND THE *ANCHORAGE TIMES*

NAOMI UEMURA STANDS ON MCKINLEY'S SUMMIT IN 1970; THIRTEEN AND A HALF YEARS LATER, HE REACHED THE MOUNTAIN'S TOP WHILE CLIMBING ALONE IN WINTER, BUT DIED WHILE DESCENDING.

Carrying a pack that seemed twice the size of his body, Waterman followed a series of frozen rivers into the foothills of the Alaska Range. He ended his long-distance trek on the Ruth Glacier, at an elevation of only 2,000 feet, and returned to Talkeetna. A faulty stove was blamed, but other climbers were convinced Waterman could have repaired it if he'd wanted to. And they suspected that the real problem went deeper.

Rather than give up his quest, Waterman began preparing for a third attempt. After weeks of indecision, he left for the mountains in early March. On departing, he told Cliff Hudson, "I won't be seeing you again."

He traveled back up the Ruth Glacier, but once more seemed plagued by indecision and spent a couple of weeks hanging out near the Sheldon Mountain House (named after its builder, bush pilot Don Sheldon), a small cabin perched above the Ruth. Friends later reported that he'd seemed run down and less cautious than usual.

In late March, Waterman called Hudson over the two-way radio he carried and asked the pilot to fly in more supplies. Then, on April 1—already too late for a winter climb—he began his final journey.

Traveling up the Ruth Glacier's Northwest Fork, the twenty-nine-year-old climber carried about fourteen days' worth of powdered milk, honey, sugar, and flour. But he took neither a tent nor a sleeping bag.

Jay Kerr, the last person to see Waterman, watched as he took a straight-line course through a heavily crevassed area. Later Kerr said that although Waterman had been acting strangely, he didn't show any signs of being suicidal.

When he hadn't been heard from for more than two weeks, Park Service rangers initiated a search. On April 22, ranger Roger Robinson and guide Mike Covington flew over the area in a helicopter and found an abandoned campsite in the middle of a crevasse field. But they never found Waterman.

A few days later, while removing the rest of Waterman's gear from the Mountain House, Cliff Hudson found a note attached to one of the climber's cardboard boxes. It read: "3/13/81 My Last Kiss 1:42 P.M."

In death as in life, John Waterman remained an enigma, even to those who knew him best.

Thirteen and a half years after completing the first solo ascent of McKinley, Naomi Uemura returned to the mountain. Again he planned to climb alone, this time in winter.

If successful, Uemura would become the first to complete a winter solo ascent of McKinley. But reaching the peak's 20,320-foot summit was not an end in itself. This expedition was merely a prelude to an even greater undertaking: a solo trek across Antarctica, culminated by an ascent of that continent's highest mountain, 16,860-foot Vinson Massif.

Since his 1970 climb of McKinley, Uemura had devoted his energies to long-distance solo treks. His journeys included a 3,700-mile raft trip down the full length of the Amazon River and a three-year, 7,500-mile dogsled trip from Greenland to Alaska. In 1978, mushing a team of seventeen dogs, he became the first person to reach the North Pole while traveling alone.

At age forty-two, Uemura was widely recognized as perhaps the greatest explorer and adventurer of his time. Jonathan Waterman describes him in *High Alaska*:

> [Just as remarkable] as his solo achievements was his sincere modesty and unassuming nature. Another part of his greatness lay in his deep interest in everyone he met. He was tremendously acclaimed in Japan, revered by thousands, much like an American sports hero. His adventure books were read by all Japanese schoolchildren.[13]

Uemura arrived in Talkeetna in January 1984 and began his trip up McKinley's West Buttress on February 1. His plan, as usual, was to go light and fast.

Wearing a forty-pound pack and pulling a sled, he hauled only the absolute essentials needed to survive a winter ascent. He would sleep in snow caves, which eliminated the need for a tent, and would subsist on a diet of raw caribou meat, seal oil, and whale blubber. As a precaution against crevasse falls–the greatest threat to a solo climber–the five-foot, four-inch climber strapped two long bamboo poles across his shoulders. The poles' function was simple: if Uemura fell into one of the glacier's many hidden fissures, the poles would span the crevasse and stop his fall. In theory, at least.

On the morning of February 13, Uemura talked by radio with two Japanese photographers being flown over the mountain by Talkeetna bush pilot Lowell Thomas Jr. and informed them that he'd reached McKinley's summit at seven the previous evening, on his forty-third birthday.

The climber was not visible because clouds covered the mountain's top. Radio communications were also poor, but the Japanese said Uemura had descended to about 18,000 feet and planned to be at his Kahiltna Glacier base camp by February 15.

News of Uemura's achievement soon reached Anchorage and the national media. Because Uemura was a highly respected mountaineer, word of his achievement was accepted even before proof could be offered.

Climbers, park officials, and reporters anxiously awaited Uemura's return, but he failed to arrive for his scheduled rendezvous.[14] A search of the West Buttress Route by Thomas and another pilot, Doug Geeting, failed to produce any sign of the climber, except for his two bamboo poles. Confident that crevasses wouldn't be a significant hazard at higher elevations, Uemura had left the poles at about 9,500 feet. The fact that they were still there convinced the pilots he was probably higher on the mountain.

Skies were clear and visibility good, but Geeting and Thomas reported extreme turbulence near the summit. They speculated Uemura had taken refuge in a snow cave while waiting for improved conditions; even at 10,000 feet, windchill temperatures had dropped below −50°F. And while hidden in a cave, he probably would have been unable to hear any planes flying overhead, particularly in high winds.

On February 16, Geeting reported that he spotted Uemura at about 16,600 feet, waving from an ice cave where he'd taken shelter from the wind. But a thick cloud mass moved in and hid the mountain the next day, making it impossible to check on the climber's progress for three days. And pilots had no luck in contacting him over the radio.

Though Uemura was now several days overdue and almost certainly running low on fuel (he'd taken only three liters of white gas, enough for about two and a half weeks total), climbers, pilots, and park officials were reluctant to launch a rescue mission out of respect for his extensive mountaineering experience. He was known to be a cautious, well-organized climber, one who didn't take unnecessary risks. Bob Gerhard, Denali National Park's chief mountaineering ranger, was among those who didn't want to diminish the accomplishment. And Geeting admitted, "If it was anybody else, we'd have somebody on the mountain already."

Most Alaskan mountaineers seemed to agree with McKinley guide Nic Parker's assessment that "he knows his limits. At least I think he does. He won't take any chances. He won't try to push it."

Attitudes began to change, however, when pilots failed to spot Uemura on February 20, despite clear, relatively calm weather that allowed them to thoroughly search the mountain. Park rangers also examined the area at 16,600 feet where Geeting had earlier spotted the climber, but failed to find any evidence he'd stayed there. Gerhard said they'd found no equipment, no dirty snow, no debris of any kind. And nearby supply caches left by previous climbers were undisturbed.

"You bet we're concerned," admitted Tom Griffiths, chief ranger at Denali National Park. "We should have been able to find him." That same day, two experienced climbers, Jim Wickwire of Seattle and Eiho Otani of Tokyo, were dropped at 14,000 feet to begin a search.

The good weather lasted only a day. Clear skies were replaced by thick clouds and wind-driven snow that once again obscured McKinley. And officials admitted their hopes were dwindling. Gerhard told the press:

> We believe the odds are extremely slim that Mr. Uemura has survived. We are continuing the search as weather allows because of his past-proven, exceptional survival skills. We've been very concerned since Monday (February 20). That's a day he should have been moving. There are many things that could have happened.

On February 26, two weeks after Uemura reached McKinley's summit, Wickwire and Otani ended their search. In a snow cave at 14,000 feet, they'd found bits of caribou meat, a nearly empty fuel can, snowshoes, socks, and a diary. But there was no trace of the climber. "In my opinion, it is almost conclusive he is dead," Wickwire said, after spending six days on the mountain. "The passage of time is so great . . . it appears there was a fatal accident." Wickwire speculated that the Japanese adventurer had fallen while descending the steep headwall between 16,200 and 14,000 feet, and that his body had been covered by later snowstorms.

The Park Service called off its air and ground search. But a team of four Japanese climbers from Tokyo's Meji University, the college Uemura had attended, flew into the Kahiltna Glacier against officials' warnings, intending to find and recover the body.

The Meji University team abandoned its search about ten days later. Though they failed to find Uemura, they located much of his gear–including a sleeping bag liner, fuel, food, and some climbing tools–in a snow cave at the 17,200-foot level of McKinley. Despite Geeting's reported sighting at 16,600 feet, the Japanese climbers concluded Uemura had probably died somewhere between 17,200 and the summit. However, park superintendent Bob Cunningham, noting that the Japanese recovered a sleeping bag liner, not the bag itself, said Uemura may have bypassed the cave on his descent.

Over the next fifteen months, several other Japanese parties searched for the remains of their country's hero. None was successful, though a flag he'd left at the summit was discovered.

Numerous theories were proposed to explain his death. Perhaps he'd gotten lost in whiteout conditions and tumbled off a cliff. Or been blown off the mountain by high winds. Or fallen into a crevasse. Or frozen to death while hidden in a snow cave.

Despite all the theories, one thing remained certain: Uemura, like Waterman in 1981, had disappeared.

The diary found in the snow cave at 14,000 feet couldn't solve the mysteries surrounding Uemura's death, but did shed some light on the final days of a man who had become a legend. In February 1985, the Japanese magazine *Mainichi Graph* reprinted Uemura's journal (later translated into English), in which he described the challenges of climbing McKinley alone in winter:15 The temperature was −22°F and snow was falling when Uemura left his Kahiltna Glacier base camp on February 1. By midday, a heavy fog had formed, making it nearly impossible to see the terrain's ups and downs. Once he dropped through the snow into a hidden crevasse, but the bamboo poles stopped his fall.

The sled didn't pull easily through the fresh snow, making progress slow and difficult. But despite the cold, the crevasses, and his frustratingly slow movement, Uemura remained optimistic: "This trip to climb Mount McKinley will be successful as long as I keep my pace."

The second day passed without difficulty, but the next morning Uemura awoke to a blizzard. Confident the storm would let up, he resumed his journey in near-whiteout conditions and severe winds. If anything, the weather deteriorated further. As he approached Windy Corner that afternoon the wind was so strong Uemura could barely stand. Even worse, his face was becoming numbed by the bitterly cold windchill.

To dig a snow cave while battered by such severe gales would be impossible. So Uemura took off his pack, weighted it down with rocks, and struggled past Windy Corner seeking shelter from the wind. After some searching he found a crevasse nearly filled with wind-drifted snow. Here he could dig in for the night.

He went back to his pack to get a shovel and snow saw and upon returning to the crevasse spent two and a half hours digging out a pit just barely big enough to crawl into. Inside the tiny hole, Uemura rested and warmed himself. Then, afraid to leave his gear exposed to the wind all night, he left the security of the shelter.

By now it was evening. Barely able to see and battered by high winds, he crawled through the darkness in search of the pack. Fortunately—almost miraculously—Uemura found his equipment, then began the torturous task of crawling back to the cave. Using his ice axe to pull himself along, he inched his way toward the crevasse while looking "from right to left, from left to right, all over" for some sign of the life-saving shelter.

He admitted, "I thought that I was going to die for sure." But he persevered. He found the hole and quickly ducked inside with his gear. "Finally I was safe," he wrote. "Then I know I am not going to die. Then I started to sing a song called Blue Mountain."

The storm continued for two more days, so Uemura remained holed up in his tiny cave. When he wasn't sleeping, eating, or resting, he found other tasks to occupy his time. He leveled the cave bottom, changed clothes, fixed his weather-beaten gloves, and tied American and Japanese flags to a pole he planned to leave on the summit.

One journal entry made during the two-day wait shows a calm acceptance of the difficulties he faced: "Seeing as how I chose the hardest season to do this, during the winter, it is inevitable I will have a hard, hard time. I feel the satisfactory feeling if I pursue this endurance of patience."

Uemura resumed climbing on February 6 in −40°F weather, and reached the 14,000-foot level where Wickwire and Otani later discovered the diary and other gear left behind to lighten the load.

In his snow cave at 14,000, Uemura described again some of his hardships and his worries:

> My face skin got peeled off because of the frostbite. In summer it takes only three days to go up to the top of the mountain from here, but how many days will it take in winter? I do not know. Foodwise, I still have six more days. . . . I can't relax. These past couple days [have been] very bad weather. I wish the weather could get a little bit better soon. The weather is very mean to me.

Because of his limited fuel supply, hot meals were a luxury Uemura couldn't afford. He ate the caribou frozen, using his stove only to melt water and make tea. He also saved his headlamp for higher on the mountain, in case he needed it during a summit assault. For light, he relied on a candle. Adding to his hardships was the sleeping bag, which had lost much of its insulating abilities because moisture had frozen within it. "I wish I could sleep in a warm sleeping bag," he wrote. "No matter what happens, I am going to climb McKinley."

That was his last entry. Less than a week later Uemura stood on the mountain's summit, just as predicted. But shortly after, he would vanish. And the entire nation of Japan would go into mourning.

Even as crowds of climbers, reporters, and friends were vainly awaiting the return of Naomi Uemura, Dave Johnston pondered his own solo expedition to the mountain.

Johnston, a six-foot-seven, red-haired and bearded Easterner who'd migrated to Alaska by way of Colorado in the 1960s, had already stood atop McKinley in winter. He, along with Ray Genet and Art Davidson, had reached the mountain's summit on February

28, 1967, then survived a terrifying week-long storm at Denali Pass. Many people, Davidson included, credited Johnston with saving the trio.

After that expedition, Johnston spent a year traveling to various corners of the globe. He visited Antarctica, New Zealand, Nepal, Europe, and Canada, and along the way, fell in love with a nurse. In 1968, he got married and two years later began building a "dream house" about two miles off the road system north of Talkeetna. He and wife Sally built their cabin on a gentle knoll that overlooked a beaver pond and offered an excellent view of the Alaska Range. Sally gave birth to two children and the couple adopted a third. To help support the family, Dave got a job at nearby Denali State Park, working as a ranger. For several years, "Life just kept getting better and better," Johnston later told the *Anchorage Daily News*.[16]

But in the late 1970s, Sally grew tired of Alaskan bush life. Missing her parents and her career, she returned to New Zealand with the children. Eventually, the Johnstons divorced. (Both have since remarried.)

In 1981, still feeling the pain of that divorce, Johnston began considering a solo trip up McKinley. But it wasn't until 1984 that he felt ready to challenge the mountain. As he was making his final preparations, he learned that Uemura had already flown into the Alaska Range. Patiently, he awaited the Japanese adventurer's return.

As the days dragged on and rescue parties combed McKinley for signs of Uemura, Johnston shifted his focus to the Wrangell Mountains. In March, he completed a solo winter ascent of 16,237-foot Mount Sanford.

Two years went by before Johnston again directed his energies to climbing McKinley. In mid-February 1986, he left his backwoods cabin and began skiing toward the West Buttress, more than eighty miles away.

To avoid worrying his parents and to remain out of the media limelight, he'd kept the departure largely a secret and shared his plans only with park rangers and a few close friends.

Unlike Uemura, Johnston was prepared for a long stay in the mountains. From his homestead he carried a pack full of gear and pulled two sleds loaded with more equipment. Additional supplies waited on the Kahiltna Glacier; he'd arranged to have a large food cache dropped off by pilot Jim Okonek and his son Brian, a McKinley guide and close climbing friend of his. Between that cache and the food being hauled, he had more than fifty days' worth of food, enough to outlast even the fiercest McKinley storm.

Moving steadily and quickly despite the heavy load, Johnston reached his Kahiltna Glacier base camp—about seventy-five trail miles from his cabin—in a week's time, a rather remarkable pace, considering the weight he was hauling, and the fact that much of his route followed unbroken trail. There, he divided his gear into two 150-pound loads, and began the slow, monotonous task of shuttling gear up the mountain.

Johnston, like Uemura, wore a device to protect himself from crevasse falls. Made of aluminum tubing and attached to the waist, his eighteen-pound creation looked like a twenty-foot ladder without rungs. He named it "Bridgit."

His ski trek up the Kahiltna Glacier may have been tedious, but Johnston made good progress and reached 11,000 feet within a few days. He carried a tent, but increased winds and temperatures to −30°F prompted him to build a snow cave, which would offer greater warmth and security. He tunneled into a snow-drifted crevasse and dug out a chamber large enough for both eating and sleeping in comfort.

Johnston's feet became numb with cold during the four-hour digging project. Once settled inside the cave, he melted some snow and placed a heated bottle on his toes.

Nineteen years earlier, during the first winter ascent of McKinley, Johnston had frozen both feet. The frostbite required a forty-five-day hospital stay and eventually he lost parts of three toes. Once they've been frostbitten, body parts become more sensitive to cold, more susceptible to freezing. So taking good care of his feet was critical.

The next day, with winds gusting to forty-five miles per hour and a windchill of −75°F or colder, the forty-three-year-old "reluctant warrior" remained inside his shelter. He passed the time reading *Clan of the Cave Bear* and listening to an Anchorage radio station. The forecast in town was for clearing skies and temperatures to −10°F.

"Lordy, what will it be here?" he wondered in his journal. "How will I keep my darn feet warm? They're my biggest obstacle, I think."

On February 28, Johnston carried one load of gear to 13,200-foot Windy Corner, then returned to his snow cave at 11,000. The morning of March 1 he awoke to clear skies, but by nine o'clock, high winds had resumed their assault on the mountain. Once again, he decided to sit tight and kill time by reading his book.

Sometime in the early afternoon, Johnston was surprised to hear a noise outside the cave. It sounded like "a pitter-patter squeak" across the snow surface—the sort of noise that's made by a footstep squeaking in the snow. He was certain the noises were real, not imagined. But footsteps? Impossible. No one could be walking out there. Maybe the skis which he'd stuck in the snow were rubbing together, or the sled was being shifted around by the high winds. He decided to go outside and look.

Working his way to the cave entrance, Johnston found the tunnel filled with wind-blown snow. The shovel was outside, so he dug with a cooking pot. When he hadn't broken out after digging through more than four feet of snow, Johnston panicked. He drove the pot through the top of the cave and hit air.

Outside, there were no footprints. Only the howling wind.

He determined the source of the noise was now less important than fixing the shelter. Wearing only fiber-filled booties on his feet, he shoveled out the front of the cave, secured the tent over the cave's damaged roof, and began to excavate a new entrance that he hoped would remain drift-free. Only then did he notice his toes were numb.

Retreating back inside the cave, Johnston pulled off the booties. Two toes on his right foot looked hard, white, and waxy. After rubbing the toes, he made a hot drink, put on socks and boots (which he'd warmed with a hot-water bottle), and returned outside to finish repairing and remodeling the cave.

Back inside the cave two or three hours later, he made dinner and again placed a warm bottle on his toes. In the early evening, Johnston began to feel an old, familiar pain in his toes. Slipping off the booties to inspect his feet, he made a horrible discovery: the big toe on his right foot was bluish-black. It was frostbite, no doubt. And up on the mountain, subjected to subzero temperatures, the frostbite would only get worse. If he continued the climb, Johnston would risk the loss of additional toes and another lengthy hospital stay.

Johnston refused to take the risk. On March 2, he retrieved what gear he could from his cache at Windy Corner. Then he began a six-day journey back to his homestead, finally arriving there twenty-three days after beginning the trip. In his journal, he wrote:

> I don't seem to feel any great disappointment at this time about missing out on the summit. . . . I feel happy, in a way, I didn't make the top—and become a story for the news hounds. Actually I hope there is a story. I'll just be a human who goofed up, instead of a homestead hero. That feels good.

Johnston's 165-mile solo trek did indeed attract media attention. But he was hardly portrayed as someone who simply goofed up. Rather, he was recognized both for his extraordinary attempt to climb McKinley in winter and for having the good sense to retreat instead of unnecessarily risking serious physical injury. Thanks to his difficult–but wise–decision to turn back, Johnston did avoid any further loss to his toes.

Watching Johnston's attempt with more than passing interest were two other notable Alaska mountaineers, Vern Tejas and Dave Staeheli. Both were highly experienced McKinley guides. And both were planning solo winter ascents of a mountain they'd climbed many times in summer.

The *Anchorage Times*

MOUNTAINEER VERN TEJAS, RIGHT, STANDS WITH BUSH PILOT LOWELL THOMAS JR. DURING A PRESS CONFERENCE FOLLOWING TEJAS'S SUCCESSFUL WINTER SOLO ASCENT OF MCKINLEY IN 1988.

Chapter Eleven

Winter Solo Ascents: Tejas and Staeheli

It may have been the wind. Or, perhaps, sounds invented by an overactive imagination. But Vern Tejas believes otherwise.[1]

In the early hours of March 5, 1988, while sleeping alone in a snow cave high on Mount McKinley, Tejas was roused by some sort of disturbance. On awakening, he sensed a presence that made his hair bristle.

"Good morning," Tejas said. In Japanese.

There was no response. Nothing else out of the ordinary happened. But Tejas is certain he received a special visit that day, from the spirit of Naomi Uemura. Just four years earlier, Uemura had become the first climber to climb McKinley alone in winter; he then disappeared while going down the mountain.

Tejas is one of many mountaineers who believe Uemura's spirit still lives on McKinley. While climbing the mountain alone in 1988, he often thought of the Japanese adventurer. Uemura, in fact, had inspired his winter solo ascent. "I never would have conceived of something like this without Naomi blazing the trail," he said after returning from McKinley.

Tejas was visiting Japan in March 1984–it was then that he learned certain Japanese phrases–when word of Uemura's disappearance reached that country. He was awed by the show of emotion, as he witnessed an entire nation mourn the loss:

> I'd heard about Naomi, read about him. I knew some of the things he'd accomplished. But I didn't realize he was such a national hero. It became very obvious that this guy was very famous, very popular. He'd caught the imagination of the Japanese people. I began to realize there's an adventurer's spirit in everyone. It just takes certain people to release it. Naomi was able to do that.

Tejas came to McKinley in mid-February 1988 carrying a Japanese flag and memories of a man he'd never met. During his climb, there were many places where he wondered, Is this where Naomi slipped? Is this where he fell?

"There were definitely places I knew I had to be especially careful," he said. "Whether it was his spirit or just my caution, I don't know. What's reality, anyway? I definitely believe his spirit lives on McKinley. I have that feeling."

The feeling was especially strong at 17,200 feet, where a search party looking for Uemura in 1984 had found some of the climber's gear cached in a snow cave. "I'm sure it's the same cave I stayed in, one that's been around for several years," Tejas said. "Certainly he was on my mind. If not consciously, then subconsciously, it weighs on you. I'm not religious or superstitious. But [in the cave] I felt I was in very close proximity to where his soul once was."

On March 7, Tejas honored Uemura's spirit by placing a Japanese flag on McKinley's summit. Eight days later, on his thirty-fifth birthday, the Anchorage climber and mountain guide was flown from the Kahiltna Glacier back to town, becoming the first person to complete a solo winter ascent of North America's highest peak and live to tell the tale.

Tejas didn't rush into his solo climb of McKinley. He was certain it would be the biggest challenge of a mountaineering career that began in 1973, after he moved to Alaska.

Tejas's path to America's Last Frontier had often been a wild and rocky one. Born in Texas as Vernon Hansel, he left home for good at age eighteen after getting into a fight with his father. He asserted his independence by traveling around North America and changing his surname from Hansel to Tejas, the Spanish word for Texas.

While passing through Canada, he caught a ride to Alaska. His third day in the state, Tejas witnessed what he calls a classic unveiling of McKinley. While at Wonder Lake in (then) Mount McKinley National Park, "the clouds lifted and I saw the mountain in stages," he recalled. "I fell in love with McKinley right then and there." He also made a vow to someday climb the peak.

Six years later, Tejas stood at the top of North America. And that proved to be only the first of many ascents. By the winter of 1988, he'd participated in fourteen McKinley expeditions–most of those while guiding for Genet Expeditions–and reached the summit twelve times (more than two decades later, in 2011, he would stand on the mountain's top for an amazing fiftieth time). During those ascents he'd taken four different routes to the top, including McKinley's classic, the Cassin Ridge. His specialty was the West Buttress; and while leading teams up this popular route,

Tejas became one of its most recognizable and best-known characters. At five feet, eight and a half inches, he's not physically imposing. But his bushy black beard, shaved head, and pigtail are guaranteed attention getters, as are the impromptu McKinley concerts he gives, with either harmonica or fiddle.

Though his mountaineering efforts were normally focused on reaching McKinley's summit, he had made other notable accomplishments as well. In 1981, Tejas participated in the first winter ascent of 14,570-foot Mount Hunter; in 1986 he led a six-member team of Anchorage climbers on the first winter ascent of Canada's Mount Logan; and later that year on McKinley he helped save the lives of two Korean climbers in a rescue effort Denali park rangers called miraculous. (Years later, he would set speed records for completing the "Seven Summits"; in 2010, he reached the highest points on each of the world's continents in 134 days.)

But experience, talent, and a thorough knowledge of McKinley weren't enough. The timing had to be right. Finally, in February 1988, Tejas decided it was time to go: there were no other climbers on the mountain. Equally important, he had the energy, conditioning, and desire to make a winter solo attempt. "I didn't want to put it off any longer," he explained. "Life is too short to pass up these kinds of opportunities."

Physically, Tejas was in the best shape of his life. He'd just returned from South America after spending several weeks on Aconcagua. During that time, he'd traveled up and down the mountain's slopes three times. First he led a group of clients to the mountain's top. Then, after descending to base camp, he returned to the summit carrying a mountain bike. And after riding the bike down to base camp he reascended to 19,000 feet, launched a paraglider, and flew it back to base.

Tejas returned to Alaska "feeling lean and mean, really strong," with his body acclimated to high altitudes. Everything was going smoothly. And then Geoffrey Lyon showed up in town. He'd come to Alaska to climb McKinley in winter. Alone. As Tejas would soon discover, Lyon's arrival "made things a little more complicated."

Lyon, a thirty-year-old East Coast lawyer, had little high-altitude mountaineering experience. He'd never climbed in arctic conditions, and his climbing resumé was limited to such Lower 48 peaks as 14,410-foot Mount Rainier and 13,766-foot Grand Teton. His greatest conquest had been a January 1988 ascent of Aconcagua, with Tejas as his guide. Lyon was between jobs at the time. He'd been hired by a company in Los Angeles, but didn't have to report for work until March 1. So after Aconcagua, he had begun looking for a new challenge.

"It seemed obvious to me that the next step was McKinley," Lyon explained shortly before flying into the Alaska Range. "It was convenient. It fit my schedule. I'm looking at it as a kind of bonus."

Tejas, however, believed that he may have put the idea in Lyon's head by talking about his McKinley plans while in Argentina. Lyon, the first member of the guided party to reach the top of Aconcagua, may have decided he could also beat Tejas to McKinley's summit. Tejas admitted that Lyon's presence was an unwelcome intrusion:

> The fact that someone from an expedition I was guiding shows up here to make a winter ascent—the chances of that being coincidental seem about a million to one.
>
> It's like he was making a challenge. McKinley is not a good place to get into a competition.

Tejas flew into the Alaska Range February 16 with bush pilot Lowell Thomas Jr. As part of their arrangement, Thomas would also conduct periodic flybys to check on his passenger's progress up and down the mountain.

During the flight in, Tejas looked for signs of Lyon, who'd been scheduled to start his trip a few days earlier, but saw none. His spirits rose; perhaps the lawyer had wised up and gone home. But no such luck. Lyon arrived at the Kahiltna Glacier a few hours later. Wishing to avoid a feud, and realizing that they might need each other's assistance higher on the mountain, Tejas chose to be friendly and asked Lyon if he wanted any help unloading gear. It was a strained congeniality, however.

Tejas left the 7,000-foot base camp first. Even this low on the mountain, the temperature was zero. For the next month, he would have to endure temperatures in the minus range. Such constant cold is one of the great differences between summer and winter climbs. In May, June, and July, daytime temperatures below 14,000 feet often rise above freezing and mountaineers can bask in warm sunshine. But not in February or March. After his climb, Tejas admitted he was "always cold," even though he'd brought much more clothing than is normal for a summer expedition.

His winter wardrobe included two pairs of heavyweight polypropylene underwear, a pile jacket, pile overalls, down pants and parka, and a wind-shell oversuit with fur-ruffed hood. To protect his face and head from extreme cold and high winds, he carried a balaclava, ski mask, goggles, and fleece cap. On his feet, he wore nylon and wool socks, vapor barrier booties, bunny boots and nylon overboots. For his hands, he brought polypropylene inner mittens, pile outer mittens, and wind shells.

For sleeping comfort in the extreme cold, he used a three-bag system: a light down bag was stuffed inside a synthetic one rated to −20°F; those, plus an insulating pad, were encased by a Gore-Tex shell. When outside his sleeping bags, Tejas later recalled, he spent nearly one-third of his time just trying to stay warm, by kicking his feet, shaking his hands, or even doing jumping jacks.

Because he would need more calories to burn in the constant cold, he also carried more food and fuel than would be necessary in summer. Like the extra clothing, they added weight to Tejas's load. Traveling on skis, he hauled about 150 pounds of food, fuel, and gear up the Kahiltna Glacier. The load was split between his pack and a small plastic sled of the type popular with climbers. At his waist, he had attached a sixteen-foot aluminum ladder to minimize his chances of being gobbled by a crevasse.

Lyon's load was much lighter, about a hundred pounds in all. He, too, carried a crevasse-protection device, but his was made from a pair of two-by-two boards. "It wasn't too strong looking," Tejas said. "Fall in a crevasse with that thing and chances are it would snap like a pencil before it would stop your fall." Sizing up Lyon's gear, he made one other mental notation:

> I realized right then and there, it wasn't going to be a race. My load was about fifty percent heavier. Anytime it got steep, I'd have to double-hump it [make two carries]. Geoff could do it in one. When we were both carrying full loads, he moved away from me pretty quickly.

It was already getting late, so Tejas set up camp about a mile from where he'd been dropped off. Rather than carry a tent as in summer, he'd decided to build snow shelters, which afford more protection from the wind and offer greater warmth in extreme cold. As he dug his first shelter—a narrow, horizontal, rectangular snow cave known as a skier's trench—Lyon passed by and continued another half mile up the glacier. There he set up a tent.

On February 17, the two soloists resumed their journey up the Kahiltna, taking slightly different routes. Tejas hugged the glacier's eastern side. Lyon traveled up the middle. By day's end, they'd each traveled about a mile and a half.

The next day, a storm moved in. Tejas remained huddled in his trench—which was covered by a tarp and protected by a two-foot-high snow wall—for two days while a fierce wind roared down the glacier accompanied by heavy snowfall and whiteout conditions. While waiting out the storm, he wondered if his rival might push on despite the difficult traveling conditions. But Lyon, too, stayed put.

The climbers resumed their independent journeys February 20, their fifth day in the mountains. They stopped at the bottom of Ski Hill, about five miles from their starting point but only 500 feet higher than the base camp elevation of 7,200 feet.

The air was calm that night, so Tejas didn't bother windproofing his trench by erecting a wall. He built it quickly, faster than usual, and was inside the shelter before Lyon got his tent set up. While building the trench, Tejas noticed Lyon watching closely.

Lyon was evidently impressed with Tejas's shelter, because he cached his tent at Camp III, intending to dig snow shelters the remainder of the trip.

The next day, both climbers headed up Ski Hill. Because of the moderately steep incline, Tejas had to make two carries. He moved about a mile and a half up the glacier, finally stopping to set up Camp IV at 9,000 feet. Lyon, carrying a single load, continued on for another mile or so and settled in at about 9,700 feet.

That night, the winds picked up again. For two days Tejas remained in his shelter. As the storm continued, his anxieties grew. What if Lyon had moved on? He might be gaining ground that could never be made up. Despite his desire not to race up the mountain, Tejas found himself getting caught up in the competition. "It was like Lyon was challenging me to a duel," he said. "I know he's a strong climber. And he doesn't know what his limits are. That's a scary combination. If he gets lucky and doesn't mind suffering, there's a chance he can make it. I knew that if he got up there first, I was gonna be depressed."

On February 24, gale-force winds continued to blow. But they'd shifted directions and were now blowing up the glacier, so Tejas made his move. Forced to rely on compass bearings and his knowledge of the West Buttress Route, he slowly worked his way through whiteout conditions up to 9,800 feet. He saw no sign of Lyon. Tejas later guessed that he passed within a hundred feet of Lyon, who was still waiting out the storm at 9,700 feet. But with high winds and near-zero visibility, the chances of noticing the snow shelter would have been almost nil.

If he had run across Lyon, Tejas's worries almost certainly would have vanished. The transplanted Bostonian was learning all about snow-shelter life, the hard way. From watching Tejas and asking questions, Lyon knew the basics of trench building. But he wasn't aware of several critical details, such as the correct way to construct a ventilation system. After returning to Anchorage, he said:

> Getting rid of my tent and relying on snow holes was unbelievably dumb. I didn't realize how dangerous they can be. Every four or five hours, the wind would blow enough snow in and it would shut off the air. I had to keep digging out to keep a breathing-hole open. That was the most dangerous part.

By February 25, Lyon had had enough. He was already behind schedule and the three-day stay in the trench had drained much of his enthusiasm. He returned to base camp for pickup. Unfortunately, poor flying conditions kept him stranded for several more days. He finally left the range February 29.

During his wait, Lyon had removed the boots he'd worn for five straight days, only to discover that three toes had been frostbitten. Doctors back in Anchorage, however, later told the climber he shouldn't lose more than his toenails. Despite his trench-building and frostbite problems, Lyon remained convinced that "it's a doable climb. All it would have taken was more time and slightly different gear."

Back on the mountain, Tejas wasn't feeling quite so optimistic. The winter storms were playing havoc with his climbing schedule. Already he was rationing food, and there was no indication the foul weather would end anytime soon. So on February 25, he again chose to travel in whiteout conditions, despite moving through a section of glacier known to contain several large crevasses.

The world surrounding him was fuzzy gray; it was difficult to make out any details. To get some idea of the immediate terrain, he would take a wand, throw it out ten to twenty feet, and observe whether it landed higher, lower, or disappeared from view. With the slope in front of him more clearly defined, he'd ski to the wand, pick it up, and repeat the process. Using that slow, cautious technique, Tejas traveled from 9,800 to 11,000 feet, setting up Camp VI at the base of a slope named Motorcycle Hill. Beyond that point, the glacier became considerably steeper and more crevassed. He didn't dare continue in poor visibility.

Again he was forced to sit tight for two days. On February 28, the wind let up and the whiteout cleared, allowing him to continue on his journey. He cached his skis at 11,000 feet, exchanging them for crampons. But because of the crevasse danger, he kept the ladder attached at his waist.

Tejas had hoped to make it from 11,000 to 14,000 feet in one day, but progress was slowed by the cumbersome ladder and his crampons, which kept slipping off his boots. By nightfall, he'd made it only to 12,500 feet. The weather had been nice for most of the day, but began to deteriorate rapidly as Tejas struggled to dig a shelter. He later recalled:

> Here it is, already dark, and I'm in the middle of a full-blown storm. I can't take my crampons off because I'm afraid of being blown off my feet and down into a crevasse. I'm tired, I'm cold, so the trench I dig is a real quickie. Then I get in. And pray.

By four in the morning, the wind had almost completely eroded the wall protecting his trench. Most of the snow holding down the tarp which served as the trench's roof had blown away. Realizing that a couple more blasts of wind might rip away the top of his shelter, Tejas left the trench to make emergency repairs. While being blasted by winds stronger than he'd ever before experienced, he cut blocks of snow for a new wall. At times he was forced to crawl between the trench and his snow-block quarry.

The wind was so fierce it cut through all his layers of clothing. His hands, feet, knees, and elbows all grew numb. The air temperature that night was about −20F–not especially cold for McKinley in winter but much more chilling than summer, when temperatures often rise above zero during storms. The windchill temperature that night fell to nearly −90F. In addition to the intense cold, wind-blown snow and ice created a sand-blast effect. Once Tejas was hit in the head with a chunk of ice the size of a baseball, a blow that nearly knocked him unconscious.

When the tarp had again been loaded with snow and a new wall built, Tejas returned to the calm and relative warmth of his shelter. There he stayed for the next two days, in a trench eight feet long, three feet deep, and three feet wide. He described his time in the trench as "kind of like staying in a freezer pushed on its side. About that comfortable. And about that cold."

On March 2, the wind died down to about twenty miles per hour and the sky cleared enough for Tejas to again safely find his way up the mountain. Before moving on, he noticed a group of three wands sticking out of the snow, about twenty feet from the trench. Tejas guessed correctly they might be marking a supply cache. After some probing and digging, he found four days' worth of food and a gallon of stove fuel.

It was exactly the sort of discovery Tejas needed. Slowed by the storm, the cold, and limited daylight, he'd been on the mountain fifteen days already, but was still far from the summit. At most, he had enough food for six more days, even using half rations. "I'd started to wonder if maybe this wasn't the right year. Maybe I should go down," he said. "Then I discover the cache. It's like a good omen, a sign that it's OK to go forward."

Feeling rejuvenated, he made his way around Windy Corner, found a protected spot, and set up Camp VIII. Along the way he had to maneuver past several crevasses. The deep, wide chasms seemed to be waiting for him to make a mistake.

Tejas reached 14,200 feet on March 3. It was his ninth camp and sixteenth day in the Alaska Range. No one had seen or heard from him since February 21, when he last crossed paths with Lyon. (Tejas's two-way radio operated on line-of-sight and the surrounding mountains made it impossible to communicate outside the Alaska Range.) The series of storms that put him behind schedule had also prevented bush pilots from flying into the range to check his progress.

The next morning Tejas heard a welcome sound: a plane flying overhead. He quickly grabbed his radio, stuffed it with fresh batteries, and tuned in to "the cheery voice of Roger Robinson," a seasonal mountaineering ranger for the Park Service, who'd accompanied pilot Eric Denkewalter. Tejas immediately made it clear that he was all right and had enough food for a summit attempt. He'd be going for the top. Then came a question that had bothered him for days: Where was Geoffrey Lyon? The news that Lyon was both safe and off the mountain "was music to my ears," Tejas admitted.

Tejas also knew that word of his well-being would quickly spread once Robinson returned to Talkeetna, thus easing the concerns of friends back home. But he had no idea just how far the news would spread. Two days later, while listening to Anchorage public radio station KSKA on his transistor radio, Tejas was surprised to hear a report that described his conversation with Robinson.

Relieved of these concerns, he moved out of Camp IX packing only the essentials; from this point on there would be no double carries. Among the gear left behind was the aluminum ladder. From 14,000 feet, he had to climb the 2,000-foot-high slope leading to the top of the West Buttress ridge. The lower portion of that slope is crisscrossed by several large crevasses, while the upper 1,000 feet consists of hard-packed snow and ice, rising at angles of forty-five to sixty degrees. Carrying a ladder up that headwall would have been next to impossible.

Progress was painfully slow, because Tejas again took the extra precaution of triple-roping while crossing the crevasse fields. But on reaching 16,200 feet, he was rewarded for his effort. While digging out a camp he uncovered a huge emergency cache containing six gallons of gas and several bags of food. Suddenly he was "back in hog heaven."

The discovery provided extra insurance. But like the cache at Windy Corner, it also presented a philosophical dilemma:

> My approach has always been to go under your own power. Idealistically, if you're going to do something like this, you shouldn't have to rely on outside help. You should be self- sufficient. If you can't, maybe you should go down. But looking those candy bars in the face, some of your ideals don't seem so important anymore. For the amount of time and energy I'd invested in this climb, it seemed reasonable to make a compromise. In some ways I had to swallow some pride.

The compromise made, Tejas celebrated with a feast.

While at 16,200 feet, he also began thinking about his father, whom he hadn't seen, or talked to, in sixteen years. Sixteen years was far too long. Suddenly it seemed important to reestablish a relationship. He decided that upon returning from the climb, he would call his father and express his love. He headed up the West Buttress ridge, tears streaming down his face. This snow-covered, knife-edge ridge, which climbers follow from 16,200 to 17,200 feet, can be intimidating even in summer; but in winter, caked with slippery ice, it's especially unnerving. A misstep along some sections of the ridge could produce a fall of more than a thousand feet.

At 17,200 feet, the site of his high camp, Tejas settled into the snow cave he believes Uemura also used in 1984. He was now in position to go for the top.

March 6 brought more stormy weather. Whiteout conditions and high winds made a summit attempt unthinkable. But after hard climbing the previous two days, he enjoyed taking a rest day.

The next morning, only a slight breeze disturbed the air. Tejas woke up at 6:30 after ten hours of sleep and tuned in KSKA to get the statewide weather report. There was no mention of wind warnings. Visibility remained poor, but Tejas could see a few hundred yards, which was enough to navigate.

Having traveled the West Buttress many times before, he knew the route almost by heart. Even as visibility dropped to twenty or thirty feet, he could almost feel his way up to Denali Pass at 18,200 feet. From there, he followed a series of rock outcroppings, using them as handrails at times. Occasionally he came upon wands marking the trail. It almost seemed as if "they were there to congratulate me for being on course," he thought.

At The Archdeacon's Tower, elevation about 19,550 feet, Tejas lightened his load as much as possible. From there he carried only two quarts of water, a camera, a handful of granola, and a couple of chocolate bars. Although protected by insulated, cold-weather footwear known popularly as bunny boots, his feet had started to grow painfully cold in the −20°F air. Several times he stopped to swing them for five to ten minutes, to get the circulation going and prevent freezing.

He crossed the Football Field and reached the base of an 800-foot-high wall that leads to the summit ridge. Everything was looking rosy. But less than thirty feet from the ridgeline, Tejas made a horrible discovery. He was standing in the middle of a snow pillow—a deposit of soft, loose snow susceptible to avalanche. By not paying close enough attention, he'd walked into one of the mountain's many traps. If the snow slid, he would almost certainly be killed.

For perhaps three or four tension-filled minutes, a stunned Tejas debated whether to retreat or continue on. Because there was no quick or safe way out and he was already halfway through the trap, he finally decided to keep moving ahead. The slope held firm, and he made it to the edge of the loose snow, where he felt a rush of relief. Then, gaining the ridge, he climbed slowly upward. And fifteen minutes later Tejas reached the summit.

The temperature was −25°F and visibility was still poor at the top. A disappointed Tejas said, "You couldn't see anything. In that respect, it was real anticlimactic. I kept thinking, 'Nobody will be able to tell [from photographs] it's the summit.'" And at the same time there was a sense of intense satisfaction that he'd accomplished his goal.

Tejas stayed at the top for about twenty minutes, despite poor visibility. He took photos and planted a Japanese flag in Uemura's honor. Then, with the summit quest completed, he began to concentrate on his main priority: getting back safely. He left the summit at about 5:00 in the afternoon, giving himself less than two hours of light to make it back to 17,200 feet.

"Practically sprinting," Tejas reached Denali Pass within an hour. But from there to camp, he forced himself to go slowly, while sidestepping along a thirty- to forty-degree slope of ice and snow. In summer, there's usually a well-defined trail through soft snow along this portion of the route. But now, frozen and packed by high winds, it was like a highly polished sheet of glass. Stopping a fall on such a surface would be extremely difficult; if not impossible. Below him were several large, gaping crevasses. Unroped and alone, a slip here would likely mean death. It may have been on this portion of the West Buttress Route that Uemura's life had ended.

"Basically I crawled down," he said. "I was very meticulous about doing things correctly. I was checking my feet each step, checking the snow in front of me. And I was breathing deeply to keep the oxygen flowing." The cautious descent from Denali Pass to the snow cave at 17,200 lasted another hour and a half. Reaching camp at twilight, he crawled into his sleeping bag, forced himself to eat and drink, then went to sleep.

March 8 dawned clear and calm—an excellent day to begin heading home. As Tejas descended along the West Buttress ridge to 16,200 feet, Thomas flew over. After extending his congratulations, the pilot delivered some bad news over the radio: another low-pressure system was on its way and would probably arrive within two days.

In a race against the storm, Tejas descended all the way to 11,000 feet (picking up his ladder en route), arriving there after dark. Quickly he dug a crude trench and climbed into his sleeping bag. The next morning, he woke at about five, ate a quick, hot breakfast, took his skis from the cache and lashed them to his pack, and resumed his journey. But it soon became obvious that he wouldn't reach base camp that day. The storm had arrived sooner than predicted.

Out on the main fork of the Kahiltna Glacier, Tejas ran into whiteout conditions and a headwind of fifty miles per hour or more. It took him three hours to travel a distance he would normally cover in one. He had to take shelter.

Tejas was forced to hole up for three days, from March 9 to 11, while the wind roared above his trench like a freight train. He later called it his most depressing, desperate camp on the mountain. "Those were some of my lowest moments. As far as I was concerned, I was still in Naomi's position. I could still die. At times I felt like I'd go bonkers."

To preserve his sanity, he kept himself busy. Cleaning his fingernails. Playing the harmonica. Repairing clothes and equipment. Doing calisthenics. Listening to the transistor radio. And just when things seemed darkest, Tejas began to feel an outpouring of emotional and spiritual support. "While lying in my snow cave, I could feel the warmth and vibrations of many, many people," he said. "I knew people were praying for me, wanting me to get back safe and sound."

By March 11, Tejas had about one day's supply of food left—maybe enough for two or three days, with careful rationing. That night, while listening to a KSKA interview, he learned Thomas had left a food cache at the 7,000-foot base camp. Knowing that supplies awaited below, he was willing to risk freezing some flesh. The need for food outweighed possible frostbite to his face or extremities. So on March 12, he resumed his march down the glacier, still heading into the teeth of a fierce gale.

About midway down Ski Hill, at an elevation of about 8,500 feet, the wind let up and snow conditions improved enough for Tejas to ski down the slope, which is exceptionally free of crevasses. Wearing his ladder for protection, he went into a tuck position and descended a thousand feet in about five minutes. Once on the flats below, he settled into a steady rhythm and felt a sense of exhilaration: the areas where he'd expected to have problems were finally above him on the mountain.

Then the crevasse opened up. One moment Tejas was gliding along. The next, he put his ski pole down and hit nothing but air. The snow fell away on both sides, leaving a gaping hole about two and a half feet wide and fifty feet long. He stopped in mid-stride, his skis straddling the crevasse. "I could see black on both sides of me," he said. "It was the stuff that bad dreams are made of. It could have eaten me if I'd gone in."

Tejas's reaction was instantaneous. Fueled by adrenaline, he poled himself across the crevasse in one quick motion.

Though the ladder would have provided him with some security in a fall, Tejas was understandably unnerved by the incident, especially since there had been no sign of a crevasse, nothing to warn him of danger. His familiarity with the route, his eagerness to reach base camp, and his assumption that McKinley's greatest dangers had been left behind all caused him to get careless. Later he admitted, "It woke me up. It was like 'Whoa!' Pay attention. Go slow. You might feel you know an area, but don't take anything for granted. Those crevasses are subtle, sneaky traps, just waiting for someone to let down their guard."

His senses back on red alert, Tejas continued, now skiing with greater caution. About two and a half miles from base camp, the weather again deteriorated. Caught in the middle of a crevasse field, he stayed put, unwilling to take any more chances. After waiting thirty minutes in high winds and whiteout, he reluctantly began digging a shelter. But shortly after, the storm broke up. He carefully worked his way through the crevasses, struggled up the slope leading to base camp—known appropriately as Heartbreak Hill—and arrived at his pickup spot by early evening.

Tejas dug out the "love cache" left by Thomas, gobbled down some frozen sausages, then snuggled into his sleeping bag. Temperatures were mild and the air calm enough that he didn't bother digging a snow shelter.

The next morning, clouds again covered the Alaska Range. Realizing it might be a few more days before pickup, Tejas built a trench of Olympian proportions. Then he relaxed, feeling comfortable and filled with sausage, and settled in for the weather to clear.

On March 14, his twenty-seventh day in the mountains, the waiting finally got to Tejas. Feeling homesick and anxious to be back in the company of friends, he "came unglued." In an agitated state, Tejas paced around camp. In desperation, he called on the CB radio, trying to reach someone–anyone–despite knowing that the surrounding mountains would block his transmissions. And he began to imagine the worst. If someone like Uemura could die in the mountains . . .

Mother Nature seemed to be teasing him. The clouds would begin to lift, then settle back down. By early evening, Tejas resigned himself to at least one more night on the Kahiltna. He went to sleep with hope in his heart and tears in his eyes. And with enough food for about a day and a half.

Tejas woke at 5:30 on the morning of March 15, but the clouds were still hanging low so he went back to sleep. A couple of hours later, he checked again. Much to his surprise and delight, the sky was bright blue, and surrounding peaks were bathed in sunlight. Frantically, he began packing his gear, but after a few moments noticed his hands becoming numb. He forced himself to slow down and take things one at a time. Light the stove. Heat some water. Make breakfast. Then pack. No need to rush or panic.

About midmorning, the loud noise of a plane's engine echoed up the valley. His ride was on the way. Tejas grabbed his radio and as nonchalantly as possible said, "Good morning, Lowell, how are you?"

Thomas answered back, "Never mind me. How are you?"

Tejas later recalled, "I could hear the joy in his voice. I think he'd been quite worried about me. I know I made the right choice going with Lowell. He took real good care of me."

Within an hour, Tejas was back in Talkeetna, greeted by many of his friends and treated to a grand welcome. Later that day he flew into Anchorage and after hugging girlfriend Gail Irvine, patiently endured a barrage of questions from print and broadcast media. He'd returned home a hero.

In retrospect, Tejas called his time spent alone on McKinley a superb test. He'd been pushed to the limits of his abilities "skill-wise, strengthwise, survivalwise, mentally and emotionally." Tejas passed his self-imposed test. And in doing so, he, like Uemura before, helped release the adventurer's spirit in all those who stayed behind yet supported and celebrated his lonely journey to the top of North America.

Vern Tejas's mountaineering triumph was followed by a tragic loss. Less than two months after returning from his winter ascent he was back on McKinley, guiding a group of clients up the West Buttress Route. And in mid-May, one of those clients, Anchorage resident Lynne Salerno, died at 19,500 feet after reaching the summit, succumbing to what doctors later diagnosed as exhaustion-hypothermia.[2]

Tejas led his Genet Expeditions party out of their 17,200-foot high camp at 9:30 A.M. on May 17. The sky was clear, temperatures were above zero, and the air was calm–ideal for a summit attempt. As usual on summit day, the climbers traveled light. Each team member carried personal clothing, lunch, two bottles of water, and one piece of group gear, which included a sleeping bag and pad, stove and fuel, cooking pot, bivy sack, ice saw, shovel, medical kit, and CB radio. Even before reaching 18,200-foot Denali Pass, Tejas realized it would be a very long day. The team was moving at the slowest pace he'd ever traveled on summit day. At the pass, he checked the condition of each person, and all seven clients confirmed that they wanted to continue. "They were," Tejas recalled, "psyched to go."

Two of the clients were obviously capable of moving at a much faster pace than the others, so Tejas sent them ahead with Denali National Park ranger Steve Winslow, who was also making a summit attempt. Because progress of his group was so slow, Tejas also chose to lighten his team's load. He left several pieces of group gear near the pass, including the sleeping bag, stove, fuel, pot, shovel, medical kit, and radio.

Twelve hours after starting its ascent, the party reached the Football Field, just under the summit massif. There, the team split up. Two climbers unable to continue were sent back to high camp, accompanied by assistant guide John Schweider. Tejas continued on with three others: Mike Moss of Minnesota, David Kazel of California, and Salerno.

The foursome crossed the Football Field and prepared to scale the 800-foot wall leading to the summit ridge. But Salerno began to drag and show signs of exhaustion. "It was pretty apparent that Lynne ran out of gas," Moss said. "She wasn't able to move any further."

Tejas stopped the team, unhooked Salerno from the rope, and told her "this is not going to be your day" to reach the summit. While Moss and Kazel proceeded up the slopes, Tejas and Salerno rested and talked. "It wasn't a debate," he later commented. "But Lynne clearly didn't appreciate my decision to hold her back."

After fifteen to thirty minutes, Salerno showed signs of recovery. "During the time we talked, Lynne had time to recuperate. She rallied, looked stronger. She was still highly motivated," Tejas said.

"I began to realize how important this was to her. She expressed a strong desire to go to the summit. And I, too, had a strong desire to get her to the summit."

There was one other factor in favor of Salerno's continuing. She could easily become chilled while waiting for Moss and Kazel to return. Retreat at this point was out of the question; Tejas couldn't abandon his other clients. So as long as Moss and Kazel continued to ascend, it made sense that Salerno, too, should proceed toward the summit if she were able. Ranger Bob Seibert observed:

> With a guided group, you can't let people get too spread out at the summit. In no way could Vern take Lynne down and leave his other climbers behind. The only alternative I could see would have been for everyone to descend. But being so close to the summit, that would have been a real tough decision to make.

Moss admitted, "Going down was something I never considered. We [he and Kazel] felt confident, excited once we started up the summit ridge. We knew Vern was nearby. We felt no concern whatever."

Given the circumstances, Tejas changed his mind. He agreed that Salerno should continue toward the summit. As she moved up the steep wall, Tejas noticed that she was climbing well, if not better, than before. "She was proving she could do it," he said.

Thus encouraged, Tejas climbed to the summit ridge to check on Moss and Kazel. He clipped into their rope and followed them to McKinley's top. It was 10:40 P.M. and the weather was beginning to deteriorate. Storm clouds and high winds were moving in from the north. Tejas descended to Salerno, who expressed appreciation for the opportunity to climb alone and at her own pace. He then returned to the summit, where Moss and Kazel waited for their partner. They were becoming chilled, so he told them to move down the ridgeline, out of the wind.

Salerno reached the summit sometime between 11:15 and 11:30 P.M. She said nothing and showed no emotion, while kneeling down as if to pray.

The wind started to pick up and visibility was diminishing rapidly. After a brief stay, Salerno and Tejas began their descent. They hadn't gone more than a few feet when Salerno became ataxic and lost the ability to walk. "It was like a switch being turned off, like she'd run her tank to empty and didn't have anything left," Tejas said. "I've never had someone go downhill so quickly." Despite the lack of physical coordination, her mental faculties seemed unimpaired; conversing with Tejas, she made complete sense.

Tejas gave what support he could, but even with his help, Salerno stumbled or fell every five or ten feet. Finally they joined with Moss and Kazel and roped together. Travel along the summit ridge was becoming impossible, both because of Salerno's condition and the deteriorating weather. The wind now gusted thirty to forty miles per hour, daylight was fading, and the climbers were faced with near whiteout conditions. Tejas decided it would be best to glissade from the ridge down to the Football Field, a rapid, sliding descent of several hundred feet.

Once on the flats, the climbers again tried to carry Salerno, but she'd become so weak, it was nearly impossible to move her. In windchill temperatures that approached −85°F, the climbers decided it would be best to stop and try to stabilize her condition. Kazel's pack, left on the Football Field, contained a sleeping pad. While Moss dug a snow trench, Tejas placed Salerno on the pad and put his down jacket around her.

Normally, there would have been other group gear cached nearby. But several items, including the sleeping bag, stove, and fuel, had been left at Denali Pass to save weight. Other items, including the bivy sack, had been sent down with the assistant guide. Tejas later commented, "Were we adequately equipped? In retrospect, no. We could have used another forty or fifty pounds of gear. Oxygen and a sled [normally not carried by summit teams] would have been nice. But in reality, we probably could have had a hospital up there and it wouldn't have helped."

Seibert agreed, "Probably nothing would have helped at that stage. There was no way to replace her energy reserves. At that point, the whole scenario was set. With a complete physical collapse in those temperatures, that high on the mountain, you really don't have any options."

Peter Hackett, a high-altitude medicine specialist and director of the Denali Medical Research Project that operated on McKinley for much of the 1980s, said Salerno fell victim to exhaustion-hypothermia: "She pushed herself too hard. She used all her energy getting to the summit and had none to get down. When she became chilled, her body could no longer produce heat; there was no fuel to burn. The result was that she became hypothermic very quickly."

Salerno's condition rapidly grew worse. Her speech became slurred and barely intelligible. Moss remembered it as a kind of mumbling or babbling, like baby talk. Tejas yelled at her, pleaded with her, trying to maintain some connection. "She was still responding," he said, "but you could see the writing on the wall. We had to get heat to her. That was her only chance."

The team's stove and fuel were nearly a mile away and more than a thousand vertical feet below. Tejas made that descent in less than a half hour, all the while second-guessing the decisions he'd made that night: "I was 20-20ing myself to death. Why did I let her get this high? Why didn't I turn the whole group back? Should I have spent more time learning about her? It was a nightmare. All kinds of questions and doubts were running through my head."

As Tejas descended, Moss finished digging the trench and built a snow wall. Kazel, meanwhile, tried to keep Salerno talking, while shielding her with his body. When he no longer could get a verbal response, Kazel tried mouth-to-mouth resuscitation. But he could find no sign of breathing, no sign of life. Refusing to give up hope, the two climbers placed Salerno in the trench, where Moss huddled over her body and periodically talked to her, trying to get some response. But there was nothing.

Tejas returned to the Football Field at 4 A.M. after being gone nearly two hours. As the emergency shelter came into view, he spotted a standing figure. That alone was cause for some relief. "I know at that point that I have at least one live one," he said. Both Moss and Kazel were hypothermic and marginally coherent. Tejas instructed them to swing their arms and legs, to increase blood flow to their extremities.

Salerno, however, was completely unresponsive, with no sign of a pulse. Both her hands and wrists were frozen, and a purplish froth was coming out her nose and mouth. There was no doubt she'd died, so Tejas turned his attention to the others. At that point, the most important thing was to get Kazel and Moss safely to camp. "I didn't want to lose anyone else," he said.

The climbers left Salerno in the trench and arrived back at camp early on the morning of May 18, nearly twenty-four hours after beginning their summit ascent. Tejas and Kazel suffered minor frostbite on their noses, toes, and fingers, while Moss had suffered severely frostbitten toes and fingers. He required hospitalization and eventually lost parts of several toes.

In the weeks following Salerno's death, Tejas re-ran the tragedy through his head dozens of times, wondering what he might have done to prevent the death. He recalled that Salerno had coughed throughout the trip; that might have been an early warning sign of pulmonary edema, a type of altitude sickness in which fluid accumulates in the lungs. But Salerno had explained it away as a cold-weather cough, one that she'd experienced many times before—nothing to be concerned about.

Only later did Tejas learn that Salerno had a respiratory problem, for which she was taking medicine. She'd also received some chest injuries when caught in an avalanche only a week before the start of the McKinley climb. Could such complications have made her more susceptible to pulmonary edema and contributed to her death?

At 14,000 feet, Salerno was held back in camp for a day because of a high pulse rate–another possible warning signal of developing mountain sickness. But thereafter, the pulse rates she reported were in the acceptable range. Again, no apparent cause for alarm.

On her approach to the summit, Salerno clearly struggled. But that's not uncommon on McKinley. "A lot of people are right on the edge [when they reach McKinley's top]," said Hackett. "People are stretching their limits, pushing themselves close to exhaustion."

The cough, high pulse rate, and Salerno's weariness on summit day didn't seem critical at the time. "They're all signs that a guide has to listen to," Tejas said. "But they are also signs that you see in a lot of people. You have to make a judgment. What's an important message? What's not?"

Perhaps more important than Salerno's physical condition was her mental attitude. In conversations with Salerno's family after the climb, Tejas discovered that there was a lot he didn't know about the thirty-one-year-old physical therapist.

As an eighteen-month-old baby, Salerno caught the measles. There were complications and she developed encephalitis, an inflammation of the brain. Salerno was almost six before she could speak. She also suffered from dyslexia, a reading disorder in which letters and words appear upside down or backward. In grammar school, Salerno flunked several grades, but she and her family refused to give up. After more than a decade of therapy and struggle, she overcame her handicaps. Eventually, she went to college and graduated with a B.S. in physical therapy. All the while, "she had a tremendous drive to learn, to do what everyone else was doing," said her brother Mark.

Lynne's early struggles and triumphs set the tone for the rest of her life. "I can't think of anything she couldn't do once she made the decision to do it," said Mark. "She was extremely dedicated, an extremely hard worker. If she failed at something, she kept trying until she did it."

Salerno moved to Alaska in 1985 and took over as director of Chugach Physical Therapy in Anchorage. Always an outdoor enthusiast and adventurer, she got hooked on the idea of climbing McKinley in 1986. As usual, she expended a great deal of time and effort preparing for this newest challenge. She went climbing in the Chugach and Talkeetna mountains and took a series of courses at the University of Alaska Anchorage. What impressed UAA climbing instructor Bill Ennis the most was her determination: "Lynne had an enormous strength of will. She took a single-minded approach. Lynne decided she was going to climb that mountain—and she did."

At five feet, two inches and 145 pounds, Salerno was not one of the strongest or biggest members of Tejas's team. But he said, "Lynne was one of the most experienced members. She'd obviously done her homework. She knew what she was doing."

Unfortunately, Tejas didn't know of Salerno's overwhelming desire to achieve goals she'd set. "I don't think there was any way of knowing beforehand how committed she was to the climb. Lynne was unique. She was the big unknown." Only afterward did he learn of her high threshold for pain and extreme determination, which enabled Salerno to push beyond her physical limits. Ultimately, it was a deadly combination.

On her final approach to the summit, Salerno apparently climbed on willpower alone. Said Seibert:

> We believe it was only mental desire that kept her legs moving. But that drive vanished when she reached her goal. What happened with Lynne is very unusual. Most clients holler "Uncle" before they get to that stage. From talking to her parents, it's clear she'd been an overachiever all her life. She's always poured herself into things totally. And that's apparently what she did on McKinley. Her total mental commitment exceeded her physical ability to match it.

At the request of her parents, Salerno's body was left on the mountain and buried at 19,500 feet. "I can't think of a more fitting memorial to her effort than McKinley itself," Tejas said. "Although it's tragic Lynne died, at least she died doing something she loved."

In retrospect, he added, "It was a mistake to let Lynne continue climbing. Though she reached her goal, it cost her dearly. The mountain will always be there; there will be other chances. One's life is more important."

The Park Service organized a board of inquiry to investigate Salerno's death, as it does following any death within a national park. According to Seibert, the board concluded that Tejas's decisions to leave some of the group's safety gear near Denali Pass and to send the bivy sack back with his assistant guide when the group split up were:

> . . . definitely a shortcoming on Vern's part; he has to shoulder that responsibility. . . . Additional survival gear may or may not have made a difference, but clearly it wasn't available. Some safety considerations fell through the cracks. There was also concern about Vern's decision to leave his client alone (while traveling back and forth between Salerno and Moss and Kazel).
>
> However, it's very questionable whether Vern should have been able to pick up on Lynne's condition, without knowing about her internal motivation and drive. Guides often rely to some degree on what their clients are telling them. So Lynne had to shoulder that responsibility.[3]

DAVE STAEHELI

ANCHORAGE CLIMBER DAVE STAEHELI WEARS HIS CREVASSE-PROTECTION DEVICE WHILE HAULING GEAR UP THE KAHILTNA GLACIER DURING HIS WINTER SOLO ASCENT OF MCKINLEY IN 1989. MOUNT FORAKER IS BEHIND HIM.

Despite any mistakes in judgment, Moss said, "Vern wasn't to blame. He kept his head. He did the best he could do under the circumstances. Climbing mountains is a risky business. Lynne knew the risks; we all did."

Before her climb, Lynne Salerno vowed she would reach the summit "no matter what it takes." In the end, it took her life.

Like Tejas, Anchorage mountaineer and climbing guide Dave Staeheli found inspiration in Naomi Uemura's 1984 solo winter ascent of Mount McKinley. But it wasn't until the summer of 1987, while climbing up the Kahiltna Glacier with a group of clients, that he began making plans for his own winter climb. From that point on, whenever he had a free moment, he would think about wintertime food requirements, equipment needs, and route selection.[4]

Staeheli, too, was well acquainted with the mountain. Since first hiring on as a McKinley guide in 1982, he'd participated in fifteen expeditions and reached the summit thirteen times. Most of those trips had been along the West Buttress.

But Staeheli wasn't interested in climbing the West Buttress alone in winter. As far as he was concerned, Uemura had already accomplished that in 1984. Staeheli wanted to do something different–something that would present a new and significantly more challenging test. He chose a solo attempt of the Cassin Ridge, widely recognized as one of North America's most difficult routes.

The Cassin had been climbed once before in winter, by the team of Roger Mear, Mike Young, and Jonathan Waterman. The climbers decided to ascend alpine style; that is, they moved continuously upward rather than relaying food, fuel, and gear up the mountain. Despite personality conflicts, the group reached McKinley's summit in eight days. Mears and Young made it to the top on March 7, 1982. Waterman, suffering from altitude sickness and numb feet, was forced to turn around a few hundred feet from the summit.

Staeheli, thirty-three, was confident of his ability to ascend–or at least attempt–the Cassin route alone. He did, after all, bring nearly two decades of climbing experience to the mountain.

Born and raised in the Pacific Northwest, Staeheli first felt the lure of high places at age nine, when he attended an exhibit on the 1963 American expedition to Mount Everest. Right then and there, Staeheli knew his calling: he would be a mountaineer. He began climbing in his midteens, and in 1973 took a mountaineering class. Four years later, while visiting Alaska, he joined an expedition to climb Canada's Mount Logan. That ascent moved him "into the big time." Over the next several years, he climbed extensively in the Wrangell–St. Elias Mountains and the Alaska Range, where he found a niche guiding people to McKinley's summit. He had indeed become a mountain man.

Staeheli had also grown up to be a private man. Not wishing to become part of any media circus, he kept his planned solo expedition as secret as possible. Only park rangers and a few close friends knew of the attempt when he flew into the Alaska Range in late February 1989. He'd even asked Denali National Park officials not to spread word of his plans.

Hauling two sleds loaded with 120 pounds of gear and wearing a fourteen-foot aluminum ladder to protect against crevasse falls, Staeheli struggled up the Kahiltna Glacier to its Northeast Fork, about two and a half miles from his drop-off at 7,000 feet. Unlike Uemura and Tejas, he carried a tent, because once on the steep, wind-scoured Cassin Ridge, there probably wouldn't be enough snow to build a natural shelter.

Staeheli's progress was slowed considerably by head winds that gusted to forty miles per hour and drove the windchill temperature to −90°F. He was knocked to the ground a few times and found it difficult to get into any sort of traveling rhythm. He'd hoped to travel six hours a day, but that schedule proved impossible to keep. One day, after traveling only a half mile in an hour's time, he stopped in frustration and set up camp.

The wind had been a big problem at 7,000 feet, but it was even worse up high. McKinley's summit was capped by a lenticular cloud. Somewhere on the mountain's upper slopes was a team of three Japanese climbers, who'd begun their own winter attempt up the West Buttress Route in early February. Concern for the Japanese had begun to grow; no one had seen or heard from the team in several days.

Wind wasn't Staeheli's only difficulty, however; he was having equipment problems as well. A shoulder strap on his pack had busted and zippers had malfunctioned. Chief among his equipment woes was the failure of his new, high-tech boots. Supposedly good to temperatures of −40°F, the boots weren't doing the job even in −20° to −25°F weather. Traveling up the glacier he'd had foot problems almost continually. "There just wasn't enough insulation on the soles," he said. "It was like standing on cold concrete. Each day I had to go through a ritual of warming the boots, and even then it would take a couple hours to get my toes warm. Some days I got real frantic, trying to warm the feet."

The boot-warming ritual would begin shortly after waking in the morning. He'd light the stove and, while heating water, place the toes of his boots near the flame. After bringing the water to a boil, he'd pour some of it into a water bottle, which was then inserted into the boots to warm their interiors. Yet even with that start-of-the-day boot warming, Staeheli's feet would sometimes become so cold while traveling that he'd have to stop, pull out the stove and sleeping bag, boil water and apply a hot-water bottle to his feet while he was inside the bag.

Staeheli's struggles with the wind—but not his gear—eased up once he left the Kahiltna's main branch and headed up the Northeast Fork. Here he was protected from the full force of the wind. But there were other dangers and obstacles to face. "The Northeast Fork is probably the most hazardous part of climbing either the Cassin or West Rib Routes," said then-chief mountaineering ranger Bob Seibert. "It's a very dangerous approach, a place where several people have died."

Entire teams have vanished up the fork, which mountaineers have nicknamed the Valley of Death. In 1980, a four-member Canadian expedition disappeared without a trace. Their bodies were never found despite a thorough search of the valley. One year later, three Japanese climbers disappeared. Only their tent was later discovered.

Not only must climbers cross crevasse fields, but their path up the Northeast Fork takes them below overhanging glaciers and across avalanche chutes. And the valley's chief obstacle is an icefall that must be traversed. "What a mess," Staeheli said. "It was a jumble of big ice blocks. I'd be going sideways half the time. Right, then left, then back to the right . . . and sometimes I'd have to climb down into a crevasse to get anywhere. Luckily nothing happened."

Once through the icefall—which took three days of strenuous work—and back on relatively safe ground, Staeheli faced a difficult decision: continue on to the Cassin Ridge or climb the West Rib:

> It took me about a day to make up my mind. I kept waffling back and forth. One of the biggest problems I had was dealing with expectations. I'd already told people that I was going up the Cassin. The West Rib is a good climb, but it's a lesser project than the Cassin. But I'm a firm believer in instincts. And with all the equipment problems I'd been having, it seemed stupid to go up the Cassin. There was no sense taking chances.

Of special concern to Staeheli was the inadequacy of his boots. The Cassin is a longer and technically more difficult route than the West Rib. Should he get in trouble, retreat would be extremely tough, if not impossible. "Going up the Cassin would have been pretty dumb, given the situation," he reflected. "My odds of getting frostbite seemed pretty good. And on that route, the consequences could have been disastrous." As it turned out, a few toes did become frostbitten, though not severely.

The Grade 4 West Rib (on a scale of 6) may not be as challenging as the Cassin, but it's still considered a technically difficult route, with several thousand feet of steep ice and snow, that requires considerable ice-climbing expertise. (The West Buttress, by contrast, is considered a Grade 2 climb.) It had been attempted only once before in winter, by a four-member party in 1983. Two team members, Charlie Sassara and Robert Frank of Anchorage, made the top in −45°F weather. The ten-hour summit climb had exhausted both men. And on their way back to camp, while descending a forty- to fifty-degree slope unroped, Frank slipped on the ice. Moments later he slid into Sassara, knocking him down as well. Sassara managed to dig his ice axe into the snow and stop his fall after sliding about thirty yards. Frank, however, plunged down the slope to his death. His body was never recovered.

Once Staeheli accepted his change of plans and headed up the West Rib without the ladder—which would have been impossible to carry up the steep snow and ice—he began enjoying his adventure. Traveling up the Valley of Death had been grim work, but ascending the rib was "fun," though it involved several thousand feet of strenuous and dangerous ice-axe and crampon climbing on sheer ice and snow faces.

Again hauling his gear in two loads, Staeheli carried about ninety pounds up the steep ridge. His first technical challenge was a 2,000-foot-high, snow-filled gully with angles of up to fifty degrees. Snow conditions were ideal for kicking steps into the slope, and Staeheli ascended the steep ravine in two and a half days, setting up a camp at 13,300 feet on March 8. Despite carrying a 300-foot rope, he free-climbed about half the couloir. Without any protection, a slip would likely have meant death. But to him, that was part of the challenge. "That's when the juices started flowing," he said. "You know you cannot fall, or that's the end."

Above the couloir was the rib itself: a ridgeline of mixed rock, ice, and snow that's steep at both ends with a relatively flat middle section. As Staeheli ascended this portion of the route, above him search parties looking along the West Buttress Route for the missing Japanese team found the three climbers dead below Denali Pass. They'd apparently been blown off the mountain by winds estimated at 100 to 200 miles per hour.

Staeheli was largely protected from the wind, though he occasionally got hit by gusts, and he traversed the rib without any major problems. He did, however, get a big scare while caching supplies at his 16,200-foot camp. Staeheli had just set his pack down and begun to bury some gear in the snow when a big gust of wind sent the pack flying. He turned around just in time to see it drop over the edge.

Scolding himself for the sort of mistake a beginning climber might make, Staeheli watched as the pack cartwheeled down the fifty-degree slope; along the way it disgorged a ski pole, fuel bottle, and some climbing hardware. He was certain it would keep rolling and bouncing until finally coming to rest on the Northeast Fork, some five thousand feet below. But luckily it stopped about 800 vertical feet beneath him. Staeheli counted his blessings, then climbed down, retrieved the pack, and made himself some lunch.

Summit day began at eight in the morning on March 12. Traveling light, Staeheli followed the rib to 19,300 feet, where it joins the West Buttress. The most breathtaking–and frightening–section of the ascent was a thousand-foot, steeply sloping gully where Frank had fallen to his death in 1983.

While ascending the precipitous wall of hard-packed snow and ice that filled the couloir. Staeheli realized he couldn't afford a single misstep:

> This was the most dangerous part of the climb; it demanded total concentration. It was the kind of situation where if you slip or stumble and start to slide, you might not stop for thousands of feet. You have to be prepared for something to go wrong. Mentally I was rehearsing my moves ahead of time, in case something did happen.

Once off the rib and on the buttress, he became exposed to the winds that had echoed above him throughout his ascent of the rib. No longer was the wind gusting to one hundred miles per hour or more. But it was blowing up to seventy miles per hour, which would have produced a −70°F windchill in the −10°F weather. Evidence of the recent hurricane-force gales was carved in the mountain's snow. "You could see the place had been absolutely blasted," he said. "The way the snow was eroded, it was like being on a different planet."

Staeheli reached the top at 1 P.M., becoming only the thirteenth climber, and third soloist, to reach McKinley's summit in winter. And he was the first to ascend a route other than the West Buttress while climbing alone in winter. During his ascent, Staeheli encountered temperatures down to −28°F, not much different from what he'd experienced on some summertime McKinley expeditions. He'd been lucky to avoid the extreme winds that may have blown the Japanese off their route. What impressed him most about his winter ascent was the absolute solitude he enjoyed—and sometimes endured.

> As far as I knew, there was no one else on the mountain. I did carry a radio, but that didn't make much difference. For two weeks, no one was flying because of the high winds; during that period I had no contact with anyone. If I'd had any trouble, my chances of getting help were slim to none, especially since I'd changed my route at the last minute. If I'd slipped, fallen down a couloir, and injured myself, there was nobody to come and bail me out. I was totally self-supporting.

During his short stay on the summit, Staeheli gazed out over the Alaska Range, took a few photographs, and then headed down. "I was happy," Staeheli later recalled. "But I was also very aware that my day was only half over. There was still the matter of descending to camp, and I wanted to stay focused on that. The euphoria [of reaching the summit] didn't hit me until later."

Two days later he was back in Anchorage, in excellent spirits and good shape except for minor frostbite. News of his ascent still hadn't spread beyond Alaska's mountaineering community. Unlike Tejas's well-publicized arrival in town one year earlier, Staeheli's return was unheralded, largely unnoticed, and certainly overshadowed by the deaths of the Japanese climbers.

The lack of public and media attention paid to Staeheli's solo climb bothered many Alaskan mountaineers, who considered his ascent to be a more significant feat than Tejas's solo because he had followed a more technically difficult path to McKinley's summit. Anchorage mountain guide Gary Bocarde said: "The West Rib is a beautiful, technical climb. It's a longer and more committing route, much more difficult than the West Buttress. To me, a technical climb like that is more of a major deal."

And as Anchorage mountaineer Steve Davis noted:

> Reaching McKinley's summit in winter while climbing alone is remarkable in itself. But the fact that the West Rib is so technically difficult makes it something to really applaud. I think the entire Alaska climbing community is proud of what Dave accomplished.

Staeheli, however, was much less disturbed by the lack of public notice and media hype. A shy person who doesn't seek attention, he'd kept a low profile, trying to stay out of the public's eye. Only reluctantly–with urging from his girlfriend and climbing partner Gretchen Reeve (now Gretchen Staeheli)–did he agree to be interviewed by reporters.

Peer recognition, not public acclaim, is what he sought. "The only people I want to get admiration from are those who've already done [McKinley in winter] and other climbers," he said.

In the two decades following Staeheli's ascent of the West Rib, only one other climber successfully soloed McKinley in winter: following the West Buttress Route taken by Uemura and Tejas, Japanese mountaineer Masatoshi Kuriaki reached the mountain's top on March 8, 1998, and then safely descended. On a previous attempt in 1997, Kuriaki spent forty days on McKinley before being turned back by severe cold and high winds. In 1998, he was graced by one of the mildest Denali-area winters on record. As of spring 2012, no other soloists have reached the mountain's top in winter.

Courtesy of the National Park Service

RANGERS AND VOLUNTEERS REMOVE A BODY FROM MCKINLEY DURING THE "DEADLIEST SEASON," 1992.

Chapter Twelve

The Deadliest Season, 1992

Denali National Park ranger Daryl Miller breathed a long sigh of relief as he listened to the radio call. Fellow climbing ranger Roger Robinson, flying in a chartered airplane near Mount McKinley's uppermost slopes, had just located an overdue team of Canadians.[1]

The Canadians had been reported missing on the morning of May 31, 1992—just one day after they'd made an attempt to reach the 20,320-foot summit. But now, at 2:30 P.M., they were at 19,000 feet, near the top of the Messner Couloir, roped together.

Neither Miller nor Robinson understood why the four climbers would be crossing that steep and often treacherous gully on McKinley's western face. It wasn't the path climbers normally take when descending thc West Buttress. But any sense of alarm was overshadowed by joy at sighting them.

The rangers were still recovering from a horrifying three-week period in which seven climbers had died and thirteen others were evacuated from the mountain because of illness or injury. The accidents had largely resulted from one of the worst spring storms in years.

The last thing any of the rangers wanted was another team in trouble. From his camp at 14,200 feet, Miller watched through binoculars while the Canadian team slowly worked its way across the Messner—a steep, snow- and ice-covered ravine that plummets more than a vertical mile. The couloir demands a climber's full attention. One slip could lead to a fall of several thousand feet.

Miller's line of vision was partly obscured by clouds. But up at the 17,200-foot camp, about twenty other climbers enjoyed a better view. They watched the Canadians proceed, step by step. Then they stood transfixed, horrified, as the man at the rear of the rope slipped and fell, pulling everyone else off their feet.

"The whole team went down," climber Cliff McCuskey reported later. "Just swoooosh! They went over the rock band and just kept going. It was sickening."

The Canadians would fall 3,000 feet to their deaths.

Poor weather prevented rangers from finding their bodies until the next day, at 16,000 feet. Simon and Christian Proulx, Alain Potvin, and Maurice Grandchamp had become McKinley victims eight, nine, ten, and eleven for the year. It was—and still remains—the highest seasonal death toll ever on the mountain. The eleven included ten foreigners—a Swiss, two Italians, three Koreans, and four Canadians. They also included Terrance "Mugs" Stump, one of the most accomplished mountaineers in America.

It began like most other climbing seasons in recent years. By the first week of May, a few hundred people were already trudging up McKinley's various slopes. Only a handful had reached the summit. The late-April and early-May weather was typically windy and cold, with nighttime lows at −30°F to −40°F. But mountaineering ranger Ron Johnson recalls it wasn't stormy. "You could travel," he says.

Through May 9, only one climber had been evacuated from the mountain: a National Park Service volunteer from Vermont, suffering minor frostbite. No one had been seriously injured. Then came the warning call from Fairbanks.

Every mountaineering season since 1982, Denali Park's rangers have received daily forecasts from the National Weather Service office in Fairbanks. The predictions begin in late April and continue through mid-July. On the morning of May 10, the forecasters issued an ominous warning: a massive storm system born off the coast of Japan was heading Mount McKinley's way, carried by a westerly jet stream. It would arrive within the next day or so, bringing extreme winds and heavy snowfall.

"We had a very high degree of confidence that the whole mountain would be blasted with a terrific wind-and-snow storm," says Ted Fathauer, who then supervised the Weather Service's Fairbanks office. "We anticipated that winds on the upper mountain could exceed one hundred miles per hour for several days."

Even more frightening than the storm's intensity was its duration. Meteorologists expected it to last a week, maybe longer. "It was an extraordinary event for this time of year," Fathauer says. "The 'Mother of Storms,' if you will. In ten years of doing forecasts for Denali, I'd never seen anything like it during the climbing season, which is a comparatively gentle time of year.

"This was more typical of a winter storm. I'd say it was a once-in-fifteen- or maybe even a once-in-fifty-years event, perhaps comparable to the one that struck the Wilcox group in 1967." (Recounted in Chapter 9, that expedition's disaster is still the single worst tragedy in Alaska mountaineering history.)

On May 11, while updating his agency's "gloom and doom" prediction, Fathauer also recommended that "people get to as low an elevation as possible, dig in, and be prepared for a long, long wait."

Soon afterward, the rangers initiated an unprecedented early warning program to notify climbers of the storm. Circling the mountain in a plane, chief mountaineering ranger J. D. Swed issued the warning over citizens-band radio (carried by many Denali expeditions) on a variety of frequencies. Informed of the danger, Talkeetna's air-taxi services also flew to the mountain and contacted as many of their clients as possible.

Fortunately, few expeditions were high on the mountain. Rangers camped at 14,200 feet on McKinley's most popular route, the West Buttress, knew of only a couple parties higher up. One of those was a three-person French team. By midday on May 11, the French climbers had reached 17,200 feet, where most West Buttress teams establish high camp. Two members then descended to 16,000 feet, where they'd cached several items of gear, including the expedition's stove and fuel. Too weary to join her teammates, twenty-six-year-old Edwige Segment remained alone at 17,200.

The storm had not yet arrived in full force, but the two Frenchmen still found the West Buttress ridge too windy for safe travel. Growing weary and frightened and unable to retrieve gear needed for their survival, they descended to 14,200 feet and told rangers about their partner, now stranded high above. Totally alone, with no means of melting snow to make water, Segment would never survive a weeklong storm, ranger Johnson knew. So he quickly organized a rescue team and headed for high camp, hoping to "get up there before the brunt of the storm hit."

The four rescuers found Segment at 7:15 P.M. The woman was tired, but otherwise in good shape. Wasting no time, the climbers quickly descended to the 14,200-foot camp, in a bowl that offers some protection from the wind. Already, gusts were blowing forty miles per hour and visibility had diminished to 200 feet or less. "Iffy weather," Johnson called it. An hour or two later and rescue would have been impossible. The Frenchwoman had been lucky.

Also lucky to leave the mountain alive was Korean climber Seok Hyun-song, who suffered severe head injuries in a fall on May 11. Seok and his partners had been trying to put in a new route on McKinley's South Face when the storm's arrival prompted them to retreat. The Koreans were rappelling down the face at about the 15,000-foot level when Seok fell nearly a thousand feet. Knocked unconscious, he was carried back to the Kahiltna Glacier base camp at 7,200 feet. Doctors with another Denali expedition tended the Korean's wounds for two days, until a lull in the storm allowed a military helicopter to fly in and retrieve the still-comatose climber. After several weeks at an Anchorage hospital, he recuperated enough to fly home. Seok's survival, one physician says, was "miraculous."

Less fortunate were Italians Giovanni Calcagno and Roberto Pimbo, the first climbers to die on McKinley in 1992. Calcagno and Pimbo had come to climb the Cassin Ridge. Named for Italian climber Riccardo Cassin, who pioneered the route in 1961, it is the most popular of McKinley's difficult routes.

Anchorage guide Gary Bocarde, who met the Italian duo at base camp in early May, says they planned to do an alpine-style ascent of the Cassin. Traveling light and fast, the two men left their tent and much of their gear at the base of the ridge. Whether Calcagno and Pimbo reached the summit is unclear. Nor are the circumstances of their deaths known. "We really have no idea what happened," Johnson said afterward. "Nothing has been reconstructed."

One thing is certain: the Italians died on the Cassin Ridge while McKinley was being battered by stormy weather. One body was first spotted at 15,000 feet on May 15, by a group of Koreans also attempting the Cassin. The second body was found a day later at 11,800 feet, wrapped in a sleeping bag.

A Swiss climber named Alex von Bergen was next to die. Unlike most—and perhaps all—of McKinley's other May deaths, his had nothing to do with the weather. Part of an eight-person team following the West Buttress route, Bergen began to suffer severe headaches and to have difficulty breathing while camped at 14,200 feet. Rangers were contacted at 10 A.M. on May 17; he died a half hour later from cardiac arrest.

Except for the short time spent with von Bergen, rescuers' attention and energies on May 17—the seventh straight day of stormy weather—were focused on two groups of Korean climbers.

During this weeklong storm, the ranger camp at 14,200 feet was buffeted almost continuously by winds blowing thirty to forty miles per hour. Occasionally gusts of seventy to eighty miles per hour would roar through camp. Ranger Johnson once stepped outside his tent and was knocked to the ground by a blast of wind, then driven several feet. He had to crawl along the ground to get back to his tent. Up high, the winds were even more extreme. At places like 18,200-foot Denali Pass, which often acts as a wind tunnel, the strongest gusts almost certainly exceeded 100 miles per hour and may have reached 150.

It was on May 16, with the storm at its peak, that three Koreans high on the Cassin Ridge first sent out a radio call for help. Extreme winds had torn up their tent and forced them to take shelter in a snow cave at 17,700 feet. The team had run out of food several days earlier and one member suffered from both altitude sickness and frostbite. Unable or unwilling to move either up or down the Cassin, the Koreans said they would wait until help arrived. But the same conditions that kept them pinned inside a snow shelter also prevented their rescue.

Park rangers in Talkeetna decided that a Lama helicopter, used in many high-altitude rescues during the 1990s, would have the best chance of saving the trio. But winds gusting to seventy miles per hour or more, in combination with near-zero visibility, thwarted rescue attempts on May 16 and 17. It wasn't until the afternoon of May 18 that a temporary window of calm air allowed Lama pilot Bill Ramsey to pick the Koreans off the Cassin one at a time and carry them to safety. Severely weakened by their week without food, Kang Hyun-doo, Kim Jae-chul, and Jun Bong-gyoo were then taken from McKinley's 14,200-foot camp to Anchorage and treated for frostbite, exhaustion, and dehydration. Except for a timely break in the weather and Ramsey's high-altitude heroics, Kang, Kim, and Jun would likely have become McKinley victims four, five, and six. They, like Edwige Segment and Seok Hyun-song, had been lucky.

Also benefitting from good fortune was another group of three Koreans, this one on the West Buttress. While nearly everyone else on the mountain had followed the National Park Service's advice to "dig in" and wait out the storm, that particular team decided to travel on May 17 despite continued high winds, heavy snowfall, and poor visibility. The reasons for their movement remain unclear, but ranger Johnson suspects the Koreans were retreating to 14,200 feet from a higher camp. In any event, the three climbers apparently became disoriented in whiteout conditions and decided to set up camp at about 15,000 feet. In the blowing snow, they failed to note that they were on a snow bridge. While the Koreans worked on their tent, the bridge collapsed and all three dropped into a crevasse. One climber, who'd fallen only to his armpits, managed to extricate himself and somehow stumbled through the storm to the rangers' camp.

Within the hour, an eleven-member rescue team that included ranger Johnson, veteran Denali guide Brian Okonek, and world-class mountaineers John Roskelley and Jim Wickwire were on the scene. Both Koreans still in the crevasse were safely removed from the deep fissure. One was unhurt but the other, who'd fallen sixty feet, was seriously injured. After being placed on a stretcher, he was hauled by sled to camp and later flown off the mountain to an Anchorage hospital. Roskelley, who's climbed several of the world's highest and most difficult peaks, was amazed that anyone would attempt to travel in such weather. "The smart people stayed put," he says. "If you had a good tent and were in a protected area, the best thing you could do was sit tight. Why would people be outside when the wind is gusting to fifty or seventy miles per hour and the temperature is below zero? It's crazy."

Both Roskelley and Wickwire had come to Denali intending to climb the Cassin Ridge. But unlike the Korean and Italian teams, they chose to play it safe when the weather got nasty. Caught by stormy weather at the West Buttress's 14,200-foot camp, where they were adjusting to the altitude, the two Americans had chosen to forego their Cassin attempt.

"The Cassin is no place to be in a storm," Roskelley says. "It's easy to get stuck, unable to go up or down. And on that route you're traveling lighter, so you don't have as much food or fuel. Being on the Cassin in that kind of storm didn't seem like such a smart thing."

Being on the West Rib wasn't such a good idea either. Not quite as challenging as the Cassin Ridge, the West Rib is nonetheless a technically difficult route, with several thousand feet of ice and snow. On May 19, park rangers received a radio call from yet another Korean party, which reported it had been stuck on the West Rib at 18,000 feet for seven days. Even after rationing their supplies for a week, Yung Soo-yang, Hong Sung-tak, and Jin Seong-jong had only enough food and water for one more day. The Koreans told rangers they planned to descend to the West Buttress's 14,200-foot camp via a long, moderately steep couloir know as the "Orient Express."

One day later, Park Service volunteers Julie and Matt Culbertson found the men's bodies at 15,000 feet. Still roped together, the Koreans had apparently fallen to their deaths while retreating down the Express, which was given its name in the 1970s after claiming the lives of five Asian climbers. Although not technically difficult, the Express is steep enough (thirty-three degrees to fifty-five degrees) and long enough (several thousand feet) to cause life-threatening injuries if a climber falls. Since the early 1970s, sixteen people have died in the Express (as of summer 2012).

McKinley's 1992 toll was now six, all foreigners. Only two other years had been more deadly: eight people died on the mountain in 1967, the year of the Wilcox disaster, and again in 1980.

By May 21 the storm had passed, leaving clear skies and relative calm. Still, gale-force winds occasionally blasted McKinley's uppermost slopes. In the storm's wake, the mountain claimed its seventh victim in seven days: Mugs Stump, one of America's foremost mountaineers, died while guiding two Californians on the South Buttress Route.

Ironically, the Utah-based guide had made all the right moves upon learning eleven days earlier that a major storm was on its way. First, he descended with clients Nelson Max and Robert

Hoffman to a protected camp at 12,500 feet. Then, after getting extra food from a cache lower on the mountain, Stump and his clients sat out the storm. When the weather finally cleared, the team established high camp at 16,000 feet. On May 20, Stump and Max made a try for the top. They got within one hundred yards of the summit before being stopped by high winds. Spotting a patch of white on Max's nose–the first sign of frostbite–Stump decided to retreat. Back at their high camp, the climbers discovered Max had frostbitten feet as well.

Wanting to get Max back to Anchorage as quickly as possible, Stump led his clients down the South Buttress the next day. First on the team's rope was Hoffman, followed by Max and then Stump. Early in the afternoon, at a steep jumbled section of glacier known as The Ramp, Hoffman came to an open crevasse. Unsure what to do, he stopped and requested Stump's help. Approaching from the rear, Stump passed his clients and approached the crevasse's lip. He was standing a couple of feet from its edge when the snow and ice gave way. As Stump fell from sight, Hoffman and Max were jerked off their feet and pulled several feet before stopping.

After tying off the rope, Max rappelled into the crevasse. About ten or fifteen feet down, he found the rope passing into a jumbled mass of ice and snow. The plug extended sixty feet down. Below it, there was nothing but darkness. No sign of the rope. Or Stump.

Max was certain Stump was either entombed in the ice and snow, or that the rope had snapped with the force of the fall. Still he yelled Stump's name over and over. No response. Finally giving up, Max climbed out of the crevasse and rejoined Hoffman. Without their guide, their radio, or their stove (which Stump had been carrying), the climbers were faced with the frightening task of descending a challenging mountain slope they barely knew. After a day of "floundering," they encountered two Washington state climbers heading up the buttress. Don Preiss and Mark Bunker provided an escort down the mountain, then radioed the Park Service for help. Within hours, the two Californians were back in town—and lucky to be alive.

Though Stump's death occurred after the May storm's departure, Fairbanks meteorologist Ted Fathauer speculates there could be a connection between the two: "Snow bridges are unlikely to break during Denali's normal climbing season. Mugs may have been standing on a snow bridge formed by new, blowing snow during the recent storm. It hadn't had the time to stabilize and strengthen."

The four Canadians who died in the Messner Couloir left their West Buttress high camp sometime on May 30. Park rangers figure they reached the summit late that night or early the next morning while battling subzero temperatures and fierce winds. Rangers could only guess why the Canadians attempted to cross the dangerous couloir on their descent, when the standard West Buttress Route from the summit to high camp was much easier and safer.

J. D. Swed, then Denali's chief mountaineering ranger, suspects they were probably trying to stay out of gale-force winds blowing across the exposed upper slopes. He adds that they made at least two errors in judgment. By leaving their tent and sleeping bags at high camp—something that many McKinley mountaineers do on summit day—the Canadians had no shelter from the extreme wind and cold. Instead, they may have been forced to risk a more difficult path. The second fateful decision (one the Koreans also made while descending the Orient Express) was to remain roped while traversing a dangerous snow and ice chute. In such steep terrain, all climbers are at risk if one member of a roped team slips. The alternative is to belay each other across, or climb unroped.

"Where they were," says Swed, "if you don't self-arrest [using an ice axe to stop sliding] in the first two seconds, you won't be able to self-arrest."

Looking back at the tragedies of May, rangers and other McKinley veterans agree that the number of fatalities and rescues was extraordinary. But they also say the death count could have been much higher. Swed credits meteorologist Fathauer and his Fairbanks staff for saving "half again as many people" with their forecast of the once-in-a-quarter-century storm. He also praises the performance of Ramsey, the Lama helicopter pilot: "The Lama was invaluable. Without it, we're forced to expose a larger number of rescuers to risk, for a longer period of time. The Lama involves a minimal amount of risk and is much quicker. There's no doubt it saved a lot of lives this year."

Fathauer, in turn, credits the performance of ranger Ron Johnson, who was stationed on Mount McKinley for the entire storm, and all those who volunteered as rescuers. "Had the National Park Service and their volunteers not taken the heroic measures that they did, I'm convinced there could have been many more who would never have returned. How many more is anybody's guess, but I'd say at least a dozen."

The timing of the storm saved lives too. When it showed up on May 11, few teams were on McKinley's uppermost slopes. Nearly everyone was in a position to dig in and wait out the weather.

Besides poor weather, 1992's fatalities can be explained in part by poor judgment at high altitude. All of the deaths occurred at 14,000 feet or higher, where the weather is fiercer and it takes more energy to survive. At the same time, people are carrying fewer supplies and their ability to make decisions is diminished by the lack of oxygen. Yet as Johnson has pointed out, the specific circumstances surrounding most of the deaths remain unknown. The best anyone can do is speculate. Of special concern to rangers was the disproportionate number of foreign climbers involved in rescues and fatalities, a trend that the Park Service began to track in the mid-1980s. Though they comprised only 41 percent of all McKinley climbers in 1992, they accounted for two-thirds of the rescues—and ten of eleven climbers to die were from other countries. (A more complete discussion of foreign-climber rescues and safety issues is included in Chapter 13.)

Because of the extreme cold so characteristic of May, both Hackett and Bocarde believe even a "normal" May storm can have deadly repercussions. And Bocarde, for one, doesn't believe that the 1992 storm was even a once-in-a-decade event. "Every time I hear the phrase 'storm of storms,' I ask myself what that means. I've been on McKinley every year since 1976 and this year's storm didn't seem much different than any others. There's been hundred-mile-per-hour winds up there for years."

Bocarde, who was on McKinley's West Rib in mid-May, thinks the difference in 1992 was that people got caught in the wrong place at the wrong time. "People hang out," he says. "Then a storm comes in and they end up not being ready to deal with it. So they pay the price. I just look at this year as maybe a lot of bad luck. I can't buy the fact that the weather was so much worse than usual."

One final thing to consider: the number of climbers on Mount McKinley has grown dramatically since the 1970s. More fatalities can be expected due to statistical probability alone. In 1992, for example, about a thousand climbers attempted the climb in May and June, compared to less than a hundred per season twenty-five years earlier.

The 1992 deaths-to-climbers ratio—one fatality for every ninety-three climbers—actually compares favorably to some years in the past. In 1967, eight of sixty-seven climbers died, or one of every eight; in 1932, when Allen Carpé and Theodore Koven became McKinley's first fatalities, two of nine climbers perished.

Although the number of 1992 fatalities shocked the public, many of those who know the mountain best argue that years like 1991 and 1999–when no one died on McKinley–are the real anomalies. "We expect deaths on this mountain," J. D. Swed admitted. "That's just the nature of mountain climbing. Eleven is too many, but it's not all that impressive. We average several deaths per year. To have no deaths at all is much more impressive."

Hackett agrees: "A large number of climbers put themselves right on the edge when they go for the summit. They're hypoxic, cold, dehydrated, and exhausted. But most squeak by. Most luck out–most of the time. In a way, 1992 made up for all the good luck of other years."

Peter H. Hackett, M.D.

A MEMBER OF THE DENALI MEDICAL RESEARCH PROJECT TEAM SHOVELS SNOW AWAY FROM THE PROJECT'S TWO HUTS AT 14,200 FEET AFTER A STORM.

Chapter Thirteen

Climber Self-Sufficiency and Rescues

Climbing McKinley is risky business. It always has been, and it always will be.

Advances in high-altitude gear, techniques, and medicine may improve climbers' chances for success, but they'll never guarantee safety. The mountain's hazards are too numerous, too unpredictable. Hidden crevasses, avalanches, steep ice and rock walls, severe storms, extreme cold, and high altitude all can kill.

In the 109 years (through 2012) since Judge Wickersham's party first attempted to reach McKinley's summit in 1903, 120 climbers have died on the mountain; more than three-quarters of those fatalities (93) have occurred since 1980. Hundreds of other adventurers have suffered severe injuries: broken legs, cracked ribs, torn ligaments, concussions, frostbite, exhaustion-hypothermia, or acute mountain sickness.[1]

McKinley's pioneer climbers didn't fully understand the risks they were undertaking in attempting to reach the summit. They knew very little about altitude sickness, avalanches, or proper diet, for example. And by modern standards, their equipment, mountaineering techniques, and first-aid skills were crude.

The pioneers, nevertheless, had one important edge over many present-day mountaineers: they were completely self-sufficient. There were no rescue groups to call on, no government agencies watching over the mountain, no helicopters or planes capable of flying injured climbers off the mountain's slopes. To survive a McKinley expedition, the earliest climbers knew they had to rely strictly on their own skills, knowledge, and good judgment. And they succeeded extremely well. From 1903 to 1913, forty-seven men attempted to reach the top of North America. None died and by all accounts none was seriously hurt.

The first McKinley group to depend on outside help was Allen Carpé's cosmic-ray expedition in 1932. That team was the first to be flown onto the mountain and to request airplane assistance to evacuate a seriously ill climber.

Reliance on planes increased dramatically during the 1940s and 1950s, when scientific expeditions to McKinley routinely received airdrops of gear, food, and fuel (airdrops within the park were finally outlawed in 1964, except in emergency situations). In 1951, the air-supported team led by Bradford Washburn became the first group to reach the summit without following the Muldrow Glacier Route. That West Buttress ascent launched a new age in which the large majority of McKinley expeditions would depend on bush pilot services for easier access to the mountain.

Helicopters also entered the McKinley scene during the 1940s to assist scientific expeditions. But since the early 1950s, they've been used almost exclusively for search-and-rescue missions, rather than for transportation or hauling supplies (the prime exception is the use of helicopters to set up the mountaineering rangers' 14,200-foot camp each spring). The first helicopter rescue occurred in 1953, when a climber with frozen feet was flown to the Wonder Lake ranger station after he'd descended to the tundra. The following year a helicopter helped save the life of climber George Argus, who'd broken his hip during a fall along Karstens Ridge (another member of the team, park ranger Elton Thayer, was killed in the fall). The pilot dropped a seven-person rescue team at 6,000 feet, then evacuated Argus after he'd been carried from 11,000 to 5,000 feet.

Helicopters were used for rescues again in 1960 and 1967. But through the end of the sixties, most McKinley climbers continued to take care of their own needs, depending on outside help only in cases of extreme emergency.

Another midcentury change that diminished climbers' independence, and to some degree their self-reliance, was the National Park Service's strict control of McKinley expeditions from the mid-1940s until 1970.[2] The system made some mountaineers unhappy, but seemed to work well. Until 1967. Despite the Park Service's safeguards, eight climbers died on McKinley that year, including the seven members of the Wilcox expedition. After that tragedy, McKinley National Park chief ranger Arthur Hayes admitted in his annual report:

> The problem of evaluating mountaineers' qualifications remains a severe one. Climbers with an impressive list of ascents . . . sometimes fail totally to cope with the conditions on Mount McKinley, while relatively inexperienced mountaineers, who happen to have rugged constitutions and a good attitude for expedition work, sometimes perform beautifully. . . . While every effort is made to increase climber safety by a fair and rigorous screening, it is impossible to be sure that correct judgments are made in all cases.[3]

The following year, Park Service officials added yet another climbing regulation to their already long list of McKinley restrictions: expeditions would be required to carry a two-way radio. In 1970, however, the agency abruptly liberalized its mountaineering policy largely because of the system's inadequacies, which Hayes had outlined after the Wilcox tragedy. The doctor's certificate and radio requirements remained intact (until 1980). But expeditions no longer needed the Park Service's permission to attempt a McKinley ascent: simple registration replaced the application/approval system. Preclimb inspections, team-size restrictions, and the requirement to have a rescue group on standby were also eliminated.

The relaxation of climbing restrictions reflected a change in management direction and style. It didn't mean, however, that the Park Service would adopt a laissez-faire attitude toward McKinley expeditions. During the 1970s and 1980s, the government became increasingly involved in efforts to protect both the mountain (from trash and human waste) and its mountaineers.

Park officials began placing greater emphasis on climber education. And they assumed greater responsibility for climber safety. If an individual or team got in trouble, the Park Service would not only organize and coordinate search-and-rescue efforts, it would pay the bill as well. Previously, because of the Park Service's limited involvement in rescue operations, costs had normally been paid by rescue groups or other government agencies, such as the Army or the Air Force.

The government's shift in priorities, combined with growing bush pilot and guide industries, opened McKinley to a new breed of mountaineer—the adventurer traveler—and set the groundwork for a climbing boom.

The yearly number of climbers on McKinley rose steadily and dramatically through the early and mid-1970s. In 1969, seventy-one people tried to climb North America's highest peak; in 1976,

508 made attempts, a sevenfold increase. Many of the newcomers had little or no high-altitude experience, and no concept of self-sufficiency.

Jim Hale of Talkeetna, who retired from the mountain-guiding business in 1980, has observed:

> You could really see a big attitude change in 1976. Back in the '60s and even the early '70s, there was more of an understanding that people were on their own. They didn't rely on others for help. But in '76, word got out that the National Park Service would pay for rescues. The prevailing attitude seemed to be "Don't worry. If we get in trouble, the Park Service will rescue us."[4]

The new attitude was reflected by some startling statistics. The Park Service coordinated twenty-one rescue missions, involving thirty-three climbers, during the 1976 season. Or to put it another way, about one out of every eighteen people to attempt the mountain had to be evacuated by plane or helicopter. As ranger Bob Gerhard noted in his annual report on McKinley mountaineering, "Watching a helicopter fly in to evacuate another climber became nearly a routine activity for many parties."[5]

By comparison, the Park Service helped evacuate a total of fifty-seven McKinley mountaineers during the previous forty-four years. And only thirty-five of those were rescued prior to 1970.

The 1976 rescue missions cost the government, and taxpayers, $82,200. Not surprisingly, that price tag provoked considerable public controversy. Many people–mostly non-climbers, but also some mountaineers–demanded that those rescued pay their own costs. Others suggested climbers be required to post a bond, or show proof of insurance, before being allowed on the mountain. Some outdoors organizations proposed that government agencies other than the military stop providing rescue assistance. (While the Park Service coordinates McKinley's rescue missions, evacuations may involve volunteer climbers, mountain guides, contracted pilots, and military personnel and aircraft, as well as rangers.) A large number of citizens also recommended that the Park Service reinstitute its pre-1970 McKinley climbing restrictions. And a few climbers argued that guiding be disallowed, because it attracted inexperienced climbers to the mountain.

Most, if not all, of these arguments and ideas have been periodically recycled since 1976, but without any significant effect. The Park Service continues to organize, coordinate, and pay for McKinley rescue missions (except for military expenses), though it emphasizes to climbers that its highest priority is rescuer safety and there may be situations where rescue is impossible.[6] The agency's rescue costs are not passed on to McKinley mountaineers—or those who climb in other national parks—for one simple reason: the federal government has a strict national policy of providing search-and-rescue services without charge. Bonding or climber-insurance programs aren't acceptable as alternatives either, because they would also violate the government's no-pay policy. As then-chief mountaineering ranger Bob Seibert explained in 1990, the system isn't likely to change anytime soon (more than twenty years later, his prediction still rings true):[7]

> Rescue costs on McKinley are an amazingly emotional issue. But if you look at our costs for the past few years, they're almost insignificant compared to Air Force and Coast Guard search-and-rescue costs [between 1985 and 1989, McKinley rescue costs ranged from a low of $18,113 in 1985 to a high of $86,336 in 1987]. The government spent one million dollars to find a group of missing walrus hunters [in 1988] and nobody complained. And as long as the Air Force, Coast Guard, and Civil Air Patrol *don't* require payments for rescue, neither will we. There's absolutely no reason to single out climbers. Why not boaters or pilots?

Rescue costs did increase substantially during the 1990s and into the 2000s in part reflecting the National Park Service's decision to rely more heavily on helicopter support during search-and-rescue operations. Since 1991, the agency has annually leased a high-altitude helicopter during the climbing season; for nearly two decades, the NPS leased a Lama helicopter but in 2010 it went to a model that is more fuel efficient, both to reduce the aircraft's environmental impact and to save money. On standby in Talkeetna from mid-April through mid-July, the Lama's pilot rescued sixty-nine climbers between 1991 and 1999, some from as high as 19,300 feet on McKinley, and was credited with saving numerous lives. And since 2000 "there have been very few rescues [high on McKinley] that *don't* require helicopters," South District Ranger John Leonard noted in 2012. Leonard, whose job includes overseeing Denali National Park's mountaineering program, added, "It's hard to say exactly how many lives have been saved, but in some cases there's no question it's made the difference between life and death. This past year, without a doubt, at least a couple of people would have died if we didn't have that helicopter."[8] One of the 2011 helicopter evacuations occurred at 19,500 feet, a record on McKinley.

It's also a fact that personnel and other costs of organizing search-and-rescue missions have increased, chief mountaineering ranger Daryl Miller said in 1999. And rescue costs at the time were reported for Denali National Park's entire South District, without McKinley being separated out, though in most years McKinley certainly accounted for the large majority of rescue operations. Total South District expenditures for the Park Service and military during the nineties ranged from a low of $55,000 in 1990 to a high of $431,345 in 1992, McKinley's deadliest season.

Costs have continued to escalate since the start of the new century. In 2012, Leonard did separate McKinley's search-and-rescue (SAR) costs from other South District rescue expenditures for the preceding eight years (2004–11). The total for that period: 112

SAR "events" on the mountain cost the government $1,449,161. That averages out to more than $181,000 annually.

High costs do not necessarily reflect a large number of rescue missions. For example, in 1987, a single rescue operation involving a US Army helicopter cost the government $33,754. And in 1999, the rescue of climbers from a British expedition cost the Park Service and military a combined $128,019. But those numbers pale in comparison to the costs of a 2011 rescue operation, following the fall of a guided and roped four-person team along the West Buttress Route, near McKinley's summit. By the time a climber with a broken leg had been airlifted from 19,500 feet and another climber's body was recovered from near 18,000 feet (the death was confirmed only after pickup) the combined efforts of Park Service rangers, the high-altitude helicopter pilot, an Alaska Air National Guard HC-130 aircraft, and a Chinook helicopter crew from Fort Wainwright military base ended up costing the government some $269,000.

Instead of bonding or insurance, some climbers have suggested that every person attempting McKinley contribute a nonrefundable fee—perhaps $50 or $100—to a rescue fund. Then rescue costs would be shared by all the mountain's users. But Denali's mountaineering staff fears that climbers would be more inclined to ask for help, rather than take care of themselves, if they paid money into any kind of rescue account. The end result could be even greater dependence on the Park Service. Rangers emphasize that the required payments McKinley mountaineers have made to the Park Service since the mid-1990s is a "special use fee," not a rescue-fund charge. Originally $150, the fee had increased to $350 by 2012, with climbers twenty-four and younger required to pay $250. In Europe, where climbing insurance is a normal part of mountaineers' expenses, rescues are a common, everyday occurrence. That's something park rangers want to avoid on McKinley.

It's also unlikely that the Park Service will ever reinstate the more restrictive application/approval system employed during the 1950s and '60s, suggested by some people to reduce rescues. As Seibert commented in 1989, "What we've seen is a movement toward keeping the mountain as open and free to individual choice as possible. We don't want to create new [or reestablish old] restrictions."

From the late 1980s through the end of the nineties, the Park Service's more open system seemed to work well. In the fall of 1989, Seibert said:

> I think people did take advantage of the system for a while. But the number of rescues has declined noticeably since the mid-1980s. To have only four organized rescues [in 1989] when people spent 19,000 to 20,000 visitor nights on McKinley is incredible to me. Maybe we've just been lucky, but I don't think so. It seems climbers are helping each other more now, instead of depending on the Park Service. They're better informed and better prepared. Plus we're not responding to rescue requests when it's obvious we're not needed. The whole operation has been greatly professionalized the last six or seven years.

Park Service rescue statistics seemed to back up Seibert's claims that McKinley mountaineers were exhibiting increased self-reliance—and perhaps better judgment. From 1979 to 1983, the agency organized nearly nineteen rescue missions per year, with a high of twenty-three and low of thirteen. But from 1984 to 1989, the number of government-coordinated-and-paid-for rescues ranged from three to six per year, with an average of five.

Rescues rose substantially during the 1990s, averaging nearly twelve per year that decade, largely because of a three-year period

(1992 to 1994) in which rescue and recovery missions ranged from fourteen to twenty-two. Still, at the end of the nineties, Miller said that Seibert's 1989 comments largely held true: overall, McKinley mountaineers were a self-sufficient bunch. But over the next decade, climber dependence on the Park Service once more began to increase; as mentioned above, the Park Service had to organize 112 search-and-rescue operations over the eight-year span from 2004 through 2011, an average of 14 SARs per year. At the same time, increased numbers of climbers began to request ranger assistance, and some demanded to be airlifted off the mountain for relatively minor injuries or illness. In 2012, Leonard admitted, "as manager of the program, one thing I really struggle with is that our rescue system does have the unintended consequence of making [McKinley's] mountaineers less self-reliant. Our main job is visitor and resource protection; we're not just here to bail people out if they get in trouble. But a lot of people seem to believe that is our only job.

"In a way, our rescues act like advertising. People see us help other climbers off the mountain and they think we'll bail them out too. We get people with minor injuries requesting help and evacuation. It becomes a huge drain on our resources when people who don't really need our help demand it. This has become a much bigger problem than it was in the 1990s. It's very frustrating at times."

Even when the overall system seemed to be working well, Denali's mountaineering rangers were disturbed that foreigners accounted for an inordinately high percentage of rescues—and deaths. In 1986, for example, about 25 percent of the mountain's crowd was from overseas, yet nine of ten evacuations and all four fatalities involved foreign climbers. In 1988, 36 percent of McKinley's climbers came from outside the United States, but seven of twelve rescue missions (58 percent) involved foreigners. And in 1989,

PETER HACKETT, M.D.

THE DENALI MEDICAL RESEARCH PROJECT CAMP AT14,200 FEET SERVED AS MEDICAL LABORATORY, COMMUNICATIONS BASE, AND RESCUE CENTER FROM 1982 UNTIL 1990.

overseas climbers again accounted for 36 percent of McKinley's total count, yet half the people needing some sort of organized rescue assistance (seven of fourteen climbers) were from other countries. And all six 1989 fatalities were foreigners.

That worrisome trend continued into the 1990s. Between 1991 and 1994, foreign climbers comprised 33 percent of McKinley's mountaineers, yet they were involved in 62 percent of the search-and-rescue missions and accounted for fourteen of seventeen deaths.

Seibert believed that such statistics reflect different climbing attitudes:

> What it comes down to is that foreigners seem willing to accept a higher level of risk, despite our warnings. Foreign parties travel lower glaciers unroped. They travel portions of their routes without the use of ice axes and ropes. And they ascend at a faster rate than is recommended to allow proper acclimatization.

> We're giving good solid information [made available through pre-expedition briefings and in mountaineering brochures produced in several languages]. And in most cases, we believe communication with climbing parties is not a problem. It seems to be a clear and conscious decision on the part of foreign climbers to adopt travel modes we don't recommend.

Others offered additional reasons. "Too many people who've climbed in other parts of the world underestimate Denali," suggested Peter Hackett, a high-altitude medicine specialist who ran the Denali Medical Research Project from 1982 through 1989. "They don't seem to understand it's a whole different ball game, climbing in a polar environment; people come here not realizing how cold, how vicious, the weather can be. The first two weeks of May at 14,000 feet, you can count on −40° temperatures every night."[9]

Many climbers from other nations tend to view McKinley as merely a stepping stone to Himalayan expeditions, when in fact its weather and physical demands rival those of the highest Himalayan peaks. Europeans–and Asians–used to climbing smaller mountains in the Alps come to McKinley expecting to "dance right up it," mountaineering guide Gary Bocarde once commented. "When the weather's good, it's usually not a problem. But if a storm comes up, that's when bad things start to happen."

Others point to language barriers. It's true the National Park Service for years has offered pre-expedition briefings in a variety of languages, up to nine by 2012. But once on the mountain, non-English-speaking climbers miss out on the word-of-mouth survival tips and weather updates often passed from team to team.

The role of cultural influences–which run far deeper than climbing techniques or language difficulties–was tragically demonstrated in the early 1990s by Korean mishaps on McKinley. In 1991, only 5 percent (50 of 935) of McKinley's mountaineers were

Koreans, yet they accounted for six of eleven people who needed rescue. In 1992, the number of Korean climbers dropped to forty. But six of those required rescue–including four who were hospitalized–and three others died.

The rash of rescues and deaths–several of them apparently tied to poor judgment–led park rangers, mountaineers, and many non-climbers to openly wonder: just what is the problem with Korean climbers? In hopes of finding some answers to that pressing question, South District chief ranger J. D. Swed traveled to Seoul in November 1992, as a guest of the Korean Alpine Federation. He left the Asian country ten days later with a much better understanding of the cultural forces that push Korean climbers.

"Koreans are driven by a set of pressures that are, for lack of a better word, foreign to us," Swed explained afterward. "They have a lot more invested in their trips to Denali than [Americans] do."

For starters, he found that Koreans as a rule received only five vacation days per year. That meant they either had to quit their jobs, or receive company sponsorships, to participate in McKinley expeditions. But company support brings its own special pressures. Failure to reach the summit is often considered an embarrassment, shameful. And it likely meant the end of corporate support. Conversely, success on big-name peaks like McKinley could lead to fame and riches in a country where climbing is a national passion.

Another contributing factor had nothing to do with cultural pressures. Traditionally, climbers wishing to join McKinley expeditions had to get special permission from the Korean Alpine Federation. And only the country's most skilled mountaineers received such approval. But that policy ended, resulting in a surge of Koreans to the Alaska Range. According to Swed, the number of Koreans attempting Denali jumped from three in 1990 to fifty in 1991. It made sense that increased numbers and decreased expertise would equal more rescues and deaths.

Unsure of how he'd be received by Korea's climbing community, Swed was delighted by the spirit of cooperation that surrounded his visit. In ten days, he explained the Park Service's concerns—and the nature of McKinley mountaineering—to hundreds of people: members of the Korean Alpine Federation, climbing instructors, magazine editors, and climbing club representatives.

"To their credit, they agreed there's a problem that requires a solution. Everyone seemed dedicated to the fact that there have to be some changes," he said. "The people I talked to were quite embarrassed by Korea's rescue and death rate on Denali. We all realize there won't be a quick fix; we're talking about cultural issues. It's going to take a continuing education program and further exchanges. In the long run, I'm hoping my visit will help save lives, or even fingers and toes."

He further emphasized, "This isn't just a Korean problem. There have been other periods [on McKinley] when we've had a rash of German accidents, or French, or Japanese. Maybe we could travel to other countries, conduct similar exchanges. I think we'll have to be less reactive and more proactive, if we're going to solve this problem."

A shift did in fact begin to occur in the mid-1990s. Between 1995 and 1998, foreign climbers comprised 39 percent of all McKinley mountaineers and were involved in 41 percent of the rescues—a dramatic drop from the early 1990s. During the same four-year period, six foreigners died, another significant decline. Rangers attributed the change to improved communication and climber education; revisions of the Park Service's mountaineering booklet, with an increased emphasis on climber self-sufficiency; and the sixty-day advance registration, which helps them reach out to mountaineers long before they get to Talkeetna or the Alaska Range.

That hopeful trend continued into the first years of the twenty-first century. In the nine years between 1999 and 2007, four of McKinley's seven fatalities (57%) were foreign climbers, but only two of those came from countries where English is not the primary language. And only one Korean died during that period, suggesting that Swed's visit to Korea made a difference. No more than one climber from any country outside the US died during that span. In four of the nine years (1999-2001 and 2003) no climbers died.

After that heartening thirteen-year stretch from 1995 to 2007, fatalities jumped again beginning in 2008, with an average of more than four deaths per year through 2012. More than two-thirds of those who died—fifteen of twenty-two—were foreigners. Six climbers died in both 2011 and 2012, the most since 1995; three who died in 2011 were members of guided parties, the most ever in one season, and ten of the twelve who died during those two seasons were foreigners. That toll, like the increased number of rescues—and rescue requests—served as a reminder that even with improved communications between park staff and climbers, plus efforts to increase climber awareness of McKinley's dangers, climber safety, good judgment, and self-reliance will always remain key challenges.

Whatever degree of success the Park Service has had on McKinley, some Alaskan mountaineers and guides have insisted that its policies inevitably foster dependency rather than self-help. Fairbanks-area climbers belonging to the Alaskan Alpine Club, a group devoted to the defense and preservation of mountaineering freedoms, have been especially critical. Chief spokesperson Doug Buchanan frequently and regularly attacked Park Service management of McKinley during much of the 1980s and 1990s and into the 2000s; in 2011, the club's website (maintained by Buchanan) continued to express its support for "self-responsibility, mutual assistance, and the rights of climbers" while decrying the intrusion of the Park Service on climber's rights.

One of Buchanan's longstanding objections has been the regulation that requires climbers to register with the Park Service before any McKinley expedition. Park officials have noted that registration is needed for safety and climber-education reasons, but Buchanan has argued that such an explanation implies that the government will come to the rescue if climbers get into trouble:

> There's an inherent human tendency to prepare less well, or take more chances, if you know there's assistance available. Whether consciously or subconsciously, in your mind you know you're covered in an emergency situation. You're given a false sense of security and no amount of warnings or cautions can negate that.
>
> But the thing is, there's no way the Park Service can back up its implication of safety; it can't always provide adequate emergency services to people who need it. Nobody except God could guarantee that kind of help. So in essence, the Park Service has made McKinley a more dangerous, deadly place. The registration system is the basic cause of most [McKinley] accidents, but no one will acknowledge that.

In response, Daryl Miller in the late 1990s emphasized that McKinley is "more than just a mountain. First and foremost, it's national parkland and rangers are charged with protecting visitors." Leonard, his successor, also has pointed out the Park Service's mandate to protect both the mountain and the people who come to climb it.

Buchanan in 1990 also accused the Park Service of refusing to cooperate with Alaskan volunteer mountain-rescue groups. Calling the claim ridiculous, Seibert countered that the Park Service has used such volunteer groups on a few occasions and once even enlisted Buchanan's help. But normally when rescue help is needed, park officials recruit people already on the mountain, because they're acclimated to high altitudes and in a position to provide immediate assistance.

Since the mid-1970s, a large percentage of rescue teams have included professional guides (though the Park Service has become less reliant on them in recent years) and Denali National Park's mountaineering rangers have many times praised McKinley's guides for their invaluable assistance. But over the years, even some of the mountain's best-known and most respected guides have admitted that they can become annoyed or frustrated by other climbers' frequent and sometimes unnecessary calls for help.

Gary Bocarde, the founder and longtime owner of Anchorage-based guide service Mountain Trip, once observed:

> So many people up there expect someone to take care of them if they get in trouble. I've been involved in rescues where people say, 'Thanks for taking care of our partner,' then they're gone and we're left to take over. That's happened too many times. In fact some of our expeditions have failed to reach the summit because our guides have been so busy helping other people.

And Brian Okonek, cofounder of Alaska Denali Guiding and its director for nearly two decades before he and his wife, Diane, sold the business in 2000, has noted, "Too many [McKinley] climbers don't have the experience or training–or both–to rescue a buddy if they get in trouble. So what happens is that guides are asked to help. It's interesting that people feel a need to ask for help instead of taking care of themselves."

Not much had changed in that regard by 2012. Like Bocarde and Okonek before him, Colby Coombs of the Alaska Mountaineering School admitted his frustration that "I spend so much time helping people [from other parties] in over their heads, instead of trying to summit."

Leonard agrees that unnecessary calls for help can be exasperating, for both guides and park staff, and he acknowledges the crucial contributions that McKinley's guides have made over the years. But in 2012, Leonard also noted that Denali's mountaineering rangers are "less dependent on guides than we once were. There was a time when we were overwhelmingly dependent on them; now they're a key component, but we have many other resources," including the increased presence of ranger-led volunteer patrols and high-altitude helicopter assistance.

"We continue to have great partnerships with McKinley's guides and value their help," Leonard added, "but in recent years their role has been over-portrayed. We get help from everyone we can, whether guides or private climbers or volunteers."

Yet another source of rescue assistance, and of debate, was introduced in 1982, when park officials allowed a group of scientists to establish the Denali Medical Research Project at McKinley's 14,200-foot level. The research camp was originally funded by a state grant given to Anchorage physician Dr. William Mills, a pioneer in the study and treatment of cold-related injuries and chairperson of the University of Alaska Anchorage's Center for High Latitude Health Research.[10]

In promoting the project, Mills emphasized that McKinley is an ideal laboratory for investigating cold-weather injuries or high-altitude illnesses. Each year, dozens of McKinley mountaineers fall victim to the cold and altitude, suffering frostbite, hypothermia, or mountain sickness. A mountain medical camp would enable doctors and other scientists to get frequent, first-hand looks at those ailments. And the knowledge gained from their research could help government, private industry, and private individuals save millions of dollars in rescue and medical costs. At the same time, Mills argued, "It's a sheer, absolute waste not to benefit from the price [McKinley climbers] pay in the form of sickness, injury and death."

Still, his proposal was initially greeted with skepticism. Many McKinley mountaineers, guides, and park rangers worried that the presence of such a camp would encourage climbers to take greater risks or become even more dependent on outside assistance. The Park Service also felt it might be too "high-tech" for average climbers and intrude on their wilderness experience.

Despite their reservations, park officials agreed to experiment with a research camp. In 1981, a site search was initiated and two locations were chosen: the 7,200-foot Kahiltna Glacier Base Camp; and the 14,200-foot basin located along McKinley's West Buttress Route. (The lower medical camp was eliminated in 1985.) "Fourteen thousand is definitely the primo spot," said project director Peter Hackett. "It's high enough to be in on a lot of the action and low enough so that we get most of the sick climbers coming down. Plus it's a safe spot; it's protected. And there's plenty of room."

The mountain laboratory at 14,200 feet was set up in May of 1982. By the end of the climbing season, the researchers had clearly demonstrated their worth. More than one hundred people had been treated for illness and/or injury. And project workers were credited with saving the lives of two Japanese climbers who suffered major injuries in a fall at 16,000 feet. For the first time in four years, no deaths were reported on the mountain, and air-supported evacuations were reduced. "That first year proved our value for rescue as well as research," Hackett said.

There's no question McKinley's researchers made climbers more aware of high-altitude sickness, its prevention and treatment. While the medical camp was in place, no one died from mountain sickness and the number of air evacuations dropped dramatically. From 1974 to 1981, thirteen aircraft rescues involved climbers suffering from high-altitude illness; from 1982 to 1989, only two people were flown off McKinley because of mountain sickness. "When the medical team tells people they need to drop down a couple thousand feet [to recover], most people take the advice," ranger Bob Seibert said in 1989, "whereas in the past, they would try to continue climbing and frequently get themselves in trouble."

Park Service statistics also show that air-supported evacuations of frostbite victims dropped sharply in the mid- to late 1980s. Rangers attributed this fact to improved climber education, both by park staff and the research camp's medical staff.

While mountaineers clearly benefitted from the researchers' presence, Hackett argued that there was no evidence climbers had become overly dependent on the camp, or taken greater risks. "People realize we're not there to babysit," he said. "They still have to be prepared."

Seibert agreed that the Park Service's early concerns about the medical camp's creating climber dependency and carelessness didn't materialize. Ironically enough, it was the government that relied heavily on the research project's services and life-saving capabilities. Because of its location, the camp made an ideal communication platform. Improved radio contact made rescue operations more efficient. Seibert admitted:

> One of our biggest problems before the camp was very poor radio communications with expeditions that were in trouble. Time and again, we were unable to determine the extent of the problem, so we'd have to anticipate a worst-case scenario. Often, we'd end up discovering that people didn't really need to be rescued. Now, with the improved communications, we're able to accurately assess the nature of the response needed.

In addition, the camp served as a base of rescue operations. Researchers and/or rangers stationed at 14,200 feet were already acclimatized to high elevations and thus better able to deal with high-altitude emergencies.

Though the Park Service clearly became attached to the research project, some mountaineers and guides still had second thoughts about the medical team's presence. Harry Johnson, owner of Genet Expeditions in Anchorage, said in 1987:

> There's no clear-cut answer. Over-dependence is still a concern. I think maybe some climbers have gotten spoiled knowing the camp is there. I think it's attracted some climbers who aren't qualified to be on the mountain, or made some climbers more careless. At the same time, it's been a real life-saver for a helluva lot of people. And as the owner of a guide service, it's nice to have them there, to deal with medical problems when necessary. Certainly there have been no environmental or visual problems. The camp is well located, it's clean. There's both good things and bad things about it. But overall, I'd have to say it's probably been good for McKinley.

Despite some lingering questions about its impact on climber self-sufficiency, the Denali Medical Research Project received worldwide acclaim. The camp, like the mountain, was unique, with nothing else quite like it in the world. Each May, Hackett and his coworkers would load several thousand pounds of food, fuel, and gear onto Army helicopters and fly in to 14,200 feet, where they remained for about two months. Activities centered around two red Quonset-style huts. One was for cooking and eating; the other was a laboratory, filled with a quarter million dollars' worth of medical equipment, ranging from exercise bicycles to computerized gas analyzers and oxygen saturation detectors.

After starting up the project in 1982, McKinley's researchers pioneered several high-altitude and cold-weather studies, with the help of a large volunteer force. They measured and analyzed fluid buildups in sick climbers' lungs and brains, tested various drugs for their effectiveness in treating mountain sickness, experimented with biofeedback techniques to keep toes and fingers warm, and checked climbers for signs of stress. "We get more data for the dollar than anywhere," said Hackett. "And the big thing we have going for us is sick people; we hang out where it's happening, where people keep getting themselves in trouble. Not many scientists are willing to do that."

Despite its proven value, the medical camp closed down in 1990, partly because of funding difficulties, but also because Hackett, the prime force behind the project, decided to pursue other interests. Park rangers, however, have continued to use the 14,200-foot camp as a base of operations from which they conduct patrols and rescues and provide other assistance where and when appropriate. The first patrol arrives at McKinley in late April. During the mid-May to mid-June peak of the season, anywhere from two to four teams will be on the mountain, at least a couple of them at 14,200 feet or higher. Each patrol consists of a ranger with paramedic training plus four volunteers, one of them a physician whenever possible.

Rangers, guides, and other McKinley climbers expressed mixed feelings about the research project's absence. Certainly the doctors' expertise and treatment would be missed. But without the medical facility, the mountain had again become a little wilder, affording modern-day mountaineers the opportunity to better follow the example set by McKinley's self-sufficient pioneers. Whether or not they do so is an entirely different matter. For several years after the facility's closure, climbers did show increased self-reliance; but entering the second decade of the twenty-first century, it seems too many McKinley mountaineers are once again asking for help when they don't need it, or taking risks they shouldn't. And the question, once more, is how to reverse that dangerous trend.

BILL SHERWONIT

MCKINLEY'S INCREASED POPULARITY IN THE LATE 1900S AND EARLY 2000S LED TO TRASH AND SANITATION PROBLEMS THAT DENALI NATIONAL PARK'S MOUNTAINEERING STAFF HAVE ADDRESSED WITH A SERIES OF EFFECTIVE POLICIES THAT HAVE LEFT THE HIGH ONE CLEANER IN 2012 THAN IT HAS BEEN IN CLOSE TO HALF A CENTURY. FOR SEVERAL YEARS, THE PARK EMPLOYED LATRINES, LIKE THE ONE SHOWN IN THE PHOTO, AT POPULAR CAMPSITES ALONG THE WEST BUTTRESS ROUTE, BUT THOSE HAVE BEEN REPLACED BY A SYSTEM THAT UTILIZES "CLEAN MOUNTAIN CANS."

Chapter Fourteen

Mountain of Trash

THE TRASHING OF Mount McKinley began in the early 1900s, when geologists, explorers, and climbers first walked the mountain's slopes. Back then, before the age of environmental awareness and governmental regulations, expeditions typically lightened their loads when departing the mountain by leaving behind any excess items not required on the journey home.

In 1903, while approaching the Peters Glacier on McKinley's north side, Frederick Cook's party was surprised to find the Wickersham Expedition's abandoned base camp, which had been deserted two months earlier. Among the items left behind was a coffee can full of salt, which the Cook team happily salvaged. The rest, presumably, was left to slowly decay or rust. It certainly didn't benefit other explorers, since nearly a decade passed before another expedition passed that way.

Perhaps the most candid and illuminating description of the pioneers' leave-it-behind philosophy was provided by Hudson Stuck in his 1914 book *The Ascent of Denali*.[1] During its ascent of Karstens Ridge, the Stuck party discovered the remains of a camp made by members of the Parker-Browne Expedition a year earlier. Scattered on the discolored snow were an empty biscuit carton, a raisin package, brown paper, and other trash—all "as fresh as though they had been left yesterday instead of a year ago." At another campsite above the ridge, the team found a shovel and an empty alcohol can.

Stuck's description of how his team discarded their supplies on their descent is even more revealing. On leaving high camp at 18,000 feet, the climbers left behind a pile of gear with no concern for littering the mountain. As Stuck matter-of-factly noted:

> Perhaps never did men abandon as cheerfully stuff that had been freighted as laboriously as we abandoned our surplus baggage at the eighteen-thousand-foot camp. We made a great pile of it in the lee of one of the ice-blocks of the glacier—food, coal-oil, clothing, and bedding—covering all with the wolf-robe and setting up a shovel as a mark; though just why we cached it so carefully, or for whom, no one of us would be able to say. It will probably be a long time ere any others camp in that Grand Basin.

A similar pattern was followed down the mountain. The climbers departed their upper Muldrow Glacier camp, leaving tent, wood supply, and unneeded gear behind. And back in the foothills below the glacier, "we made our final abandonment, leaving the tent standing with stove and fuel and many articles that we did not need cached in it."

Such abandonments remained the rule rather than the exception for several decades. Some groups simply left unneeded or unwanted supplies sitting on the ground, while others buried fuel, food, and equipment in the snow. Some of the largest caches were made by scientific expeditions supported by airdrops.

In his *National Geographic* account of the 1951 West Buttress expedition, Bradford Washburn recounted how he and teammates found caches left four years earlier at Denali Pass:

> A shapeless bundle appeared ahead. . . . This was the cache of cosmic ray apparatus that was left there by our 1947 expedition, which had climbed the other side of McKinley. It was still neatly covered with the yellow rayon cargo parachutes with which it had been dropped to us by the 10th Rescue Squadron.[2]

While the cosmic-ray equipment remained neatly packaged, another cache left by the 1947 expedition was in shambles. Washburn wrote:

> A shocking scene of confusion met our eyes. The party which had climbed McKinley in 1948, probably in desperate need of supplies, had ripped off the tents and parachutes with which we had covered the cache and left it unprotected. Snow and ice, driven by screaming gales, had penetrated every crack and cranny. The whole heap was frozen into a solid, rigid mass. Only about a third of the supplies remained.

Remnants of the scientific caches were still highly visible two decades after being left behind. The large cache that Art Davidson, Ray Genet, and Dave Johnston found during their 1967 winter ascent was scattered on the snow at Denali Pass. Starved for food after surviving a weeklong storm, the climbers' search through the rubble revealed a shredded tarp, smashed wooden crates, torn clothes, and silverware. They suspected the cache was most likely one that Washburn had carefully prepared at the conclusion of a scientific expedition, but, as Davidson noted, "Twenty years of storms and curious climbers had left it a trash heap half buried in the ice."[3] Digging deeper into the cache, Davidson had found rotted rope, pots, socks, boots, ladles, several boxes of clothes, and, at the bottom, life-giving food.

Though the twenty-year-old cache helped to save three climbers' lives, it also demonstrated one of the problems with leaving supplies on the mountain. Sooner or later, many caches have been either scavenged by ravens, torn apart by storms, or left in a mess by other climbers. Particularly at elevations above 14,000 feet—where high winds scour the mountain and hinder burial by snow—supplies, trash, and human waste could litter McKinley's slopes for decades, possibly centuries.

Nonetheless, the gradual accumulation of garbage and human waste wasn't a pressing issue through the first five or six decades of McKinley mountaineering. Even into the mid-1960s, no more than a few dozen people attempted to climb the peak each year. "People figured the mountain's so vast, the glaciers are so huge, that the garbage they left wouldn't make any difference," says Anchorage mountaineer Steve Davis.[4] But as steadily increasing numbers of climbers continued to show disregard for McKinley's environment, the once-pristine mountain was gradually turning into North America's highest garbage dump.

One of the first to publicize the mess and to do something about cleaning it up was Gary Grimm, head of the University of Oregon's Outdoor Program. Climbing the West Buttress Route in 1971, Grimm discovered a one-hundred-square-foot garbage heap at 16,000 feet. Dumped on the snow was a conglomeration of cans, plastic bags, aluminum foil, paper bottles, new and broken equipment, underwear, half-burned parachutes, human feces, and even some lightweight plywood boards (probably used in airdropped crates).

According to a report in the National Wildlife Federation's *Conservation News*,[5] Grimm and six companions burned what garbage they could, buried whatever couldn't be moved or burned, and carried the rest down the mountain. The climbing and clean-up team recovered about 380 pounds of junk from McKinley's slopes–a good haul, certainly, but it was only a small, first step.

Grimm placed much of the blame for the accumulation of trash on commercial guides, "who seem to be more interested in profits than in environmental quality. They won't bother to bring [their trash] back because their clients don't pay to carry garbage."

Upon returning to Eugene, he created the Denali Arctic Environmental Project and proposed that twenty climbers from Pacific Northwest schools, including his own, return to McKinley in 1973 for a massive trash pickup. The American Alpine Club provided partial funding for the project, as well as the use of four tents and communications equipment, but most costs were paid by those participating in the program.

Between 1973 and 1976, Denali Project teams cleared tons of garbage from the West Buttress, while criticizing "the irresponsibility of previous expeditions in the pollution of this route."[6] Their efforts and commentary stimulated a greater environmental awareness within the climbing community. But many mountaineers continued to either ignore the problem or argue that it didn't exist. Ray Genet, well on his way to becoming a McKinley legend, told the *Anchorage Daily News* in 1974:

> It used to be called caching and now it's called trashing. It's not a major problem. Most of the expeditions just need to be better organized and need to have the guide tell them to dig latrines. People bitch about other people's garbage but all they need to do is pick up their own.

Despite Genet's protestations, many climbers making their first trip to McKinley were disgusted by what they found. Anchorage resident Peter Blewett told the paper that he'd planned to sleep in an already-built snow cave at 17,200 feet, but he "took one look inside the cave and decided to sleep in the tent. It was just absolutely a garbage dump. People had left every conceivable item in there." Blewett also reported finding a rolled-up mattress stuffed in the snow with an empty beer can on top:

> It does ruin the aesthetic experience. You're up there, so far away, and the purity of the mountain and glacier is what you're going there to experience. But it was like going over some camping trail and stumbling over someone's beer cans. It was a great shock.

The National Park Service, charged with managing McKinley, agreed a serious problem existed. In 1964, park officials had enacted a regulation prohibiting airdrops on the mountain. They already had a pack-it-in, pack-it-out policy in place, but rules against littering were difficult, if not entirely impossible, to enforce. A park official explained in 1974, "It's impossible to have rangers scampering all over the mountain making sure each climber picks up his dehydrated chili con carne packages."

Park rangers put much of the blame on inexperienced climbers who packed in more equipment than needed, then discarded it. They also pointed to increasing numbers of foreign climbers, who hadn't developed a "Keep America Clean" consciousness.

Though the West Buttress Route had become McKinley's most obvious eyesore, other paths to the summit were gradually being trashed as well. By the early 1980s, technically difficult routes used by a relatively small number of climbers had their own garbage dumps. In *Surviving Denali*, Jonathan Waterman noted that a burned-out tent was visible at 15,200 feet on the West Rib and that human feces dotted the snow both there and at the 16,500-foot campsite.[7] And at 16,500 feet on the Cassin Ridge:

> Climbers have jettisoned excess weight from their packs; looking around in the obvious, sheltered tent site, one can find assorted hardware, a new climbing rope, a pair of long underwear, books, and various pieces of trash. . . . One must select cooking snow very carefully from among the wasteland of brown turds.

On the Muldrow Glacier, meanwhile, climbers can find remains of old canvas tents, sardine cans, and rotted clothing.

Increasingly frustrated with garbage and sanitation problems on McKinley, the Park Service finally initiated its own clean-up campaign in the late 1970s, with an emphasis on climber education. Since then, rangers have refined and expanded the ways in which they communicate the need to "climb clean." One of their tools is a mountaineering booklet sent to anyone expressing interest in climbing McKinley. Printed in nine languages (English, Japanese, German, French, Spanish, Korean, Russian, Polish, and Italian), the booklet outlines the Park Service's leave no trace policies. Under waste disposal, climbers are informed:[8]

- Everything brought into the park must be brought out Abandoning surplus gear, food, fuel, or wands is not allowed Violators will be issued citations.
- (Other than on the West Buttress), fixed lines and protection should be removed on descent.
- Caches must be properly labeled with expedition, name, permit number, and return date. Permanent caches are illegal Mark caches with 5 to 6 foot (1.5 to 2 meter) wands.
- For human waste, use latrines at 7,200 feet (2,200 meters) and 14,200 feet (4,300 meters). Use CMCs (Clean Mountain Cans, dis-

cussed below) to remove waste elsewhere. [The latrines where eliminated in 2011.] Use biodegradable bags and crevasse human waste if CMCs are not available.
- Use a central urine spot and mark it with a wand.

Another avenue of education is the pre-expedition check-in required of McKinley mountaineers. Assisted by computer graphics and interpreters when necessary, rangers discuss the how-tos and whys of clean climbing.

By the late 1980s, the majority of climbers had taken the anti-litter message to heart. Despite much larger crowds, particularly on the West Buttress, "The mountain is cleaner now than when I first went there in 1973," McKinley guide Brian Okonek said in 1989. But he noted, "There are still too many people who don't police themselves. It just takes a few to make it unsightly. Littering is one of my personal pet peeves; I can't believe someone would go to such an incredible place and leave their garbage."

Another source of frustration was the widespread practice of dumping garbage into crevasses, rather than hauling it off the mountain.

Guides and rangers agreed that much of the littering and crevasse-dumping was being done by climbers from other countries. "I don't want to point fingers, but the fact is that foreigners in many cases don't seem as environmentally aware," ranger Bob Seibert said in the late 1980s. "They leave more trash and don't dispose of feces." On the cusp of the new millennium, chief mountaineering ranger Daryl Miller said Seibert's comments remained "a fair assessment of the situation."

Those who continued to trash the mountain were subject to fines. In 1984, a European team was fined $500 in federal court ($250 was suspended) after being cited by park rangers for leaving a garbage heap at 17,000 feet, and in 1989, two fines, of $150 each, were levied against American parties for littering. More recently, six mountaineers were each fined $100 in 1997 and nine climbers–all of them Europeans–were cited and required to pay $100 each in 1999. Because such penalties were for many years few and far between, Fairbanks mountaineer Doug Buchanan criticized the Park Service for inadequate enforcement of its garbage-removal regulations:

> If the Park Service really wanted to solve McKinley's so-called garbage problem–and I'm not sure there really is one–they could easily do so by arresting more people. That would stop it fast. The West Buttress should be one of the easiest places in the world to enforce littering regulations, because camping is concentrated in a few small areas.

Rangers argued that enforcement was difficult because only one Park Service team patrolled McKinley at any given time. "Making a litter case is very difficult," Seibert explained in 1989. "Either you have to see them doing it, or tie them directly to the garbage." Ten years later, Miller asserted, "That's still absolutely true." Even when citations were issued, climbers–particularly those from outside the United States–didn't necessarily pay their fines, which are misdemeanor penalties.

The situation has improved substantially since 2000, for a number of reasons. First, more Park Service teams are patrolling the mountain; between two and four roam McKinley's slopes during the mid-May to mid-June peak. Second, all climbers are now issued NPS trash bags and Clean Mountain Cans (the latter are discussed in more detail below) before they begin their expeditions, and they're checked for compliance on returning to base camp. At the same time, more citations are being issued and fines levied. In 2012, South District Ranger John Leonard said "We're fining at least a few climbers $150 every year." Violators are cautioned they could be banned from climbing in any of America's national parks if they don't pay and, Leonard adds, international mountaineers are further warned "they may have problems gaining future entry into the US" if they don't make good on the fines. New technologies have enabled the agency to compile an online database that gives its warning more bite. Consequently more climbers are paying the fines and word has spread that enforcement is stricter. Finally, as discussed in the following chapter ("Guiding on McKinley"), more people from outside the United States are climbing McKinley with American guiding companies, which ensures greater compliance with Denali National Park's climbing policies.

"Things have gotten a lot better," Leonard said in 2012. "It's still not 100 percent, but we've had success in closing the gap [between American and foreign climbers]."

As the mountain slowly grew cleaner in the last two decades of the 1900s, an even more frustrating–and worrisome–problem than garbage was the increase of human waste on McKinley. By the late 1980s, sanitation had become a substantially bigger problem than littering.

The Park Service didn't begin emphasizing human-waste controls until 1984. Over the next five years, rangers built communal pit latrines at the Kahiltna Glacier Base Camp, the starting point for most McKinley expeditions, as well as at campsites at 14,200 feet and 17,200 feet along the West Buttress Route. By the late 1990s, there were two latrines each at Kahiltna Base Camp, 11,000 feet, and 14,200 feet, and one at 17,200 feet.

Rangers advised climbers to use the communal latrines where present; elsewhere, McKinley mountaineers were instructed to dig their own latrines (or use snow pits left by other teams), line the pits with garbage bags (staked down to keep them from blowing away), and then use the set-up for both feces and food scraps. When they finished using the bags, climbers were expected to drop them into a deep crevasse.

Okonek, a proponent of the Park Service's glacier waste-control system, explained why he supported it:

> [McKinley's crevasse system] is as good as any disposal site in the United States. The waste will go deep into the glacier and eventually be ground up and buried under tons of morainal material. I don't think you have to worry about it someday showing up in streams below the glacier. Certainly it's better than bringing human feces back to Talkeetna.

Others, however, have questioned the wisdom of using glacial crevasses and have expressed concern that the human feces and plastic bags in which they're stored will survive their trip to the snout of the glacier and someday—even if it's centuries from now—be flushed into river systems fed by the mountain's ice and contribute to water pollution.

As might be expected, the human-waste rules were hard to enforce and all too often they were ignored, especially at higher elevations. At 17,000 or above, people are so tired and worn out that they're less likely to follow the instructions. "Up high, you're just not thinking as clearly," Miller noted. "People are so incapacitated that they have problems even taking care of themselves. That's especially true after being struck by a series of storms; people struggle just getting in and out of their tents."

Over the decades, campsites at 16,200 and 17,200 feet had become particularly messy. Unlike the lower mountain, which is covered with new deposits of snow each year, upper slopes are often blasted by high winds that reveal, rather than hide, what's been left behind. A common complaint by those following the West Buttress Route was the abundance of urine stains and piles of frozen feces at the high camp. Besides being an eyesore at such spots, the human waste can also create health problems if climbers happen to melt contaminated snow for consumption.

To ease the waste problem at 17,200 feet, the Park Service installed a pit toilet there in 1989. It received enough use that rangers had to dig four holes during the April-through-July climbing season. Rather than remove the waste, they buried it. Though the latrine helped, Okonek was concerned about the available space for future pits at that altitude. The high camp is located in a basin of stagnant ice that isn't moving like the glaciers below. Wastes buried in that basin "will just stay there," said Okonek, who suggested that perhaps waste from the pits should eventually be packed to glacial crevasses located 300 to 400 yards away.

In 1990, Denali's rangers began doing just that. The latrine at 17,200 feet was placed above a portable steel toilet lined with heavy-duty garbage bags. When filled with human waste, those bags were hauled down to crevasses lower on the mountain.

Though the latrines helped, they didn't adequately address the problem of fecal waste along other sections of the West Buttress, or the mountain's other routes; too many climbers didn't follow the Park Service's crevasse-drop rule. And questions remained about even that strategy and the long-term impacts of group latrines.

Longtime mountaineering ranger Roger Robinson believed there had to be a better way, and he made it his personal mission to solve McKinley's sanitation issue. In 2000, using portable toilets that had been developed for wilderness river trips, Robinson led a twenty-four-day patrol that showed it was possible to completely remove an expedition's solid human waste from McKinley's slopes. He then worked with the manufacturer to design a smaller, lighter version more suitable for mountaineers. With a grant from the American Alpine Club, Denali National Park staff purchased fifty of the prototype "Clean Mountain Cans" (CMCs), which rangers and volunteer mountaineers employed while on McKinley, with encouraging results. With the help of AAC and Access Fund grants, Robinson and Geo Toilet Systems produced an even more climber-friendly "can." And in 2002, some 500 climbers successfully used CMCs to remove their waste from the West Buttress's notoriously fecal-contaminated high camp at 17,200 feet.

The experimental program continued for a few seasons. Then, in 2007, the Park Service ended its use of a latrine at 17,200 feet and instead required climbers to remove all fecal waste from the West Buttress high camp. The agency followed that with a new policy that requires McKinley mountaineers to use CMCs everywhere on the mountain. By 2011, communal latrines were no longer employed, even at 14,200 feet and the Kahiltna Base Camp.

With an inventory of more than 1,000 CMCs, the Park Service now routinely loans them to climbers at the beginning of their McKinley expeditions. If, for some reason, a CMC is unavailable, climbers are required to "deposit" their waste into a biodegradable bag (also provided by the NPS) and dump it in a deep crevasse far from any well-used trails.[9]

At the end of the 1990s, despite considerable progress, Miller had lamented that "sanitation and garbage is still a huge problem. It's a much bigger problem than climber safety and we haven't come close to solving it. I'm not sure what the answer is, but one thing is certain: without ranger patrols it would be even worse. It makes me sad. People need to be more responsible."

By 2012, climbers seemed to be accepting that responsibility in unprecedented fashion. Mount McKinley hadn't been so free of garbage and human waste for half a century.

More than ever in modern times, the large majority of people who walk McKinley's slopes seem to understand this simple fact: though the mountain is huge, it can easily be trashed. Every person who climbs the great peak must do his or her part to keep McKinley clean.

George Wichman

RAY "PIRATE" GENET HELPED OPEN MCKINLEY TO ADVENTURE SEEKERS WITH LITTLE OR NO MOUNTAINEERING EXPERIENCE, BY ESTABLISHING THE FIRST FULL-TIME GUIDE SERVICE ON THE PEAK.

Chapter Fifteen

Guiding on McKinley

Ray "Pirate" Genet, more than anyone, made guiding a big-time business on Mount McKinley. And in doing so, he changed the nature of McKinley mountaineering forever.

As the first full-time guide on McKinley, Genet opened its slopes to those who otherwise wouldn't have the opportunity to climb the great peak. From the late 1960s through the end of the 1970s, he led literally hundreds of people to the mountain's top.

Pirate specialized in trips up the West Buttress, a climbing route that could be safely and successfully negotiated by adventurers with little or no mountaineering experience–provided they had the proper guidance, of course.

Genet had discovered the West Buttress while participating in the first winter ascent of McKinley in 1967. That expedition had been a turning point in Genet's life. On McKinley's slopes, the thirty-eight-year-old Swiss-born American found both an identity and an environment ideally suited to his aggressive personality, boundless energy, and restless spirit. No longer would he have to bounce around from job to job, searching for a comfortable niche. Always a capable salesman–he'd proved this to be true by talking his way onto the winter expedition despite marginal qualifications–Genet formed Alaska Mountain Guides, Inc. (later called Genet Expeditions) in 1968 and began promoting guided trips up McKinley's West Buttress.

Though one or two guided McKinley expeditions had been organized in the early 1960s, Genet's was the only business to operate regularly on the mountain from 1968 through the mid-1970s. With no competition and little, if any, regulatory control by the National Park Service, he had free rein to develop whatever guiding style he desired. From the start, his Pirate image was predominant.

With his closest friends, Genet felt free to show his gentle, warm, vulnerable side; in private he was often loving and sensitive to others' needs. But the public rarely, if ever, was witness to that side of his personality. What most people saw instead was the Pirate, complete with booming voice, black beard, leather vest, and bandanna-covered hair. Powerfully built, boisterous, and brash, Genet exuded machismo. And his mountaineering clients loved it.

"Ray was a very charismatic character," says Jim Hale, Talkeetna resident and Genet's assistant during the mid-1970s. "The winter ascent of McKinley gave him this heroic, tough-guy aura . . . and most of the people who climbed with him really enjoyed it."

Female clients especially found the macho mountaineer appealing. According to his friends and acquaintances, Genet was a flamboyant womanizer who enjoyed the following of a number of climbing groupies over the years, including some he hired as assistant guides.

Though he loved to have fun, Genet was all business when it came to getting his clients up McKinley. His motto "To the summit!" became his trademark. And he would do whatever was necessary to get his clients there. According to Hale:[1]

> Ray was incredibly powerful, a great judge of people, and a superb motivator. His purpose was to get people up and down and he didn't really care if his clients hated him or loved him for it. He'd do whatever it took: threaten, scream, yell. . . . His methods worked. I don't know what the exact percentages were, but Ray had a very high success rate.

Although he usually exhibited a domineering and hard-driving demeanor when pushing for the summit, Pirate could also be supportive and playful. Kathy Sullivan, who worked as Genet's assistant and later became his partner, recalls:

> You could have fear of him. But his power and his strength and his meanness and his anger and his force were just as high as his peace and his warmth and his comfort and his gentleness.
>
> If something was done improperly, he could blow his stack like an erupting volcano. But he was fun—he was a strong, fun, wild man. You could be out in the wilderness and trust him hanging on a rope with a drop of 10,000 feet below you. You could trust him to hang on to you.[2]

Joe Redington Sr., founder of the Iditarod Trail Sled Dog Race, found Pirate's often overpowering personality to be balanced by good judgment and an eagerness to share his passion for McKinley. With some guidance from Genet, Redington and Susan Butcher (winner of four Iditarod titles) mushed a team of four sled dogs to McKinley's summit. Afterward, Redington commented:

> I couldn't help but admire [Genet]. He was one of the strongest men for his size that I ever saw. He would carry a pack that I could hardly lift off the ground.
>
> I saw him work on some people that never would have made it there. Some of them he kind of abused a little bit. But his main purpose was to get them to the top. And when he got you to the summit, there was a sparkle in his eyes—he just took such extreme pleasure in helping others do what he loved to do. I never doubted his judgment in any way—not even with the dogs.

Another Genet trait was his preference for large expeditions. Groups of twenty to twenty-five were not uncommon. And once, assisted by three other guides, he led forty-three climbers up the mountain's slopes.

On a typical expedition, the Pirate actually spent little time with his clients. Assistant guides were responsible for getting the team from base camp to 16,000 or 17,000 feet. Genet, starting several days later, would then quickly ascend the mountain—traveling alone despite the dangers—catch up to the party, and lead the climbers to McKinley's summit. Once his clients had reached the top, Genet would descend ahead of the party, again leaving his assistants in charge.

When guiding large expeditions, Genet would usually divide the team into smaller parties for the final push from high camp. Then, one by one, he'd accompany each of the groups to the summit. Although he never led more than four expeditions in any given year—and averaged two or three per season from 1968 to 1979—the Pirate may have stood on McKinley's summit as many as forty-five to fifty different times during his twelve-year career.

As Genet's reputation grew and the number of his clients increased, he came to view McKinley as his private domain. In his eyes and in the eyes of many others, he was king of North America's largest mountain. So when competing guide companies began leading expeditions up the mountain in the mid-1970s, the Pirate quite naturally felt his turf was being invaded.

"Ray was very territorial about McKinley," says Gary Bocarde, the founder and longtime owner of Mountain Trip guide service. "He was real upset that there were other people guiding on his mountain, and he definitely felt it was his."

Genet did everything possible to protect his mountain kingdom. During the mid-1970s, the Pirate even convinced some rival companies that he alone owned a permit to operate on McKinley, which wasn't at all true. "Ray had a lot of people fooled; he really had 'em buffaloed," Hale recalls with a chuckle. "He had other guide services going to him, trying to work out a deal so they could work on McKinley."

Those he couldn't delude, Genet often chose to ignore. During the 1976 season, Bocarde's first as a McKinley guide, the Pirate refused to acknowledge his new rival's presence. Eventually he loosened up and the two got along reasonably well, but Bocarde always found it difficult to accept Genet's guiding methods. "Ray definitely had his own unique style," Bocarde says. "His attitude was, 'I'll get you up there, no matter what.' That kind of attitude can be dangerous."

Hale also had difficulty accepting some aspects of the Pirate's leadership style and parted company with Genet after assisting on three expeditions. "Ray was really set in his ways," Hale explains. "Things were fine as long as you did things his way. But if you challenged his ideas, look out. He was very authoritarian in that respect."

While guiding a large group of Genet clients in July 1975, Hale and another assistant, Tom Ross, decided to turn back at 14,000 feet because of extreme avalanche danger. Neither Ross nor Hale wanted to risk injury or death. While descending, the expedition ran into Genet—getting his usual delayed start—who was furious that his assistants had retreated. Hale recalls:

> It was then he told me he'd made a decision early in his career never to turn around. His philosophy was to always go to the summit, no matter what. Well, I couldn't go along with that. And I didn't like the idea that I was responsible for people's lives, but didn't have any authority to make decisions. It was obvious we couldn't work together; we'd reached an impasse. So I kind of quit and got fired at the same time.

Art Davidson, who developed a special bond and long-lasting friendship with Pirate during the 1967 winter ascent, says much of Hale's criticism is unfair:

> The very best chief guides on McKinley have strong views and are authoritarian. It's essential to be that way, with the responsibilities they have. And Ray didn't drive all his clients to the summit. He often made the judgment that they were not fit to go. He had specific criteria for determining [clients'] fitness at altitude. If they couldn't perform a certain exercise, they couldn't go to the summit.
>
> Ray may have put some people off because he was so unconventional and dared to be different, but he was an inspiration to so many people. He lived life to the fullest and on his own terms. People liked to climb with him not only because of his success record, but because he was larger than life.
>
> Once you got to know him, it was easier to appreciate his humor, his tremendous energy, and his concern for others. One thing I especially admired about Ray was his willingness to stick his neck out for people when they were in trouble. He could be counted on. He was a true adventurer. And in a mythic sense, he was the wild man of the mountain.

Despite his controversial style, Genet had a good safety record. In twelve years of guiding, while leading hundreds of people to McKinley's summit, he lost only one client, who died from high-altitude pulmonary edema, an acute form of mountain sickness. Some of Genet's critics argue that even one fatality is too many and marvel that more of his clients didn't die. But others point out that Genet's safety record was far better than that for unguided expeditions and also note that Pirate often participated in search-and-rescue operations, risking his own life to help those in trouble.

Pirate's to-the-summit obsession and sense of invincibility may have contributed to his own death in the Himalayas. In 1979, at age forty-eight, Genet joined an expedition to 29,028-foot Mount Everest. Despite being weakened by illness, he challenged the mountain and pushed himself to the summit, once again demonstrating his extraordinary drive and indomitable will. While descending, he and a teammate were forced to spend a night out in the open, unprotected from the cold and wind. That night, the legendary king of McKinley died.

Genet's death literally marked the end of an era. In 1980, National Park Service officials decided they needed to monitor and regulate McKinley's guide services more closely to ensure client safety. Their first step was to restrict the number of businesses that could run guided trips on the mountain. The Park Service announced that anyone wishing to operate on McKinley would have to apply for a concession permit. Preference would be given to guides who'd worked on the mountain prior to 1980, but anyone could apply.

The number of companies with extensive experience on the peak was small. Gary Bocarde says that Mountain Trip and Genet Expeditions were the only guide outfits to consistently operate on McKinley during the 1970s, while two others worked there off and on: the National Outdoor Leadership School in

Wyoming; and Rainier Mountaineering, Inc., based in Tacoma, Washington. The Park Service eventually granted concession permits to those four organizations (Kathy Sullivan continued to operate Genet Expeditions after the Pirate's death), plus three other businesses.

The agency supposedly based its decision on two main criteria: previous McKinley experience and financial ability to run a quality operation. But some mountaineers were convinced that political pull also played an important role. Bocarde recalls:

> It came as kind of a surprise when they issued that many [permits]. It was a joke, really. The way the Park Service had explained it, the original intent of the concession system was to keep the numbers down and emphasize quality of operation. Then all of a sudden these other companies were being added. I couldn't believe it; there had to be a lot of politics.

The concession-permit decisions didn't shock Doug Buchanan as much as they angered him. And his complaint wasn't the issuance of too many permits, but too few. An experienced Alaskan climber whose permit request was turned down, Buchanan has, over the years, accused the Park Service of establishing a monopolistic system for economic gain:

> By controlling and regulating the number of permits—and then charging for that 'service'—the government can rake in big profits off the guides. What's going on legally constitutes a form of racketeering. There's no reason to limit the number of permits. It hasn't kept McKinley from becoming more crowded, it hasn't improved the quality of guiding, and it hasn't prevented accidents from happening. The only thing it's done is make money for the Park Service.

There's no question that the concessionaire system brings in substantial revenue each year, with the Park Service charging McKinley's guide businesses a franchise fee for the rights to operate on the mountain. In 2012 that fee was equal to 4.25 percent of a company's adjusted gross income from its Denali National Park operations, with an increase expected in 2014, when new concession contracts would be renewed (they're reissued every ten years). But South District Ranger John Leonard (whose responsibilities include overseeing Denali's mountaineering program) emphasized in 2012 that "this is not a moneymaker for Denali [National Park]." Of the $97,342 the Park Service received from McKinley's six guide outfits in 2011, for example, 80 percent went to Denali. And all of that, Leonard noted, was "put directly back into the mountaineering program to support operations."

Years earlier, in response to Buchanan's criticisms, Denali ranger Bob Seibert had also explained that Congress has mandated concession-type management of businesses within national parks. He further argued that the public's interest, not financial gain, is the primary motive for restricting business operations on McKinley. "By granting special rights to these companies, we're encouraging them to invest in their business and do the best possible job of serving the public," Seibert said. "The result should be safer, higher quality trips. And the people to benefit are the clients."

To ensure that the public is being served, McKinley's rangers closely monitor guiding operations. As long as a business meets Park Service standards, its permit is renewed. Through the first decade of concessionaire management on McKinley, no permits were withdrawn, though a couple changed hands, with government approval.

Harry Johnson, who purchased Genet Expeditions in 1984, commented in 1990 that, "The Park Service watches us like a hawk. And at the end of every season, they review us very, very thoroughly. There's a lot of pressure to run a safe, quality operation, or lose your permit." Ironically, only two years later, McKinley's oldest, largest, and most famous guide service became the first–and so far only–company to lose its right to operate on the mountain.

The National Park Service revoked Genet Expeditions' McKinley permit prior to the 1992 climbing season because of what it called "a continued pattern of unsafe practices observed and documented since 1988." Johnson appealed the revocation and accused the Park Service of "armchair quarterbacking," faulty logic and unsubstantiated charges. But Park Service director James Ridenour rejected that appeal, as well as Johnson's follow-up request for reconsideration. Johnson then filed a lawsuit, seeking to have his permit reinstated, but the case never went to trial.

Under Johnson's management, Genet Expeditions had continued to specialize in ascents of the West Buttress and regained its status as McKinley's largest guide service. From the mid-1980s until 1991, Genet Expeditions accounted for about a third of all McKinley clients, while running five to ten trips during the late-April-through-mid-July climbing season.

Through 1987, Johnson's McKinley concession annually earned "satisfactory" ratings. But that ended in 1988 when the Park Service gave Genet Expeditions a "marginal" grade, mainly because one of its clients died after reaching McKinley's summit. (The death of Lynne Salerno is described in Chapter 11.) Genet Expeditions received a second straight marginal rating in 1989 because of two "significant" safety incidents. In the first, a tent containing two clients was blown off the West Buttress. The two men fell nearly 1,000 feet but miraculously survived, though one suffered a fractured vertebrae and the other lost parts of six fingers due to frostbite. The second, less-publicized 1989 incident involved a client who was left in high camp while the remainder of the expedition headed for McKinley's summit. When checked later by another Genet guide (leading a different expedition), the client was found to be suffering from acute mountain sickness. Assisted to a medical research camp at 14,200 feet, the climber was treated for moderate-to-severe high-altitude pulmonary edema.

Genet Expeditions returned to satisfactory status in 1990, but in 1991 the Park Service gave Johnson's company an unsatisfactory rating–and subsequently revoked its permit–because of several "safety incidents." No one was killed or injured in those incidents, which included the fall of a guide and client, and Alaska Regional Director John Morehead said, "None of the (1991) incidents reported, in themselves, would have convinced me to revoke the permit. But if you look at the incidents cumulatively, there's a pattern of unsafe behavior."

Johnson responded: "It's armchair quarterbacking. If you watch any expedition closely enough, you can come up with these sorts of incidents." Several other McKinley guides agreed with Johnson that the specified incidents were "pretty common" on McKinley and that the Park Service's revocation was too harsh a penalty. Others, however, insisted that the agency's action was long overdue, because of Genet Expeditions' continued overemphasis on getting climbers "to the summit."

Since Genet Expeditions lost its permit, only six companies have guided on McKinley. Nowadays owners are required to submit a plan of operation before the climbing season begins in April. The plan must include detailed climbing resumés of all guides being hired, an expedition itinerary, proof of insurance, a fee schedule, and all advertising material used in company promotions.

The client/guide ratio may not exceed four to one and no more than nine clients at a time may be taken up McKinley's southern routes, which are the most crowded. Expeditions on the north side may include up to twelve clients.

Though the Park Service uses no system to certify guides, it requires that all chief guides leading McKinley expeditions have previous experience guiding on the mountain. And all climbing resumés are carefully inspected.

Over the years, some guides have continued to complain that the Park Service is too restrictive, but most seem to agree the system is working. The quality of guides is better than ever; clients are given a better all-around mountain education; and the guide industry's safety record on McKinley has for the most part been excellent.

Back in the seventies, most McKinley guides had little, if any, formal training in mountain rescue or emergency medical treatment. Assistants were sometimes recruited off the streets, with no thorough check of their climbing backgrounds. Now, at least partly because of Park Service scrutiny, McKinley's guide services are more selective in their hiring practices and do a better job of educating their employees. Climbing expertise is only one of many requirements. Guides must also be safety conscious, environmentally aware, and skilled at dealing with people. (Most McKinley guides range in age from the early twenties to mid-forties. And while many once worked in a variety of fields during the August to March "off season"–for instance law, medicine, education, construction, and government–nowadays the majority continue to work as guides, or in some related outdoor field, throughout the year, in jobs scattered around the world. This, ranger John Leonard believes, "has advanced the profession.")

Another significant change has been the shift of guiding attitudes and philosophies. Guide services now generally emphasize that the overall experience and climber safety are what's most important, not whether a person stands on McKinley's summit.

The style of guiding varies considerably among the permit holders, however. The National Outdoor Leadership School, or

NOLS, places great emphasis on well-rounded climber education and leadership training; its students are expected to be as self-sufficient as possible, while working within the team framework. The Alaska Mountaineering School, too, stresses education, while developing leadership and teamwork skills. Other companies are more likely to "shepherd" their clients up the mountain, with little non-climbing instruction.

All of McKinley's guide outfits organize West Buttress expeditions though NOLS more frequently takes its students along the Muldrow Glacier route. The Alaska Mountaineering School, Mountain Trip, Rainier Mountaineering, and the American Alpine Institute may also do more technically challenging routes, particularly the West Rib. Some companies travel faster than others; expedition lengths normally range from fourteen to twenty-four days (weather permitting, of course). And some tend to hire Alaskan guides, who have a greater sense of the state's mountaineering history and folklore, while others chiefly employ guides from outside Alaska.

Whatever their different styles and philosophies, all of McKinley's current guide services have impressive safety records. No complete statistics are available from the 1970s, because the Park Service didn't separate climbers into guided and non-guided categories (though agency records indicate that two guided mountaineers died on McKinley, one in 1971 and another in 1976). But from the 1980s through the 1990s and the first thirteen years (2000–2012) of the twenty-first century, approximately 11,000 McKinley mountaineers hired the services of guides, and only eight of those died. (Three guides also died during those years, Terrance "Mugs" Stump in 1992, Chris Hooyman in 1998, and Suzanne Allen in 2011.)

Curiously, seven of the eight guided clients died between 2004 and 2011; even stranger, perhaps, is that four of the seven climbers collapsed and died from cardiac arrest, including onc twenty-three-year-old climber who turned out to have a congenital heart condition. In 2012, Denali's lead mountaineering ranger, John Leonard (whose responsibilities included overseeing Denali's mountaineering program) said the latter statistic is attributable in part to the fact that "it's more common now for older people to climb the mountain." The aging of McKinley's climbing crowd is reflected in their average age, which rose from thirty-four years old in 20000 to nearly forty in 2011. And with increased age comes the increased risk of heart attack.

Another of the seven deaths could be attributed to bad luck: in 2004, a huge rock fall in the Windy Corner area injured two guided climbers and killed a third. "No one could have foreseen that," Leonard noted, "It was simply a case of being in the wrong place at the wrong time."

Finally, a Park Service-appointed investigative panel of three veteran Alaska mountaineers concluded that one recent client death (Beat Niederer in 2011) occurred in part because of mistakes made by Mountain Trip guide Dave Staeheli (a veteran McKinley guide and skilled mountaineer who had soloed the West Rib in 1989). In its accident analysis, the panel (among other points) concluded that "The results of this guiding accident on Denali involving the death of one client [to hypothermia] and the extreme frostbite to another may have been prevented" if the guided team had been better prepared and carried more survival gear on its summit attempt. A complete analysis is included in "Management Evaluation Report of the Accident Investigation on a Mountaineering Accident Involving the Mountain Trip Concession Guide David Staeheli and Death of Client, Beat Niederer," available from the NPS.

During that same thirty-three-year period (1980–2012), more than 22,000 non-guided climbers attempted to ascend the mountain; eighty-two died. Some quick arithmetic shows that guided climbers are about five times more likely to survive a

McKinley trip than their non-guided counterparts. They also stand a better chance of returning from the mountain healthy: besides the fact that only ten guided climbers have ever died, relatively few have been seriously injured. But as Denali's mountaineering rangers point out, that's the way it should be. When someone hires a guide, they're trusting their safety to someone else.

And who are these people who climb the mountain, trusting their safety to McKinley guides? Back in the 1990s, Brian Okonek of Alaska Denali Guiding described his "average" McKinley client as a male, white-collar professional in his mid-thirties, with little or no previous high-altitude climbing experience. Some are natural athletes, but many are not. Okonek noted:

> A few of our clients have lots of mountaineering experience; they choose a guide because they're unable or unwilling to organize their own expedition. But the large majority are people who haven't climbed a big mountain before. They're looking for a once-in-a-lifetime adventure. And rather than work their way up to McKinley—pay their dues on other mountains, so to speak—they want to go for the gusto in one shot.

That profile still largely held true in 2012, according to Colby Coombs, codirector of the Alaska Mountaineering School, though the average age was likely a bit older. One noteworthy change: an increased number of clients climb McKinley as part of their "Seven Summits" quest (the goal being to climb the highest peak on each of the Earth's continents).

Now, more than ever, McKinley guides get inquiries from people who have never winter camped, climbed, or even backpacked—in other words, people totally unprepared for a McKinley expedition. For that reason, more applicants are being turned down.

Ideally, guides say, any prospective West Buttress client should at least be a longtime backpacker with enough cold-weather camping experience to understand its difficulties and challenges. Familiarity with snow and ice climbing–and its tools–is also a great advantage, as are mountaineering courses and experience on peaks like Washington state's Mount Rainier.

For many years, the typical McKinley-concession client was, with few exceptions, born in the USA. Since the early 1980s, 20 to 45 percent of McKinley's annual mountaineering crowd has come from overseas. But through the end of the twentieth century, only a tiny fraction of the foreigners–no more than a handful each year–climbed with Park Service–approved guide outfits. If they desired professional leadership, foreign climbers were much more likely to hire the services of what Seibert once called "bandit" guides, usually from their home country.

McKinley's bandit operations have presented a special dilemma for the Park Service. Though they're illegal, they meet a need that American companies do not. As then-chief mountaineering ranger Seibert admitted in 1990:

> The whole issue of foreign guiding has been a big thorn in our sides. Our American companies aren't able to adequately service foreign climbers. There's the language problem, plus differences in diet and climbing style. Foreigners–particularly European and Japanese–tend to be more aggressive climbers; they're willing to accept a higher level of risk. A few American companies have tried working with foreign guides but that hasn't worked out either. It's been extremely frustrating for everyone, a very awkward situation with no easy solution. We have to find a solution that's fair for everyone, but still offers adequate safeguards. So far we haven't come up with a satisfactory answer to the problem.

Daryl Miller, Denali's chief mountaineering ranger in 1999, said nothing had changed by the late 1990s: "Foreign guiding is still a big problem and there's no solution in sight."

But things began to change in the early 2000s, first under Miller and then his successor, Leonard, who in 2012 noted, "Illegal guiding is still an issue, but we've focused more of our resources on it and it's not nearly as big a problem as it used to be."

One especially valuable "resource" is the Internet. Not only does it allow the Park Service to more easily reach—and educate—the international climbing community, it has enabled Denali's mountaineering staff to more easily track down companies, or individual mountaineers, that might attempt to illegally guide on McKinley.

"Our goal is to stop illegal operations *before* they get on the mountain," Leonard says, "and it's become much easier to do that. We can contact both [suspected] guides and their clients before they travel here and give them advance warning—and also explain other options."

Namely, joining the outfits authorized to guide on McKinley.

While the NPS is legally obligated to turn away such "bandits"—or cite and remove those who are caught on McKinley's slopes, with penalties of $500 fines or appearances in court—Leonard emphasizes that "what really motivates us is that illegal guided expeditions are less safe and they're not as careful about protecting the resource. Foreign guides will sometimes take as many as ten or eleven clients; and in some cases they've never been on the mountain. Safety is a real concern."

The evidence suggests that the Park Service's proactive approach is working. While a tiny percentage of foreigners signed up with McKinley's permitted guide companies before 2000, since 2005 nearly one out of every four guided clients have come from outside the United States. That shift is a major reason that the number of guided McKinley mountaineers rose 33 percent between

2002 and 2011, while the number of "private" climbers dropped 32 percent.

While the proportion of foreign clients has grown substantially since 2000, the percentage of women on guided McKinley trips has remained small (whatever the nationality) and there's some evidence that fewer women join guided expeditions now than in the mid-1980s. Harry Johnson, for instance, estimated that as many as one-fourth of Genet Expedition's clients were women in 1984-85; but by the end of the decade, only about one in ten clients was female. For the industry as a whole, about 10 percent female clients has been the norm on McKinley for most of the past two decades (through 2011). The percentage of female clients in the first decade of the 2000s more or less mirrored the overall population of women on the mountain; between 2000 and 2011, 7 to 12 percent of all McKinley mountaineers were women, with the average for that entire period close to 10 percent. The number of female guides, meanwhile, varies from company to company, but on average ranges from 10 to 20 percent.

The women who sign up for guided climbs tend to be about the same age as their male teammates. And though they don't participate as often, Okonek found that "the women who do join us typically do very well. It's usually very obvious that they've painstakingly trained for it; they take it seriously."

In 2012, Coombs confirmed that Okonek's assessment still largely holds true, adding, "It only becomes a particular challenge with women with a small frame size. There is a minimum [amount of weight] you have to carry on Denali and above 14,000 it's all on your back. That can be crushing for 5-foot, 4-inch women. I think it is definitely more of a challenge for women with respect to hydration. Guys can roll over in their sleeping bags in the middle of a storm and pee in a bottle."

Though there are devices to help women urinate indoors, their "system" remains more complicated than men's.

Because pre-expedition training is a key ingredient to any mountaineering success, guide services give prospective clients recommended fitness programs as part of the screening/application process. The application process itself tends to weed out those who are unwilling to commit the time, money, and energy necessary to climb McKinley. But as Bocarde once noted, "You can't really know how a person's going to do until you get him out there. I've had some who looked great on paper, but turned out to be the worst climbers on the mountain. And vice versa."

Occasionally a client will go through the entire training program and still arrive in Alaska unfit to climb McKinley. Such people are told point-blank that they have no chance of reaching the summit. And they're given a choice: stay behind and get a refund; or go up McKinley and pay the full price, no matter how short the stay.

Almost always, even the most out-of-shape clients choose to tackle McKinley, though some bail out at base camp or, more rarely, even Talkeetna. Those who do make the effort are roped up with one or more guides and closely monitored when traveling along the Kahiltna Glacier. But after suffering for a few days on the lower mountain, they'll see their mistake and ask to leave. As Okonek once put it, "They'll come up to you and say, 'I'm wasted. I want to go.'" They are then escorted back to base camp, for pickup by one of Talkeetna's air-taxi services.

Adds Coombs, "Denali does the screening if we don't. We keep a healthy pace down low on the mountain. Most cases of people unprepared come to the guide and request an exit strategy before 11,000 feet. We sit down with each client, one-on-one, in Talkeetna and tell them the guide has the final say on whether they can continue. They sign [an agreement] acknowledging that."

Although physical fitness is a must on any McKinley route, mountaineering ability isn't usually required by companies offering guided trips up the West Buttress. Before beginning the ascent, guides train their clients in the basic ice-climbing, glacier-travel, and crevasse-rescue skills needed to safely travel up and down the mountain.

While some familiarity with climbing equipment and techniques is highly recommended, there's no direct correlation between climbing expertise and success in reaching McKinley's summit. Mental attitude, guides say, is just as important as physical ability–sometimes more so. Climbers who come prepared to climb, who stay focused on their goals, and are willing to deal with a certain amount of suffering, are most likely to do well.

Achieving the summit is never guaranteed, of course. McKinley's often stormy weather and climbers' ability to adapt to high altitude often determine which mountaineers reach the top and which don't. Guides can only promise their clients high adventure and the opportunity to discover new horizons. Okonek likely echoed the sentiments of most, if not all, McKinley guides, when he commented, "I haven't had a client who wasn't challenged to the extreme. For a lot of people, climbing McKinley is the test of a lifetime."

NOTES

CHAPTER ONE — THE MOUNTAIN

1. James Kari in *Shem Pete's Alaska: The Territory of the Upper Cook Inlet Dena'ina* (Alaska Native Language Center, University of Alaska and the CIRI Foundation, 1987).
2. Art Davidson, *Minus 148°: The Winter Ascent of Mt. McKinley* (Seattle: Cloudcap Press, 1986), p. 12.
3. Robert Hixson Julyan, *Mountain Names* (Seattle: The Mountaineers Books, 1984), p. 136.
4. Grant Pearson, *My Life of High Adventure* (Englewood Cliffs, New Jersey: Prentice Hall, 1962), p. 129.

CHAPTER TWO — THE PIONEERS

1. Terris Moore, *Mt. McKinley: The Pioneer Climbs* (Seattle: The Mountaineers Books, 1981), p. 1. Captain Vancouver's full account can be found in his published journal, *A Voyage to the Pacific Ocean*, Volume III (London, 1798).
2. Moore, p. 7. Dall's account is presented in his book *Alaska and Its Resources* (Boston, 1870).
3. Moore, p. 8.
4. Moore, pp. 8–9.
5. Moore, pp. 9, 12–15. See also William Dickey, "Discoveries in Alaska," *New York Sun* (January 24, 1897), p. 6.
6. The spelling of some Alaska place names has changed through time, and spellings often varied in different explorer's accounts. Examples include Tyonick (now Tyonek) and Cook's Inlet (now Cook Inlet).
7. Pearson, p. 129.
8. Moore, p. 19.
9. Moore, p. 28. See also Alfred Brooks, "The Mount McKinley Region, Alaska," *US Geological Survey Professional Paper No. 70.* (Washington, D.C., 1911).
10.Moore, p. 29. Brooks's account, written with D. L. Reaburn, is titled "Plans for Climbing Mt. McKinley" and appeared in the January 1903 *National Geographic*, pp. 30–35.
11. Moore, Wickersham account, pp. 31–40. Wickersham's own account can be

found in his book *Old Yukon Tales, Trails and Trials* (Washington, D.C.: Washington Law Book Co., 1938), pp. 203–320.

12. According to Moore, Cook "completed his medical education at New York University in 1890."

13. Moore, p. 43. Dunn's account of the 1903 climb is presented in his book *Shameless Diary of an Explorer* (New York: The Outing Publishing Co., 1907).

14. Moore, Cook's 1906 expedition and the McKinley and polar controversies, pp. 51–67. Cook's account of his 1906 climb is given in his book *To the Top of the Continent — Discovery, Exploration and Adventure in Sub-Arctic Alaska. The First Ascent of Mt. McKinley, 1903–1906* (New York, 1908, and London, 1909).

15. Moore, accounts of the 1910 Parker-Browne and Mazama expeditions, pp. 77–85.

16. Despite the abundance of evidence disproving Cook's claim, the controversy surrounding his professed McKinley ascent never completely died. Even now, there's a contingent of Cook supporters who believe he was the first to reach McKinley's summit, despite overwhelming evidence to the contrary.

17. Moore, pp. 88–104, the account of the Parker-Browne 1912 expedition. For Belmore Browne's own story of both the 1910 and 1912 expeditions, see Browne's book *The Conquest of McKinley* (New York, 1913).

Chapter Three — The Sourdough Expedition, 1910

1. The telephone survey was conducted in June 1989. The responses of four of the participants, Andy Embick, Steve Davis, Jim Hale, and Todd Miner are quoted here.

2. Terrence Cole, editor, *The Sourdough Expedition* (Anchorage: Alaska Northwest Publishing Company, 1985) presents what is perhaps the best historical overview of the Sourdough Expedition. Valuable sources of information for this chapter were the various reports, stories, and interviews in that 64-page booklet, as well as some material in Terris Moore's book *Mt. McKinley: The Pioneer Climbs*, pp. 69–75.

3. Cole, pp. 7–9, introduces the Sourdough Expedition story.

4. Cole, pp. 17–32, includes Tom Lloyd's official account of his 1910 McKinley expedition from the *New York Times Magazine* (June 5, 1910). Also included is "The Story Behind the Story," by W. F. Thompson, editor, *Fairbanks Daily News-Miner*. At the time of the Cook Expedition controversy, there were two competing newspapers in Fairbanks, the *Fairbanks Daily Times* and the *Fairbanks Daily News-Miner*.

5. Expedition member Billy Taylor was interviewed by Norman Bright in 1937; the interview was published in *The American Alpine Journal* in 1939. Bright's

interview, and a discussion of the expedition and the interview by alpine historian Francis Farquhar, are included in Cole, pp. 47–56 and 57–62.

6. Bradford Washburn, personal communication, April 1990.

7. Pearson, p. 135.

8. Farquhar, in Cole, p. 59.

9. Farquhar, in Cole, p. 62.

10. Moore, p. 104, provides Browne and Parker's observations about Lloyd's account.

11. Hudson Stuck, *The Ascent of Denali (Mount McKinley): A Narrative of the First Complete Ascent of the Highest Peak in North America* (Lincoln, Nebraska: University of Nebraska Press, 1989, reprinted from the 1914 edition), p. 87.

12. Stuck, p. 173.

13. Stuck, p. 170.

Chapter Four — Hudson Stuck and the First Ascent, 1913

1. Moore, p. 107.

2. Moore, p. 107. See also Edwin Swift Balch, *Mt. McKinley and Mountain Climbers' Proofs* (Philadelphia, 1914), p. 67.

3. The text of this chapter closely follows Hudson Stuck's 1914 account of his 1913 expedition, *The Ascent of Denali.*

4. Jonathan Waterman, *High Alaska* (New York: The American Alpine Club, 1988), p. 47.

5. This entry from Karstens's Diary was reprinted in Waterman's *High Alaska*, p. 47.

Chapter Five — The 1932 Expeditions: Carpé and Lindley-Liek

1. Stuck, p. 117.

2. Primary sources for the 1932 expedition accounts are Moore, pp. 121–42, and Pearson, pp. 125–65.

3. Edward Beckwith, "The Mt. McKinley Cosmic Ray Expedition, 1932," *The American Alpine Journal* (1933), pp. 45–68.

4. Jean Potter, *The Flying North* (New York: Macmillan, 1965), pp. 96–114.

5. Alfred Lindley, "Mt. McKinley, South and North Peaks, 1932," *The American Alpine Journal* (1933), pp. 36–44.

6. Moore, p. 132. According to Moore, Strom wrote an article for the Norsk Tinde Klub (Norwegian Climbing Club) which was later translated into English under the title "How We Climbed Mt. McKinley."

Chapter Six — Bradford Washburn and the West Buttress

1. Stuck, p. 118.
2. Bradford Washburn, "Mount McKinley from the North and West," *The American Alpine Journal* (1947), pp. 283–93. Bradford Washburn's unequalled photographs of Mount McKinley were unavailable during the production of this book, and therefore it was not possible to include complete route photos to supplement the text. See Waterman's *High Alaska* for McKinley route diagrams superimposed on Washburn's photos.
3. Nan Elliot's "Shared Horizons," *Anchorage Daily News* (June 14, 1987).
4. Washburn, personal communication, September 1989.
5. The 1951 West Buttress account in this chapter was taken from Bradford Washburn's "Mount McKinley Conquered by New Route," *National Geographic* (August 1953), pp. 219–248.
6. Washburn, personal communication, April 1990.
7. The 1987 West Buttress account is reprinted with permission of the *Anchorage Times*. It originally ran as a three-part series by the author, "Climbing McKinley," July 19 and 26 and August 3, 1987.
8. Dick Bass, Frank Wells, with Rick Ridgeway, *Seven Summits* (New York: Warner Books, 1986).
9. Glenn Randall, *Mt. McKinley Climber's Handbook* (Evergreen, Colorado: Chockstone Press, 1992).

Frostbite is a localized cold-weather injury characterized by frozen body tissue. Temperatures must be below 32°F for it to occur. During outdoor activities in cold weather, toes are most susceptible to frostbite; fingers, hands, ears, and nose are also commonly frostbitten, though usually not as severely, because they're easily checked and warmed. The earliest symptom of frostbite usually is pain in the affected tissues. But as the tissue freezes, all sensation is lost and the pain disappears. Therefore, the only symptom may be the absence of any feeling. Such numbness may not be noticed by a person involved in an activity such as climbing, which often involves great concentration, particularly if the climber is hypoxic or hypothermic, and is not thinking clearly or is unaware of frostbite's serious consequences. Frostbite symptoms are variable, however, and some individuals never experience pain, while others never lose it. Frostbitten tissues are usually very pale in color because blood vessels become constricted and the amount of blood in the tissues is reduced. Such color changes in the hands and feet often go unnoticed because they're usually covered by clothing. Frozen tissues also become firm or hard. Two factors that contribute to frostbite are hypothermia (a cooling of the body's core temperature) and clothing that restricts circulation, such as boots that are tied too tightly.

As body tissues begin to thaw, blisters will form. Depending on the severity of the frostbite, some tissue loss may occur. Tissue damaged beyond repair will eventually become black and mummified. Digits or parts of digits in such acondition often separate or break off without surgery. Amputation may be required if the affected body parts become infected or if the extent of damage includes a major portion of a hand or foot.

This information on frostbite can be found in *Hypothermia, Frostbite and Other Cold Injuries*, by James A. Wilkerson, M.D., editor; Cameron C. Bangs, M.D.; and John S. Hayward, PhD. (Seattle: The Mountaineers Books, 1986), pp. 84–96. The section on frostbite was written by Wilkerson.

Chapter Seven — Cassin's Conquest of the South Face, 1961

1. Bradford Washburn, "Mount McKinley, Alaska," *The Mountain World* (London: Allen & Unwin, 1956–57).
2. Steve Roper and Allen Steck, *Fifty Classic Climbs of North America* (San Francisco: Sierra Club Books, 1979), pp. 19–24.
3. Riccardo Cassin wrote two accounts of his McKinley expedition, both of which were sources for this chapter: "The South Face of McKinley," *The American Alpine Journal* (1962), pp. 27–37; and *Fifty Years of Alpinism* (Seattle: The Mountaineers Books, 1981), pp. 131–46.
4. Chris Jones, *Climbing in North America* (Berkeley, University of California Press; and New York: The American Alpine Club, 1976), pp 325–26.
5. Bradford Washburn, "Washburn Says Italians Are Attempting One of World's Great Mountain Climbs," the *Anchorage Daily Times* (July 13, 1961).

Chapter Eight — The First Winter Ascent, 1967

1. Washburn, personal communication, September 1989.
2. Davidson, personal communication, October 1986.
3. David Roberts, "Introduction" to Art Davidson's *Minus 148°*, pp. 5–6.
4. Davidson's *Minus 148°* was the primary source for this chapter.

Chapter Nine — The Wilcox Expedition Disaster, 1967

1. Howard Snyder, *The Hall of the Mountain King* (New York: Charles Scribner's Sons, 1973).
2. Joseph Wilcox, *White Winds* (Los Alamitos, California: Hwong Publishing Company, 1981). The expedition account presented in the text is taken from both Synder and Wilcox's accounts.
3. Snyder's reflections are presented on pp. 176–82 of *The Hall of the Mountain King.*
4. Joseph Wilcox, *A Reader's Guide to The Hall of the Mountain King*

(Gig Harbor, Washington: Joe Wilcox, 1981).

5. Wilcox's rebuttals and comments are outlined on pp. 453–77 of *White Winds*.

6. Washburn, personal communication, April 1990.

Chapter Ten — Winter Solo Ascents: Waterman, Uemura, and Johnston

1. Steve Davis, personal communication, October 1989.
2. Davis, personal communication, April 1990.
3. National Park Service, *History of NPS Requirements, Restrictions to Climb Mount McKinley* (Alaska, February 1988).
4. Bob Seibert, personal communication, December 1989.
5. For example, Gladys Reckley, "Solo Climber Carried Salmon, Rice for Food," *Anchorage Daily Times* (September 1, 1970).
6. Gary Bocarde, verbal communication, June 1989.
7. Glenn Randall "Over the Edge," *Anchorage Daily News* (August 14, 1983).
8. Glenn Randall, *Breaking Point* (Denver: Chockstone Press, 1984), p. 6.
9. John Waterman, "Mount Hunter Traversed Solo," *The American Alpine Journal* (1979), pp. 91–97.
10. This and subsequent John Waterman quotes and impressions, with noted exceptions, were taken from Randall's "Over the Edge."
11. Dave Carpenter, "Fairbanks Climber Attempts to Achieve First Winter Solo Ascent of Mount McKinley," *Anchorage Times* (January 5, 1980).
12. Davidson, *Minus 148°*, p. 230.
13. Jonathan Waterman, *High Alaska*, p. 87.
14. The account of the search for Naomi Uemura, including quoted remarks, was taken from Associated Press reports in *Anchorage Times* and the *Anchorage Daily News* by Bruce Bartley, Paul Jenkins, and Hal Spencer during February and March 1984.
15. The Uemura diary entries were taken from Craig Medred's story, "Naomi Uemura: Final Days of a Climbing Legend," *Anchorage Daily News* (May 12, 1985).
16. The quotes and journal entries for the Johnston account were taken from George Bryson's story, "Alone on McKinley in the Winter," *Anchorage Daily News* (April 13, 1986). Other sources for general information include Beth Barrett's story, "Frostbite Ends Johnston's Trip up McKinley," *Anchorage Times* (March 23, 1986); and Davidson's *Minus 148°*, pp. 240–42.

Chapter Eleven — Winter Solo Ascents: Tejas and Staeheli

1. This account of Vern Tejas's solo winter ascent was reprinted, with a few modifications, from the author's story, "Following in Uemura's Footsteps,"

Anchorage Times (April 10, 1988); some information was also taken from George Bryson's "The Tejas Triumph," the *Anchorage Daily News* (April 3 and 10, 1988) and Art Davidson's "Ladder over the Stars," *Alaska* (July 1989).
2. The account of Lynne Salerno's death was excerpted from two stories originally written by the author for the *Anchorage Times* and published May 29, 1988: "Determination to Succeed Killed Climber" and "Anguished Tejas Couldn't Have Known Climber's Trouble."
3. Seibert, personal communication, April 1990.
4. Dave Staeheli's account was taken from the author's story, "McKinley Masterpiece," the *Anchorage Times* (March 19, 1989), as well as from the author's interview with Staeheli, April 1990, and Craig Medred's story, "Alone on the West Rib," the *Anchorage Daily News* (April 23, 1989).

Chapter Twelve — The Deadliest Season, 1992

1. The account in this chapter is adapted from a story written by the author that ran in the *Anchorage Daily News We Alaskans* Sunday magazine on July 12, 1992.

Chapter Thirteen — Climber Self-Sufficiency and Rescues

1. Jonathan Waterman provides an excellent analysis of McKinley accidents for the period 1910 through 1982 in *Surviving Denali* (New York: The American Alpine Club, 1983). Updated statistics and analysis through 1990 were later provided in a second edition published in 1991.
2. National Park Service, *History of NPS Requirements, Restrictions to Climb Mount McKinley* (Alaska, February 1988).
3. Arthur Hayes, *McKinley National Park Mountaineering Summary for 1967* (National Park Service, Alaska).
4. Jim Hale, personal communication February 1990.
5. Bob Gerhard, *McKinley National Park Mountaineering Summary for 1976* (National Park Service, Alaska).
6. There is an exception to that rule. Based on a Memorandum of Agreement with the National Park Service, the US Army pays its own costs whenever Army personnel or aircraft are used in McKinley rescues. However, the Army's expenses are included in the total government cost annually computed by the Park Service.
7. Bob Seibert's comments throughout this chapter (except for the Denali Medical Research Camp discussion) were taken from interviews with the author in December 1989 and February 1990.
8. Personal communications were obtained from Doug Buchanan, January 1990; Gary Bocarde, February 1990; Brian Okonek, December 1989; Daryl Miller, September 1999; and John Leonard, March 2012.

9. Comments about foreign climbers by Peter Hackett, Gary Bocarde, and J. D. Swed are based on interviews conducted in fall 1992.
10. The following discussion of the Denali Medical Research Camp is adapted from an article by the author, "Mountain Doctors Set Up Shop on McKinley," the *Anchorage Times* (March 29, 1987), with updated information on the camp's closure.

Chapter Fourteen — Mountain of Trash

1. Hudson Stuck's references to garbage on the mountain can be found in *The Ascent of Denali*, pp. 71, 117, and 130–31.
2. Bradford Washburn, "Mount McKinley Conquered by New Route," *National Geographic* (August 1953), p. 247.
3. Davidson, *Minus 148°*, p. 191.
4. Personal communications presented below were from Steve Davis, October 1989; Brian Okonek, December 1989; Bob Seibert, December 1989 and February 1990; Doug Buchanan, January 1990; Daryl Miller, September 1999; and John Leonard, March 2012.
5. A reprint from the *Conservation News*, "Climbers Tackle Garbage," can be found in the *Anchorage Times* (July 11, 1979).
6. The 1974 material in this and the next two paragraphs can be found in Elaine Warren's article, "Highest Garbage Dump in America," *Anchorage Daily News* (June 16, 1974).
7. Waterman, *Surviving Denali*, pp. 163 and 165.
8. National Park Service, *Mountaineering in Denali National Park and Preserve* pamphlet, 2005 (downloaded from park website in March 2012).
9. National Park Service, Denali National Park and Preserve, "Trash and Waste Policies for Glacier Environments," downloaded from park website, March 2012.

Chapter Fifteen — Guiding on McKinley

1. Unless otherwise noted, comments quoted in this chapter were taken from the author's interviews with Jim Hale, February 1990; Gary Bocarde, February 1990; Doug Buchanan, January 1990; Bob Seibert, December 1989 and February 1990; Harry Johnson, February 1990; Brian Okonek, February 1990; Art Davidson, April 1990; Harry Johnson, February 1990 and April 1992; Brian Okonek, December 1989 and September 1999; Daryl Miller, September 1999; and John Leonard and Colby Coombs in March-April 2012.
2. Kathy Sullivan and Joe Redington Sr.'s comments were taken from Nan Elliot's "The Final Days of Ray Genet," *Anchorage Daily News* (November 7–8, 1981).

GLOSSARY

alpenstock — the predecessor of the modern ice axe, with a much longer staff and smaller cutting head.

ataxic — a condition in which a person has partially or completely lost the ability to coordinate voluntary body movements. It may occur at high altitudes because of insufficient oxygen to the cerebellum, the part of the brain that controls balance.

balaclava — a knitted pullover "helmet" made of wool or synthetic material that covers the head and face, with only a small opening for the eyes and nose.

belay — the procedure by which a stationary person manages the climbing rope for a moving team member to stop a fall if one should occur.

bivouac — an impromptu camp, often in the open without shelter.

bivy sack — a bag or sack intended to protect a climber from the elements when camping in the open. Unlike a sleeping bag, it is not insulated; usually it's a wind and waterproof (resistant) shell.

chute — an inclined channel or gully through which water, ice, snow, or rocks are funneled.

cornice — an overhanging shelf of snow, formed on the downwind side of a ridge. In cross section, a cornice is shaped like a breaking wave. Cornices are dangerous because they're often unstable and subject to collapse.

couloir — a mountain gully or ravine.

crampons — special spiked footgear that is strapped or clamped to the bottom of climbing boots, to provide traction on ice or hard snow. In the early 1900s, they were also called ice creepers, or simply creepers.

crevasse — a crack or fissure in a glacier, often hundreds of feet deep.

exhaustion-hypothermia — see hypothermia.

Fahrenheit — a temperature scale devised by physicist Daniel Fahrenheit in the 1700s, in which the boiling point of water is 212° and the freezing point is 32° at sea level; its abbreviation is "F." This is the temperature scale most commonly used in the United States. Most countries, however, use the centigrade scale, in which 0 is the freezing point and 100 is the boiling point for water; its abbreviation is "C." Conversion factors correlate temperatures between the two scales.

fixed line – a line of rope that is attached to a steep rock, snow, or ice slope, usually by bolts or screws. When ascending or descending, climbers connect themselves to the fixed line, for added protection.

frostbite — a condition in which body tissue has become frozen as the result of exposure to extreme cold. The condition may be accelerated by dehydration, hypothermia, and/or poor circulation. The first sign of freezing is numb, pale skin; eventually blisters will form. Most frostbite involves the feet, but the fingers, nose, and ears can also be affected. If frostbite is severe, amputation may be required.

glacier — a large mass of ice that forms in areas where the rate of snowfall constantly exceeds the rate of melting; it moves slowly down a mountain slope or valley until the ice melts or breaks away. Movement normally ranges from a few inches to several feet per day.

harness — synthetic webbing tied around a climber's waist and groin to which the climbing rope is attached.

hypothermia — a subnormal body temperature. The earliest sign of hypothermia is shivering. As the body continues to cool, a person will exhibit one or more of the following symptoms: numbness, slurred speech, lack of coordination, gray or bluish skin, lethargy, confusion, or forgetfulness. If its core temperature gets too low, the body will lose its ability to rewarm itself. If untreated, a person suffering from extreme hypothermia will sink into a coma and die. Exhaustion-hypothermia occurs when a person literally exhausts his/her energy supply; upon becoming chilled, there is no internal fuel left to burn, no internal mechanism to replace the body heat that's lost.

hypoxic — an oxygen-poor environment or condition; oxygen depleted.

ice axe — a tool used for climbing snow and ice. The bottom of the shaft has a metal spike; the head has a curved steel blade on one end and a curved, serrated steel pick on the other.

icefall — a portion of glacier that has become highly fractured as it flows down a steep gradient.

lenticular clouds – clouds capping the top of a mountain, indicating extremely high winds at the summit.

massif — the central mass of a mountain ridge.

moraine — mounds of debris deposited by a glacier. Ground moraines, deposited directly beneath retreating ice, typically produce hummocky surfaces. Lateral and terminal moraines, which are deposited along the sides and terminus of a glacier, respectively, normally form ridges.

mountain sickness (high-altitude illness) – an ailment caused by decreased oxygen in the blood and the body's inability to adjust to lower oxygen levels at high altitudes. It usually affects climbers who ascend too rapidly. McKinley mountaineers rarely suffer from mountain sickness below 10,000 feet. In its earliest stages, mountain sickness can be marked by several symptoms, including "dry" coughs, shortness of breath, bad headaches, loss of appetite, difficulty sleeping, nausea, loss of coordination, or sudden fatigue. If not treated, it can lead to high-altitude pulmonary edema or cerebral edema, which is the accumulation of fluid in the lungs and brain, respectively. Ultimately it can result in death.

pemmican — a concentrated fat-rich food, often used by explorers, that's designed for high energy yield. It usually includes a combination of dried meat and fat, sometimes mixed with sugar and fruit.

pitch — a section of a climb.

rappel — a method of descending by sliding down a rope that is tied into the climber's harness.

supergaiter — a covering for the foot and lower leg that extends from the sole of the boot to just below the knee. Often inflated, supergaitors are intended to provide additional warmth and prevent snow or ice from accumulating inside the boot.

triple roping — a technique used by solo climbers to protect themselves from a fall while crossing dangerous areas, such as crevasse fields. When crossing a crevasse, for example, a soloist would anchor his/her rope before the crevasse, cross the chasm, and set up second anchor on the far side, return to retrieve the climbing hardware used on the original anchor, and recross the crevasse a third and final time.

wand — a thin bamboo stake, usually wrapped with brightly colored surveyor's tape, used for marking routes on the mountain.

whiteout — a surface weather condition in which dense fog, clouds, or heavy snow obscures the surrounding landscape and sky in a featureless white veil, making it impossible to determine directions (without a compass) and often causing disorientation because no horizon line is visible.

windchill factor – measures the amount of body-heat loss due to convection by wind currents, at specific air temperatures. (The body loses heat in several ways; in cold air, most heat is lost through a process known as convection cooling, particularly if the air is moving. For a given temperature, the convective loss of body heat increases dramatically as wind velocities rise. In high winds, the loss can be enormous. Through research, scientists have formulated windchill charts that correlate specific temperatures and wind speeds with an equivalent calm-air temperature that would have a similar cooling effect on exposed skin. For example, at −10°F, a five-mile-per-hour wind could produce a windchill equivalent temperature of −15°F; for twenty- and forty-mile-per-hour winds, the windchill equivalent temperature would fall to −53°F and −69°F, respectively.)

Mount McKinley Firsts (through the 2011 climbing season)

First ascent, North Peak: Pete Anderson and Billy Taylor, April 3, 1910.

First ascent, South Peak: Hudson Stuck, Walter Harper, Harry Karstens, Robert Tatum, June 7, 1913.

First solo ascent: Naomi Uemura, August 1970, West Buttress.

First winter ascent: Dave Johnston, Art Davidson, Ray Genet, February 28, 1967.

First winter solo ascent: Naomi Uemura, February 12, 1984, West Buttress (died on descent).

First successful winter solo ascent: Vern Tejas, March 7, 1988, West Buttress.

First circumnavigation: Frederick Cook Expedition, May through September, 1903.

First winter circumnavigation: Mark Stasik and Daryl Miller, February 17 through April 2, 1995.

First blind ascent: Joan Phelps, May 30, 1993.

First night on top: Meiji University Team, May 4, 1960.

First woman to summit the mountain: Barbara Polk Washburn, June 6, 1947.

First female solo ascent: Miri Ercolani, July 21, 1982.

First hang glider descent: Wade, Kvalic, Burns, Hudson, June 1976.

First parapente descent, South Peak: Vern Tejas, June 1989.

First parapente descent, North Peak: Bertrand Doliez and Serge Tuaz, May 1989.

First dog-team ascent: Susan Butcher, Joe Redington Sr., Rob Stapleton, Ray Genet, Brian Okonek, May 28, 1979.

First guided trip: Richard McGown and five clients, June 1961.

First continuous ski descent of the Wickersham Wall, Adrian Nature, 1997.

Oldest male to summit: Michio Kumamoto, 76, June 29, 2007.

Oldest female to summit: Toshiko Uchida, 70, June 16, 2001.

Youngest male to summit: Galen Johnston, 11, June 17, 2001.

Youngest female to summit: Merrick Johnston, 12, June 24, 1995.

First ascent by full-leg amputee: Sarah Doherty, May 1985 (no artificial limb).

Oldest husband/wife team to summit: Norm and Kip Smith, 64 and 62, respectively, July 1992.

Most ascents: Vern Tejas, 50 ascents as of June 2011.

Winter Ascents of Mount McKinley through Spring 2012

Note: To qualify as a winter ascent, climbers must reach McKinley's summit before the spring equinox, March 20.

February 28, 1967, via the West Buttress: Americans Dave Johnston, Art Davidson, and Ray Genet. French teammate Jacques Batkin died on the ascent.

March 7, 1982, via the Cassin Ridge: Englishman Roger Mear and American Mike Young.

March 11, 1983, via the West Rib: Americans Charlie Sassara and Robert Frank; Frank died on the descent.

February 12, 1984, via the West Buttress: Japanese Naomi Uemura. He died on the descent, likely between 16,000 and 18,200 feet.

March 7, 1988, via the West Buttress: American Vern Tejas became the first soloist to reach the summit in winter and return safely.

February 20, 1989, via the West Buttress: Austrians Helmut Steinmassl, Helmut Mittermayr, and Walter Laserer.

March 12, 1989, via the West Rib: American Dave Staeheli.

January 16, 1998, via the West Buttress: Russians Artur Testof and Vladimir Ananich.

March 8, 1998, via the West Buttress: Japanese Masatoshi Kuriaki.

Denali National Park and Preserve Climbing Services

Denali National Park and Preserve maintains a ranger station in Talkeetna, Alaska. Those interested in climbing Mount McKinley are directed to contact the park's mountaineering staff using the following information:

Denali National Park and Preserve
Talkeetna Ranger Station
P.O. Box 588
Talkeetna, AK 99676
(907) 733-2231
Fax (907) 733-1465
Website: www.nps.gov/dena/planyourvisit/mountaineering.htm.

The mountaineering "home" page includes links to all sorts of valuable information, including climbing registration, the park's mountaineering booklet (in nine languages), guide and transportation services, the Clean Mountain Can program, annual mountaineering summaries, and more. E-mails can also be sent to park staff via the website.

McKinley Mountaineering Guide Services

The following six businesses are the only guide services authorized to lead commercial trips on Mount McKinley:

Alaska Mountaineering School
P.O. Box 566
Talkeetna, AK 99676
(907) 733-1016
Fax (907) 733-1362
www.climbalaska.org

Alpine Ascents International
109 W. Mercer St.
Seattle, WA 98119
(206) 378-1927
Fax (206) 378-1937
www.alpineascents.com

American Alpine Institute
1515 12th St.
Bellingham, WA 98225
(360) 671-1505
Fax (360) 734-8890
www.mtnguide.com

Mountain Trip International, LLC
P.O. Box 658
Ophir, CO 81426
(970) 369-1153
Fax (970) 728-3779
www.mountaintrip.com

National Outdoor Leadership School (NOLS)
P.O. Box 981
Palmer, AK 99645
(907) 745-4047
Fax (907) 745-6069
www.nols.edu

Rainier Mountaineering
P.O. Box Q
Ashford, WA 98304
(360) 569-2227
Fax (360) 569-2982
www.rmiguides.com

Bush Pilot Services

The following air-taxi operators are authorized to land at the Kahiltna Glacier Base Camp (as of 2012):

Fly Denali
P.O. Box 1152
Talkeetna, AK 99676
(907) 733-7768 or toll-free, (866) 733-7768
Fax (907) 733-7767
www.flydenali.com

K2 Aviation
P.O. Box 545
Talkeetna, AK 99676
(907) 733-2291 or toll-free (800) 764-2291
Fax (907) 733-1221
www.flyk2.com

Sheldon Air Service, LLC
P.O. Box 648
Talkeetna, AK 99676
(907) 733-2321 or toll-free (800) 478-2321
www.sheldonair.com

Talkeetna Air Taxi
P.O. Box 73
Talkeetna, AK 99676
(907) 733-2218 or toll free (800) 533-2219
Fax (907) 733-1434
www.talkeetnaair.com

Freight Hauling

Expeditions approaching McKinley from the north side of the Alaska Range can arrange to have freight hauled overland by:

Denali North Side Supply
(360) 313-7038
e-mail: denalinorthside@yahoo.com

BIBLIOGRAPHY

Balch, Edwin Swift. *Mt. McKinley and Mountain-Climbers' Proofs.* Philadelphia (1914).

Barrett, Beth. "Frostbite Ends Johnston's Trip up McKinley." *Anchorage Times* (March 23, 1986).

Bartley, Bruce, Paul Jenkins, and Hal Spencer. Series of stories on the search for Naomi Uemura. Anchorage, Alaska: Associated Press (February–March 1984).

Beckey, Fred. Mount McKinley: *Icy Crown of North America.* Seattle: The Mountaineers Books (1993, reprinted in 1999).

Beckwith, Edward P. "The Mt. McKinley Cosmic Ray Expedition." *American Alpine Journal* (1933).

Bright, Norman. "Billy Taylor, Sourdough." *American Alpine Journal* (1939).

Brooks, Alfred H. "Plans for Climbing Mt. McKinley." *National Geographic* (January 1903).

_____. "The Mount McKinley Region." *US Geological Survey Professional Paper No. 70*, Washington, D.C. (1911).

Browne, Belmore. *The Conquest of McKinley.* Boston: Houghton Mifflin (1956; reprint of 1913 edition published by G.P. Putnam's Sons).

Bryson, George. "Alone on McKinley in the Winter." *Anchorage Daily News* (April 13, 1986).

Carpenter, Dave. "Fairbanks Climber Drops Attempt to Achieve First Winter Solo Ascent of Mount McKinley." *Anchorage Times* (January 5, 1980).

Cassin, Riccardo. *Fifty Years of Alpinism.* Seattle: The Mountaineers Books (1981).

_____. "The South Face of McKinley." *American Alpine Journal* (1962).

"Cheers are Given as Climbers Leave." *Fairbanks Daily Times* (December 22, 1909).

"Climbers Tackle Garbage." *Anchorage Times* (July 11, 1973). Reprinted from the National Wildlife Federation's Conservation News.

Cole, Terrence. *The Sourdough Expedition.* Portland, Oregon: Alaska Northwest Publishing Co. (1985).

Cook, Frederick A. "America's Unconquered Mountain." *Harper's Monthly Magazine* (January 1904 and February 1904).

_____. *To the Top of the Continent.* London: Hodder & Stoughton (1909).

Coombs, Colby. *Denali's West Buttress: A Climber's Guide to Mt. McKinley's Classic Route.* Seattle: The Mountaineers Books (1997).

Darack, Ed. *6194: Denali Solo.* Davis, California: Ed Darack Photography (1995).

Davidson, Art. *Minus 148°: The Winter Ascent of Mt. McKinley,* third edition. Seattle: The Mountaineers Books (1999).

Dickey, William A. "Discoveries in Alaska." *New York Sun* (January 24, 1897).

"Dramatic Story of Thomas Lloyd." New York Times (June 5, 1910).

Dunn, Robert. *Shameless Diary of an Explorer.* New York: The Outing Publishing Co. (1907).

Elliot, Nan. "The Final Days of Ray Genet." *Anchorage Daily News* (November 7-8, 1981).

Farquhar, Francis P. "The Exploration and First Ascents of Mount McKinley." *Sierra Club Bulletin* (June 1949 and June 1950).

Gerhard, Bob. *McKinley National Park Mountaineering Summary for 1976.* National Park Service, Alaska.

Hayes, Arthur. *McKinley National Park Mountaineering Summary for 1967.* National Park Service, Alaska.

History of National Park Service Requirements, Restrictions to Climb Mount McKinley. National Park Service, Alaska (February 1988).

Jones, Chris. *Climbing in North America.* Berkeley: University of California Press; and New York: The American Alpine Club (1976).

Julyan, Robert Hixson. *Mountain Names.* Seattle: The Mountaineers Books (1984).

Koncour, Ruth Anne, with Michael Hodgson. *Facing the Extreme: One Woman's Story of True Courage, Death-Defying Survival, and Her Quest for the Summit.* New York: St. Martin's Press (1998).

"McKinley Ascent is Now Questioned." *New York Times* (April 16, 1910).

Medred, Craig. "Naomi Uemura: Final Days of a Climbing Legend." *Anchorage Daily News* (May 12, 1985).

Moore, Terris. *Mt. McKinley: The Pioneer Climbs.* Seattle: The Mountaineers Books (1981).

Mountaineering: Denali National Park and Preserve, Alaska. National Park Service (1987).

Mountaineering in Denali National Park and Preserve. National Park Service (2005).

Pearson, Grant. *My Life of High Adventure.* Englewood Cliffs, New Jersey: Prentice-Hall (1962).

Porco, Peter. "High Altitude, High Risks and High Costs on McKinley." *Anchorage Daily News* (July 17, 1988).

Randall, Glenn. "Over the Edge." *Anchorage Daily News*. (August 14, 1983).

______. *Breaking Point*. Denver: Chockstone Press (1984).

______. *Mt. McKinley Climber's Handbook*. Evergreen, Colorado: Chockstone Press. (1992).

Reckley, Gladys. "Solo Climber Carried Salmon, Rice for Food." *Anchorage Times* (September 1, 1970).

Roper, Steve, and Allen Steck. *Fifty Classic Climbs of North America*. San Francisco: Sierra Club Books (1979).

Rush, C. E. "On the Trail of Dr. Cook." *Pacific Monthly*, Portland, Oregon (January 1911).

Secor, R. J. *Denali Climbing Guide*. Mechanicsburg, Pennsylvania: Stackpole Books (1998).

Sherwonit, Bill. "McKinley Rangers Fight Battle with Trash on Mountain." *Anchorage Times* (May 19, 1985).

______. "Mountain Doctors Set Up Shop on McKinley." *Anchorage Times* (March 29, 1987).

______. "Climbing McKinley" (three-part series). *Anchorage Times* (July 19 and 26 and August 2, 1987).

______. "Following in Uemura's Footsteps." *Anchorage Times* (April 10, 1988).

______. "McKinley Mountaineering, 1988." *Anchorage Times* January 22, 1989.

______. "McKinley Masterpiece." *Anchorage Times* (March 19, 1989).

Sherwonit, Bill, ed. *Alaska Ascents: World-Class Mountaineers Tell Their Stories*. Portland, Oregon: Alaska Northwest Books (1996).

______. *Denali: A Literary Anthology*. Seattle: The Mountaineers Books (2000).

Snyder, Howard. *The Hall of the Mountain King*. New York: Charles Scribner's Sons (1973).

Stuck, Hudson. *The Ascent of Denali (Mount McKinley): A Narrative of the First Complete Ascent of the Highest Peak in North America*. New York: Charles Scribner's Sons (1914). (Reprinted by University of Nebraska Press, Lincoln, Nebraska, 1989).

Tabor, James. *Forever on the Mountain: The Truth Behind One of Mountaineering's Most Controversial and Mysterious Disasters*. NY: W.W. Norton & Co. (2008).

Thompson, W. F. "First Account of Conquering Mt. McKinley." *New York Times* (June 5, 1910).

"Trash and Waste Policies for Glacier Environments." National Park Service, 2012.

Warren, Elaine. "Highest Garbage Dump in America." *Anchorage Daily News* (June 16, 1974).

Washburn, Barbara, Bradford Washburn, and Lew Freedman. *The Accidental Adventurer: Memoir of the First Woman to Climb Mount McKinley.* Kenmore, Washington: Epicenter Press (2001).

Washburn, Bradford. "Mount McKinley from North and West." *American Alpine Journal* (1947).

_____. "Mount McKinley Conquered by New Route." *National Geographic* (August 1953).

_____. "Mount McKinley, Alaska." *The Mountain World.* London: Allen & Unwin (1956-57).

_____. *Mount McKinley's West Buttress: The First Ascent, Brad Washburn's Logbook 1951.* Top of the World Press (2003).

Washburn, Bradford and Peter Cherici. *The Dishonorable Dr. Cook: Debunking the Notorious McKinley Hoax.* Seattle: The Mountaineers Books, 2001.

Washburn, Bradford, and David Roberts. *Mount McKinley: The Conquest of Denali.* New York: Harry N. Abrams (1991).

Waterman, Jonathan. *High Alaska.* New York: The American Alpine Club (1988).

_____. *Surviving Denali.* New York: The American Alpine Club (1983; revised and updated in 1991).

_____. *In the Shadow of Denali.* New York: Dell (1994).

Wickersham, The Honorable James. Old Yukon Tales, Trails and Trials. Washington, D.C.: Washington Law Book Co. (1938).

Wilcox, Joseph. *A Reader's Guide to The Hall of the Mountain King.* Gig Harbor, Washington: Joe Wilcox (1981).

_____. *White Winds.* Los Alamitos, California: Hwong Publishing Co. (1981).

Wilkerson, James A., M.D., editor, Cameron C. Bangs, M.D., and John S. Hayward, Ph.D. *Hypothermia, Frostbite and Other Cold Injuries.* Seattle: The Mountaineers Books, 1986.

INDEX

About the Author

Bill Sherwonit reached Denali's summit in 1987 while a reporter at the *Anchorage Times*, an accomplishment he calls a once-in-a-lifetime experience. Although he says he's never been a hard-core mountaineer, Bill offers his own intimate knowledge of Mount McKinley in *To the Top of Denali: Climbing Adventures on North America's Highest Peak.*

A freelance writer since 1992, Sherwonit has contributed to a wide range of magazines, journals, newspapers, and anthologies. He is also the author of thirteen books about Alaska, including *Iditarod: The Great Race to Nome*; *Alaska's Accessible Wilderness: A Traveler's Guide to Alaska's State Parks*; the pocket field guide *Alaska's Bears*; *Changing Paths: Travels and Meditations in Alaska's Arctic Wilderness*; and *Living with Wildness: An Alaskan Odyssey.* He also compiled and edited the anthologies *Alaska Ascents: World Class Mountaineers Tell Their Stories* and *Denali: A Literary Anthology.*

Born in Bridgeport, Connecticut, in 1950, Bill has lived in Anchorage since 1982. He now makes his home in the city's Turnagain area, while continuing to explore and write about Alaska's wild nature, both in remote backcountry and in his adopted hometown. His website is www.billsherwonit.alaskawriters.com.

Printed in the USA
CPSIA information can be obtained
at www.ICGtesting.com
JSHW012018140824
68134JS00033B/2760